Richard Cunningham McCormick

St. Paul's to St. Sophia; or, Sketchings in Europe

Richard Cunningham McCormick

St. Paul's to St. Sophia; or, Sketchings in Europe

ISBN/EAN: 9783337167738

Printed in Europe, USA, Canada, Australia, Japan

Cover: Foto ©Andreas Hilbeck / pixelio.de

More available books at **www.hansebooks.com**

St. Paul's to St. Sophia;

OR,

SKETCHINGS IN EUROPE.

BY

RICHARD C. McCORMICK,

AUTHOR OF "THE CAMP BEFORE SEVASTOPOL," "THE
ITALIAN WAR OF 1859," ETC.

NEW YORK:

SHELDON & COMPANY, 115 Nassau Street.

BOSTON: GOULD & LINCOLN.

1860.

.

PREFACE.

THE following locodescriptive sketchings are from letters principally written at the places they describe,* during a tour through Great Britain, and from London to Constantinople, made under circumstances very favorable for accurate observation.

They are published in the present form at the instance of those for whose entertainment they were originally penned, and others of the author's friends, in the belief that from their familiar style, and frequent minuteness of detail, (and they claim no higher merit,) they will be acceptable to the public, even in this day of travel, and books of travel.

* Half a word fixed upon, or near the spot, is worth a cart-load of recollection.—*The Poet Gray to Mr. Palgrave.*

It is hardly necessary to state that they do not profess to treat of all the notable places and objects between the leaden dome of St. Paul's and the golden minarets of St. Sophia, nor yet of all that came within scope of the author's recorded observation, but simply of some of such as in his humble judgment will be most likely to interest the general reader.

New York 1860.

CONTENTS.

ST. PAUL'S TO ST. SOPHIA.

ST. PAUL'S.

A CROWNING glory of the " World of London " is
the stately and venerable cathedral of St. Paul. Its
sightly dome meets the traveler's eye from every approach to the metropolis, and serves as an obliging
beacon by which his perambulations through the
labyrinthian streets are guided, by which he starts
forth at early morn and returns at close of day, never
to cease amazement at the manifold wonders of the
largest city in the world, whose inhabitants are in in-
tercourse, commercial, political, or religious, with
almost the whole human race—" which has been the
scene of the most stirring events of history—which
has been a city of progress from its first foundation,—
which has sent forth its literature through four centuries to the uttermost ends of the earth,—and which is

full, therefore, not only of material monuments of the
past, but of the more abiding memorials which exist
in imperishable books."

Washington Irving, in his sketch of "Little Britain," which must be read here to be rightly appreciated, speaks of the great dome of St. Paul's as swell-
ing above the houses of Paternoster Row, Amen Corner, and Ave Maria Lane, and looking down with an
air of motherly protection on the antiquated neighborhood he so inimitably describes—and this motherly protection seems to extend to all London, great as
it is—for no structure, not even the classic Abbey of
Westminster, or the Royal Exchange, ventures to dis-
pute the supremacy and dignity of St. Paul's.

Certainly no ecclesiastic edifice in all Britain, is
more opulent in historic interest, or more distinctively
attractive. The very ground on which it stands has
from time immemorial been associated with memorable events in the progress of Church and State. Sir
Christopher Wren, who dug deep into all parts of the
ground in laying the foundations of the present cathedral, discovered no indications to confirm the tradition
that the site had been originally occupied by a temple of Jupiter or Diana; but he found under the choir
of the old building, a *presbyterium*, or semicircular
chancel, of Roman architecture—a structure of Kent-
ish rubble-stone, cemented with their inimitable mor-

tar, which proved that the first Christian church had been the work of the Roman colonists; and he also clearly ascertained that the northern part of the churchyard had been a depository for the dead from the Roman and British times.* The first church is supposed to have been destroyed in the Dioclesian persecution, and to have been rebuilt in the reign of Constantine. This was again demolished by the pagan Saxons; and restored in 603, by Sebert, a petty prince ruling in these parts under Ethelbert, king of Kent, the first Christian monarch of the Saxon race; who at the instance of St. Augustine, appointed Melitus the first Bishop of London.†

When the city of London was destroyed by fire in 1086 this church was burnt; the bishop Mauritius began to rebuild it, and laid the foundation which remained till its second destruction from the same cause in the great fire of 1666.

Street preaching appears to have been early sanctioned in London. "Paul's Cross," a famous pulpit of wood, mounted upon steps of stone, and covered with lead, in which the most eminent divines were appointed to preach every Sunday in the forenoon, was erected in the space adjoining the cathedral at a very early date. We hear of its being in use in the

---

* Knight's London.   † Pennant's London.

year 1259. It was used not only for the instruction
of mankind, by the doctrine of the preacher, but for
every purpose political or ecclesiastical; for giving
force to oaths, for promulging laws, or rather the
royal pleasure; for the remission of papal bulls, for
anathematizing sinners, for benedictions, for exposing
penitents under censure of the church, for recanta-
tions, for the private ends of the ambitious, and for
the defaming those who had incurred the displeasure
of crowned heads.*

The reign of Queen Elizabeth was wisely ushered
in by the appointment of good and able men to preach
from this Cross the doctrine of the Reformation and
rejection of the papal power. The last sermon here
preached was before James I., who came in great
state on horseback from Whitehall on Midlent Sunday, 1620. The object of the sermon was the repara-
tion of the cathedral, which had become quite out of
repair. In 1633 the celebrated Inigo Jones was appointed to the work, and began, (says Pennant) with
the most notorious impropriety, that of adding a portico of the Corinthian order (beautiful in itself,) to
the west end of the ancient Gothic pile, while to the
end of the two transepts he put Gothic fronts "in a
most horrible style." The great fire of 1666 made
way for the restoration of the magnificent building

* Pennant's London.

by Wren, then Surveyor General of his Majesty's works. But Sir Christopher had difficulties of all sorts to contend with, in the prosecution of his work—his plans were interfered with, his money was not paid, and his genius was undervalued. Yet he lived to see the completion of his work, and died at the good old age of 90. He was buried in the vaults underneath the church, and a fine epitaph was writ-ten on him by his son, of which the concluding words are so well known:—"If you would behold his mon-ument, look around you," and a grand and imperish-able monument it is. The first stone was laid June 21, 1675, and the building completed in 1710, but the whole decorations were not finished till some years later. In the reigns of James I. and Charles I. the body of the cathedral was the common resort of the politicians, the news-mongers, and the idle in general. It was called "Paul's Walk," and the frequenters known by the name of "Paul's Walkers." It is now more sacredly devoted to religious purposes.

Among the more interesting meetings annually held at St. Paul's, is that of the "Society for the pro-pagation of the Gospel in Foreign Parts," which So-ciety has now been engaged for more than 150 years in endeavoring to plant the Church of Christ among Englishmen abroad and among the Heathen. From North America its operations have gradually been extended to the West Indies, Australia, India, South Africa, New Zealand, Ceylon, and Borneo. When the Society was first founded, there were probably not 20 clergymen of the Church of England in these lands. There are now congregations under the pastoral care of 2,965 clergymen, of whom 447, stationed generally in the most destitute places, are assisted by the Society. There have been established in the British Colonies 17 Colleges, in which clergymen are educated : to 14 of these the Society lend aid. The demands on its resources increase year by year. The Rev. John Wesley was originally a missionary of this Society, and in that character proceeded to America in 1735, returning to England in 1738. I was successful in securing a ticket to the 153d anniversary, held few days since, and more fortunate in that the exercises were held in the rotunda under the dome, a room now but seldom used. The attendance of Bishops and state officers was very great. At the appropriate time the Lord Mayor and High Sheriff came in with their attendants, bearing the enblems of their respective offices. A sermon was preached by the Bishop of Dublin, a stout, gray-haired old gentleman. There was a full choral service ; the performers a selection from the best choirs in London. The audience was very numerous, temporary seats being arranged throughout the rotunda. At the close of the services,

I had an opportunity of seeing the Lord Mayor, Sheriff and Archbishops of Canterbury and London ride off in their pompous state carriages. The Lord Mayor's turn-out is gaudy beyond imagination. The officers of the society, the bishops, and clergy, having been invited to dine with the Mayor, the whole procession of carriages passed through Cheapside, a short distance, to the Mansion House, where the customary awning had been erected over the stairways and piazza, and the guests alighted and passed in, amid the gaze of a great crowd of curious citizens : and if reliance may be placed upon the newspaper reports of the following morning, a glorious good time was had that afternoon and evening, in the enjoyment of the Mayor's elegant hospitality.

Next to the architectural magnificence which ever charms the visitor, the monuments to those buried within the walls of the Cathedral attract his attention. They are not so numerous or elaborate as those at Westminster Abbey but commemorate not a few of Britain's most distinguished sons, whose fame reached to the uttermost parts of the earth. Those of Nelson, Pitt, and Wellington are the most striking, but besides them the visitor, from their prominence, will easily distinguish those of Lord Collingwood, Lord Heathfield, Dr. Samuel Johnson, Abercrombie, Sir Thomas Picton, Sir William Jones, and Sir John Moore who fell, at Corunna, and before which Marshal Soult is said to have stood and wept.

But passing all in its interest to my own mind, is the statue at the entrance way to the choir, to the memory of John Howard the philanthropist, the saviour rather than the destroyer of his fellows—the peaceful hero, to whose pure name all ages will do homage, and whose career, far better even than that of a Nelson or Wellington, illustrates a truly courageous and useful life. It was by a singular felicity the first statue erected in St. Paul's.

The outward appearance of the cathedral bespeaks much of gross neglect. The walls are sadly in need of sweeping, not to say scrubbing, and the many figures standing at different points should have their begrimed faces thoroughly washed. The decorative paintings and ceilings in the interior are now being carefully restored.

The great bell "St. Tom," still hangs in the southern campanile tower. Irving enumerates it among the wonders of Little Britain, and says it sours all the beer when it tolls; and many years since the inhabitants in the vicinity of the cathedral petitioned *not* to have it tolled in the usual manner, as it shook the foundations of their houses. It has been since struck on the side, without being swung like other bells by the wheel. Indeed it is now never tolled but on the death of one of the Royal family, or the Bishop of London.

The clock is quite as worthy of note as the bell; the dial on the exterior is fifty-seven feet in circumference, and the minute hand eight feet long.

The district just around St. Paul's, embracing Little Britain and Paternoster Row, the latter now the great bookselling street of the city, has ever been famed for its literary associations. St. Paul's Churchyard, as the irregular circle of buildings enclosing the cathedral and burial ground is called, was before the destruction of the old cathedral, chiefly inhabited by stationers, whose shops were then distinguished by curious signs, such as now seem·to have passed into disuse save for public houses. At the sign of the *White Greyhound*, the first editions of Shakespeare's Venus and Adonis, and Rape of Lucrece, were published by John Harrison; at *Flower de Luce* and the *Crown*, appeared the first edition of the Merry Wives of Windsor; at the *Green Dragon*, the first edition of Richard the Second; at the *Angel*, the first edition of Richard the Third; at the *Spread Eagle* the first edition of Troilus and Cressida; at the *Gun* the first edition of Titus Andronicus; and at the *Red Bull* the first edition of Lear.*

After the fire, the majority of the booksellers moved

* Cunningham's Hand Book of London.

to Little Britain and Paternoster Row, but the Yard was not wholly deserted. At No. 65 lived John Newbery, the philanthropic bookseller, with the red pimpled face, to whose kind catering for the public we are indebted for the entertaining histories of Mr. Thomas Trip and Little Goody Two Shoes. At No. 72, now the extensive drapery warehouse of Messrs. George Hitchcock & Co., lived Johnson, the publisher of Cowper's "Task," who, notwithstanding it was almost universally denounced by the literary censorship of the day, had the courage to publish it and the subsequent poems of Cowper, and the satisfaction of sustaining his own, and reversing public opinion in their favor.

This quere in "The Task," is as appropriate to-day as when first suggested:

" Where has commerce such a mart,
So rich, so thronged, so drained, and so supplied,
As London? opulent, enlarged, and still
Increasing London ?"

What an enlargement has there been since Johnson wisely undertook "The Task"! In three score years and ten, just the allotted age of man,* how have the great sides of London expanded, and its insatiate tendrils grasped the surrounding villages, till all are concentered in a still more opulent and increasing metropolis than the poet dreampt of. The population is

* " The Task " was published in 1785.

so vast that one is apt to lose sight of items which, considered separately, would appear enormous. Thus there are eighty thousand children born yearly in London, and fifty thousand persons always resident in poor-houses, prisons, and other establishments, where they are daily fed out of national or public resources. Then there are twelve hundred places of worship, in which it is supposed about one million worshippers attend every Sunday; there are also six thousand schools, on the books of which are about six hundred thousand scholars.

There are nearly thirty thousand tailors plying the needle in London, and forty thousand bootmakers cobbling or fashioning leathern understandings. The professional men amount to twenty-five thousand, with an equal number of authors and printers. The domestic servants in London, male and female, reach the almost incredible number of two hundred thousand. The ancient dames of the Gampian school, together with their co-laborers the charwomen, washerwomen, and manglers, number sixty thousand, and as many as one hundred thousand women and girls endeavor to earn a subsistence by their needle. Alas! how many of this illy requited class,

> "Stitch, stitch, stitch,
> In poverty, hunger and dirt,
> Sewing at once with a double thread,
> A shroud as well as a shirt!"

It has been calculated that if the population of London continues to increase in the same proportion it has of late, before the end of the present century London will contain six millions of souls! Gloomy forebodings occupy some minds on the subject of this large metropolis. History does not record such a stupendous civic population; and having no precedent to serve as its basis, men are at a loss to picture the possible economy of six millions of human beings living in one city.

But without waiting to dream of what may be some thirty or forty years hence, London already affords sufficient food for astonishment, admiration, and delight.

STREETS AND PARKS.

WHEN Edmund Burke spoke of London as "clean, *commodious*, and neat," he could scarcely have intended the second of these adjectives to apply to the streets, for many of them are ridiculously crooked and absurdly narrow. The modern population must not be blamed for these faults however. We must throw the censure upon their narrow minded ancestors— who must have thought cow paths and donkey trails amply convenient for the business of that unimportant creature man. It is a wonder how such great men as Johnson, Reynolds, Wren, and their large minded cotemporaries ever managed to get through such contracted lanes. But there are some wide streets in London, more than the stranger would expect to find, from general report. Portland street, Regent street, Piccadilly, The Strand, Pall Mall, Holborn, The City Road and other prominent avenues are agreeably spacious; and the city's pride, New Cannon Street, a thor-

(23)

oughfare just cut through from St. Paul's to the London Bridge, is as wide and well regulated as any street in New York. The buildings lining it on the Thames side are really noble, and much resemble the best stone stores on Park Place and Murray street. In fact it is about the only street in London appropriate for comparison with any of the new mercantile avenues on the west of Broadway.

The popular stone here is, when first quarried, of a rather pleasing hue — a sort of light drab — and when exposed to a few months of London smoke and air, it turns to a dismal brown, and all attractiveness is gone. It would be hard to tell, from outward appearance, of what material the old buildings are built. The stone of St. Paul's, Westminster Abbey, and Old Bailey, is so deeply dyed with smoke, and dust, and fringed with cob webs, that a practiced geologist would have to labor hard to make anything of a guess as to its class. The stone of which all the old buildings are made must be rather a soft one, as it appears to have been cut and carved with great readiness.

In the old portions of London, or in the city proper, for but a small part of London is known as " the city," the buildings are many of them of brick, and stand as firm as if just finished. The bricks are somewhat larger than those used in the States, and are both red and brown, or were so originally. The roofs of most of the buildings are of red tile, and the appearance of the metropolis from a housetop is exceedingly curious. The chimney tops are ornamented with " chimney pots." It being very hard to get the flues to draw, these artificial aids are almost universally applied. A chimney without " pots" is a rarety, a phenomenon. In the outskirts and suburbs of the metropolis the buildings look more cheerful, and are generally disconnected and surrounded with liberal and well arranged garden plots. The cottages are two to three stories in height, and usually nearly square— say 30 by 40 feet—and having four chimneys. They stand from 10 to 25 feet back from the street line, and are all fitted with the " modern improvements"—gas being always introduced, and in much greater use than in America.

There is not a street about London destitute of gas lamps, and for 10 to 20 miles out, you may enjoy the company of the artificial light. In fact there is hardly a city or village in England without gas, and the pipes appear to run through many of the country roads and fields. I have often wondered to see a beautiful gas light wasting its brilliancy beside some untraveled farm road, or peeping over a six foot hedge. It seems sad to think of, does'nt it ? that so much light should be spent for naught when " Gotham" sighs in darkness almost universal, when perchance the almanacs and the moon agree to disagree. But the English people lose nothing by their abundant light. Good lamps tend as much toward the protection of life and property as the most vigilant policemen.

The gas posts are several feet higher than those in New York, which is decidedly disadvantageous. I believe that *pro bono publico*, the lamps are on duty every night the year round. The moon, or almanac makers having failed to gain the confidence of the authorities. The pavement of the London thoroughfares is with an occasional exception, all of square blocks of stone, in size and color not at all unlike that used by Russ. There are no cross walks. The pavement appears to stand remarkably well, and is very smooth, yet not slippery, and kept astonishingly clean. The sweeping, for the most part, is done at night, and the dust kept quiet by frequent sprinkling, both by nature and art, during the day. It would be quite safe to do away with the sprinkling, carts, so regular and copious are the clouds in their outpourings.

The roads leading to the city are McAdamised and kept in beautiful order, so that vehicles glide over them as over a parlor floor. A few of the city streets are thus paved, and a few with the old fashioned wooden blocks, which appear to stand well.

The side walks are usually not so high above the

street as in American cities, and are well preserved. The gutters of all the streets appear perfectly free from stagnant water, slops and filth. The excellent drainage of London, with the strict police regulations, serves to make the highways wholesome and decent promenades rather than mud holes as too often in other cities. There are 30,000 or more streets in London, and you may at almost any day meet more filth in Chatham street (New York,) than you can find in the whole of this immense number of crowded thoroughfares at any one time. How much sickness, and discomfort, and inconvenience is arrested by such a creditable regard to cleanliness.

*   *   *   *   *   *

To the passionate fondness of the early English sovereigns for the chase, is probably due the origin of the noble parks of which London is so justly proud, and which amid a world of narrow, crooked, dingy, and tumultuous streets, alleys, and lanes, are as spacious and inviting as those of any city in Christendom. It is to be regretted however that they are somewhat remote from the very classes of the population most in need of the healthful recreations they so generously afford. Nevertheless they are visited by many of the poorer people who are ambitious enough to walk across the city to enjoy their pure atmosphere, and the contrast from the stifled courts of Spitalfields, Field

Lane, and St. Giles's is enough to repay a much longer walk.

Pleasant is it to the hard-working Londoner to escape at the termination of the fatigue of the counting-house and the shop, to the refreshing presence of trees, and grass, and flowers; to wide, unpaved avenues, to meadows, to the banks of quiet glassy lakes, to all the luxurious refreshings of actual country, even in the heart of the city. A day in Hyde Park is equal to a day in the retirement of Kent or Surrey; a day under the great trees in the Regent's Park will well compare with a day in any rural district I wot of.

Hyde Park boasts 387 acres of lovely landscape, picturesque in the extreme, now rolling, then smooth, and everywhere intersected with charming carriage drives, romantic footpaths, and wide spreading trees.

It is the great driving park of London, and on a fair summer afternoon thousands of fashionable ladies and gentlemen may be seen lolling in their elegant coaches, or enjoying the more active and healthful exercise of the ride on horseback. Rotten Row as the main riding avenue is strangely called, often presents a cavalcade of prancing steeds and graceful riders, both male and female, worthy a more chivalric age. There is little fast driving or riding, and London has no " Bloomingdale Road."

An attractive feature of Hyde Park is the Serpentine River, a pretty sheet of water, fringed with boats, and the sail upon its silvery bosom seems like a trip to fairy land. In winter this is a favorite skating resort and is greatly prized by "young London." •

Hyde Park is also used for military reviews, and has witnessed the mustering of real as well as of holiday warriors. It was the frequent rendezvous of the Commonwealth troops during the civil war. Essex and Lambert encamped their forces here, and here Cromwell reviewed his terrible Ironsides.

The Regent's Park, if slightly less romantic than Hyde or St. James' Parks, and without their age and historic associations, is scarcely less popular as a resort for all classes of the London people. Its vast acres are thoroughly shaded with trees, and I have often noticed large flocks of sheep contentedly grazing on its beautiful meadows. Wide, smooth, pebbled roads and footpaths intersect the Park in every direction, and when the evening twilight sheds its rich azure tints on every side, throngs of peaceful denizens, the titled and lowly, the merchant and the mechanic, mingle and linger to enjoy the rural grandeur and comfort of the ever-attractive resort.

There is an indescribable loveliness in the genial quietude that marks the hours of parting day mid the drooping foliage of the Regent's Park. The thought

of strife, the perplexities of mercantile care, seem to
pass from remembrance, and man holds happy communion with pure spirits, and bright golden visions of
peace, and plenty, joy and rest, occupy his contempla-
tive mind.

The Botanical Gardens covering a portion of the
Park are extensive, and the lovers of the rare and
exquisite in the wide botanical world, here find an
elaborate congregation of the plants of every clime
and country. Hours, days, and even long weeks may
be passed in a careful examination of the countless
varieties, and yet there is room for continued and
profitable study. To the thousand lovers of the beautiful in nature, who from the limit of acres and the
avarice of landlords are deprived the pleasure of cul-
tivating the rose or lily, the privileges of such a collection are inestimable, and I doubt not highly esteemed. It is to the credit of a nation, that a taste for
gardens and flowers, for agriculture and horticulture,
pervades its society, even from the most elevated to
the more humble ranks.

The renowned Zoological Gardens, second to none
in the world, are also located in Regent's Park.
Their extent surpassed my imagination, their interest
would have kept me within their percincts for days,
rather than hurried hours. The arrangements made
for the care and exhibition of the vast gathering of

zoological specimens, many of them very rare, are of the most complete and creditable character. Everything, from the elephant's house to the head-quarters of the chattering monkeys, shows the results of good taste and judgment on the part of the intelligent directors and keepers.

The Regent's Park is now almost surrounded by elegant mansions, fit to compare with the most luxurious and extravagant of our Fifth Avenue palaces. The aristocracy look out upon the waving grass and shadowing trees, but to enjoy the peaceful sight no more, or reap any advantage not guaranteed the poorest subject of the royal command. Thanks to the liberal laws controlling the public places throughout Britain, the lord and the boot black are allowed their equal enjoyment. Pleasantly is this demonstrated at the British Museum, where every day its valued stores are freely inspected by all, and the masses feel they have a full right to treasures of which the rich might well be proud. The fruits of such a right must ever prove potent to the best interests of the commonwealth.

With the expansion of the metropolis, new parks are being laid out. One of these is in the Eastern District, called after the sovereign, is spacious, and already very attractive. Every great city should have just as many parks as are necessary to give a

breathing space to all its denizens, and if too neglect-
ful of their breath, to frequent them of their own
accord, they should be forced by law to do so. The
English are, as a people, fond of out-door recreations;
but, even they, too often do their nature wrong by
neglecting

> " The bodily joys that helps to make them wise,
> The long day's walk, the vigorous exercise."

Thanks to the early closing and Saturday half-holi-
day movement, of late so vigorously and successfully
prosecuted, the clerks and apprentices now find time
to snuff the fresh air, and enjoy the parks and rural
districts, more than ever before. As civilization advances, shop keepers and shoppers will more and
more realize the manifold advantages of early closing
to all concerned. London finds no inconvenience
worth naming, in the now almost universal custom of
closing the shops at six or seven o'clock, and earlier
on Saturdays.

SHOPS AND MARKETS.

As a people, the Londoners do not rise early. Scarcely any shops are open before half-past eight or nine o'clock, and no one is seen in the streets at an earlier hour, save the market men, and no business at all transacted except at Billingsgate, Covent Garden, and other market places. The shops of London are generally small. Not one in an hundred is over forty feet deep, and thousands are much less, and in no way are they superior or seldom at all approaching to the myriad palaces of retail trade to be found in the thriving cities of the States.

The enormous panes of glass, found in most of the shop windows, nevertheless give them to the casual observer, a more elegant appearance than those on . Broadway. The sashes are often of brass, and kept well polished. The window glass in the modern houses is much larger than that used in the States, and many of the London buildings have but one or

(33)   2*

two panes in a large window. The shops in the
plebeian portions of the city, depend much on out-
door show, and are brilliantly illuminated at night
with outside gas lights. The largest and most
fashionable ice cream and refreshment saloon in
London, of the "Thompson" or "Taylor" order, is not
fit to be named in the same day with the elegant
establishments of either of these enterprising caterers.
I do not think the first refreshment saloon here is more
than quarter the size of Taylor's palace, and it is not
half so superb. I visited one of the best saloons here
in company with some friends a few evenings since,
and found one waiter in service, and at the most likely hour, not over a half dozen customers! Chop
houses suit John Bull far better. He don't care for
ice. His blood and climate is cold enough at all
times. He wants his beef, his mutton, his cheese, and
his *stout*. Poor fellow, how he grumbles at a slight
attack of the sun. How he'd foam under an American
August day, with the mercury near the summit of
the tube and rising!

Oysters are not popular here, nor are they as plenty,
as cheap or as good, as in New York. The chop
houses are quiet nooks, in which one may refresh the
inner man in a very comfortable manner. They are
frequently up narrow alleys and gloomy courts, and
appear to be made as unattractive as possible. Those

on Fleet street and Cheapside, in the city proper, are
many of them honored with having been patronized
by such famous men as Johnson, Goldsmith, Garrick
and their illustrious cotemporaries, who it is well
known were wont to live well. I have dined at
several of the more antique and celebrated, for the
purpose of examining the curious places. The " Che-
shire Cheese," on Fleet street, is one of the oldest and
most notorious. The building is a dilapidated one—
the kitchen at the top ; no carpet on the floors. You
lounge in, order a chop, and if an Englishman, a pint
of "'Aff and 'Aff," or Barclay, Perkins & Co. entire,
and proceed to eat and drink in the slowest possible
manner. The chops are generally well cooked. The
charge is from 12½ to 25 cents, according to the
standing of the house. Bread and butter are always
subject to an additional charge of 4 to 6 cents, and
potatoes at the same rate. The waiter's fee is a penny
on every shilling laid out. The eating tables are
placed *a la* Taylor's ice cream stands, although never
so elegant. I have been provoked at the tedious
delays to be met at these shops, but to the Londoners ·
they are not offensive. One can scarcely imagine ·
greater pokes than the waiters. To be in the fashion,
you must always take either ale, beer or stout, and
afterwards a huge piece of cheese. The plainness of
the chop houses is surprising, but by no means objec-

tionable. At one or two places the chops are served on leaden plates, and at many of the establishments nothing is cooked but chops.

On Cheapside, and other public places, there are public dining saloons in the Fulton street style, and very little if any better. At these you may get almost any kind of meat, vegetables or pudding. The charges are higher than in New York, and the waiters have to be paid extra. Coffee, tea and cocoa or chocolate may be had at all times. The latter are much more in vogue here than in the States. Butter is never brought upon the table unless especially ordered, and the commonest brown sugar is given for use on pies or puddings. At "Simpson's," Billingsgate, there is an ordinary, or *table d' hote*, at 1 and 4 o'clock daily, where for. 37½ cents you may get some half dozen kinds of fish and two varieties of meat, all decently cooked. There are many other places furnishing a table d' hote. The best place to get a dinner is at some of the hotels, where joints are served up at certain hours every day. Here you may be well served, everything clean and excellent. But you must expect to wait a full half hour or more after you have given your order, before you see any thing in the shape of " feed," and if you get half so good a variety for $1 00 as you could in New York for 50 cents, you may think yourself fortunate. There is an air of quiet ease about these resorts, however, which is certainly pleasant, yet one cannot afford to indulge in ease at such an outlay of time and money. The lady of the house (usually a very fat and polite woman) superintends in person the eating department, and the waiters are always very neatly dressed in black, with white cravats. They would be voted parsons in America.

Here too you are looked upon as a curiosity if you do not order some sort of liquor. Pies, such as are common in the States, are comparatively unknown. If you ask for a pie, you get what we would denominate a tart. The cutlery and crockery arrangements are much more complete than in America; each eater has two knives and forks, two or three plates, always warmed. A muffin, hot and well buttered, is invariably given with breakfast or tea.

When you enter a hotel your name is not asked, but you are immediately conducted by "Mr. Boots" to your room, which has over the door a number in prominent figures. To this number everything you have is charged. If you order cab, postage stamps, paper, or in fact anything, the expense is not mentioned, but quietly charged to your number, and all brought out in bold relief when you ask for your bill. Servants are allowed one to two shillings per day.

The most fashionable London hotels are at the

West End. Fenton's and Morley's are resorted to by
wealthy Americans, who stop in town but for a short
time : private lodgings are secured by all who wish
to make a long stay. To live well at these hotels,
costs about a guinea per day—double the price
charged at the best Broadway house. There is no
regular hour for meals ; you order what you please,
when you please. There is none of that bustle and
excitement about the premises always to be found at
American hotels ; no carriages or porters meet you at
the depots or wharves. If you wish to go to a hotel,
you must hire a cab. The landlords seem perfectly
indifferent as to whether they get any custom or not.
Signs of any size are seldom hung out, and he is indeed a lucky fellow who having walked out from
these sleepy and obscure stopping places, manages to
find his way safely back again.

You will feel interested in hearing something of
the wholesale warehouses or stores. There are
many of them large, and it is the custom for
the clerks to eat and sleep on the premises. I have
visited two or three establishments, where some one
hundred young men are employed, and all live on
the premises. They have dining rooms, libraries, sitting rooms, and bed rooms conveniently arranged, and
servants and housekeepers are supplied by the proprietors. At Morley's, one of the first establishments,

the accommodations for the clerks are excellent. The library and reading room is supplied with the best literature of the day. The young men have their evenings to themselves, and are obliged to be at home by eleven o'clock.

The largest Dry Goods establishment in London is not a circumstance to " Stewart's." The term " Dry-Goods," is entirely unknown. The dealers in linen, silk, and calico, are called Linen Drapers, Silk Merchants, &c. The display of goods made in the windows of the retail shops on Regent and other leading streets, is often dashing, and advertising is quite as popular, excepting perhaps in the newspapers, as in the American cities. Many novel ways are resorted to for attracting the attention of the almighty public. Men walking with banners, and at night with illuminated advertising hats, and other oddities, may be frequently seen. The custom of issuing blazing posters and attractive handbills, is quite as prevalent as with the Yankees. Every inch of unprotected wall is covered with all manner of notices. In the printing of monstrous and variegated show-bills, I thought several of my New York friends had attained perfection, but they are yet behind the printers of this country. I was satisfied of this as soon as I jump-ed on the dock at Liverpool, near to which was a large wall, completely sheeted with advertisements—bills

of shipping, of theatrical and other performances,
many of them (if my eyes be true) full five yards long
and four wide, and of the richest colors, and the type
of an amazing size. The theatre handbills are smaller
than in the States, and are sold by men and women
at the doors, for a penny each. This would not " go
down " at the Chatham, eh ? The inner sides and
ceiling of the railway carriages, on many of the
roads, are closely lined with advertisements, neatly
printed, in a style to suit the panels. " Nicoll & Co.,"
shirt makers, and Hyam, " the tailor," have their
cards prominent everywhere. They should sell gar-
ments enough to keep a regiment of sewers at work.
Messrs. Smith & Son, of the Strand, are the contrac-
tors for railway advertising. They pay the companies so much for the entire control of the stations
and carriages, and charge advertisers a good sum for
the privilege of inserting their notices, which they
agree to protect. To this end, they have large caution bills in each carriage, offering a reward of several pounds for the detection of any one caught in the
act of mutilating any of the advertisements. This
same enterprising firm has elegant book-stalls at most
of the stations, beside being the agents of most of
the London papers.

Sermons are advertised much more than in America.
Bills are circulated widely when any strange preacher

is to appear. Special prayers, whenever ordered, are hawked about the streets at a penny each! The contents of the papers of the week are announced in flaming letters, *a la* the New York Sunday press. Just at present there is a great outcry for paper. What is to be done, no one can tell. It is certain that, for a long time, the supply has not equaled the demand, and now it does not approach it. Large rewards are offered for the discovery of some new process of manufacturing the useful article. The paper used, is generally much superior to most of that used for American publications.

Of the daily newspapers, I had thought to say a few words. The *Times* stands head and shoulders above all its cotemporaries. Its mammoth pages are widely read. It circulates all over the kingdom. Hotel keepers, in announcing the features of their establishments, are sure to say " *the Times taken in.*" It is not served to city subscribers until nine or ten o'clock. The price, five-pence, (ten cents,) is no higher than that of most of the other dailies, though I believe no other has sixteen pages regularly. The supplement to the *Times* is filled with advertisements, and the paper is delivered to all dealers, by Messrs. Smith & Son, the grand agents, to whose office the copies are carted every morning. It is the custom for the proprietors of reading rooms and hotels, to sell their papers to the country folk at a slight reduction from the first cost, and deliverable the next day. So that you may scarcely ever find in any reading-room, a copy of the *Times* for a day or two back. The *Daily News* comes next to the *Times* in estimation: on many accounts it is as good, its city reports being more minute. Its editorials are not so much thought of, though, perhaps, often full as worthy.*

But to return to the shops. Every one of much · pretension has the Royal coat of arms and the mottoes, "Dieu et mon droit," and "Honi soit qui mal y pense," emblazoned in large size over the door-way, or carved on the front of the roof. Hundreds of tradesmen display after the title of their business, the words, "To her Majesty:" thus, "Carriage-maker to her Majesty," "Stationer to her Majesty;" and others thus, "Boot-maker to his Royal Highness, Prince Albert," "Hatter to the Royal family;" others, "Patronized by Royalty;" others, "Under the immediate patronage of the Nobility;" and others, "Stationers, &c., to the Honorable the East-India Company." It is evidently thought "a great card" to get the name of some scion of royalty as a patron of an establishment.

Signs like the following are met with in all parts

---

* Since the above was written, the removal of the stamp duty has led to the starting of several penny dailies in London, some of which are well supported.

of the kingdom, viz.: "Carriage Broker," "Sworn
Stock Broker," "Bacon Factor," "Poulterer,"
"Green Grocer," "Silk Mercer and Haberdasher,"
"Iron-Monger," "Assurance Company," "Linen
Draper," "Licensed Victualer," "Corn Dealer," (all
grain, such as rye, wheat and barley is called
corn,) "Purveyor," "Licensed to sell Stamps,"
"Livery and Bait Stable," "Fruiterer," "Carrier,"
"Cheesemonger."

Over a small beer-shop, just out of Liverpool, an
unpretending sign-board makes the following announcement: "Susannah Smith, licensed to sell ale,
beer, porter and tobacco by retail, to be consumed
upon the premises." Is not the word "retail"
quite superfluous, inasmuch as a customer could
hardly be expected to consume a wholesale quantity of
any of the articles on sale in the premises? perhaps,
however, it was introduced to keep great drinkers
away.

I was inclined to smile, (though, perhaps, it would
have been smiling at too solemn a business,) when
I first saw a sign announcing that "Funerals would
be performed by ———." "Funerals performed"
is a common sign, to be seen at every undertaker's
shop; and, doubtless, many funerals are heartless
performances; but it did, at first sight, appear exceedingly novel to me, to find an undertaker publish-

ing his readiness to "perform" a funeral. Custom
has rendered this expression so familiar as to
attract no special notice from the people. Under-
takers, also announce themselves as "Funeral Feath-
ermen." This means, I believe, that they supply the
feathers and other paraphernalia, for setting off a
funeral in great style. In this connection, though
I had not intended it, it will not be amiss to allude
to the manner of conducting funerals in this country.
In scarcely anything is the antiquity of the nation so
perfectly illustrated at the present time. The pomp
and show at the burial of a wealthy or noted person,
are great beyond description. Mourners march two
by two in front of the procession, carrying immense
staves, covered with deep black cloth and crape.
These men, who are not relatives of the deceased, but
furnished by the undertaker at a heavy charge, are
dressed in black throughout, and have weeds attached
to their hats, and flowing down their backs. They
march at a solemn pace, and look so sorrowful, one
would naturally suppose them to be near friends of
the departed. The hearse is usually of great size,
and trimmed in very rich style, mounted with six or
eight immense black feathers, standing some two
or three feet high. The driver is dressed throughout
in mourning, and so are the drivers of all the
coaches. The coaches are clumsy affairs, decked in

black, and used, I judge, for funerals only. (A very proper plan. I have often felt it to detract from the solemnity of a funeral, to see persons riding in vehicles in which, perhaps, not longer than twenty-four hours previous, they had gone to a party or ball.)

The horses used for funerals, have attracted my special notice. They appear a distinct breed. They are about sixteen hands high, long, and well built, not over heavy, and of ebony black, (I have not seen other than black horses attached to any funeral train,) and have shaggy manes and fetlocks, appearing something on the Canadian pony order. I have noticed them in no other service. There is, on the whole, an air of mournful solemnity attached to a funeral in England, which we never see in the States. Whether it is calculated (affected, of course, as much of it is) to impress the living with a greater idea of their frailty, and the approach of the time when they must yield to death, I am, on the whole, much in doubt.

The "Beer-shops" should, by every right, have preceded the funeral. Pray pardon the improper precedence given the corpse. It is generally granted that New York can show as great an array of drinking saloons as any one city in the world; but New York is yet far behind London or Liverpool in this unenviable point. In either of these places one can hardly walk ten yards without seeing a beer-shop, and at most of these shops, gin, whiskey, and all the strong liquors are sold. The name of "gin palaces" has been appropriately applied to these countless *depots* of intoxicating drinks. As the inhabitants are divided, so are the saloons. There are gorgeous ones, there are quiet ones, and there are miserable holes— and the latter apparently predominate. Beer, ale, porter and stout, are the principal beverages, and it is customary to display the names of those whose liquors are kept on sale in dashing letters ; so that you may see in every street huge signs on the house fronts like the following :—" Barclay, Perkins & Co.'s Entire," " Truman, Hanbury, Buxton & Co.'s Entire," " Whitbread & Co.'s Entire," " Reed & Co.'s Entire." These are among the most extensive and popular brewers in London. The word entire is probably added to signify that the liquors are kept unadulterated and of the first quality. When very often you cannot find any intimation of the name of the proprietor of a shop, you may see such signs as I have exampled stretching over the whole front of the establishment in gayly painted letters. You can have little idea of the immense consumption of beer and stout which every day witnesses in London. I have repeatedly seen notices in shop windows to the effect that a fresh barrel of beer was put on draught every twelve hours. The shops have two entrances, (the extensive ones)—one labeléd " Bottle and Jug Department ;" the other, " On Draught Department." The beer is sold for a mere song; the ale and porter, also, at a very low rate. Everybody drinks, or nearly everybody—men, women and children. I have been astonished to see respectable women quaffing their glasses in the shops, while at night the saloons will often be almost entirely filled with females, generally of the lowest character.

Brilliantly illuminated with gas, and conveniently situated, they undoubtedly attract many who would naturally abstain from drinking. I think they generally find much more patronage than in the city of New York. It is not common to see a drinking-room crowded there, except on an extraordinary occasion—the time of an election or a fire ; but here you may find them swarming with customers every day and night. There is much drunkenness, but few of the drinkers ever become so top-heavy as to attract notice. Out and out tipsy fellows are no more common than in other large cities.

I have seen parties stop their carriages before the shops and have glasses brought to them, and drink in the open street ; and I have been in an omnibus when the driver pulled up at a shop, and detained his passengers a number of minutes, until both he and the conductor went in and quaffed a glass or two. Late at night, shouts of boisterous merriment issue from these crowded establishments,. and sounds of maudlin song echo from many voices. Once or twice I think I have detected the rollicking words of bully Wagstaff's " Confession of Faith,"

> " Though I go bare, take ye no care,
> I nothing am a colde,
> I stuff my skyn so full within,
> Of joly good ale and olde."

Certain it is, that, as at the "Half-Moon and Bunch of Grapes," the whole club join in the chorus with a fearful thumping on the tables, and clattering of pewter mugs. But with all their apparent jollity, I doubt not many of these inveterate beer drinkers go far more bare and cold than consistent with their physical comfort; for while, in view of the climate, and general usage, a prudent use of malt liquors might prove harmless, if not beneficial, it cannot be gainsayed that this practice of excessive tippling is productive of the worst results, and quite sufficient to warrant legal interference, though I am hardly ready to believe, with some enthusiastic tee-totalers, I have met here, that the passage of a Maine law would be either practicable or wise. Colquhoun, in his valuable treatise on the police of the metropolis, published

about 1800—a copy of which I have been greatly
interested in perusing, says: " It is a mistaken notion
that a very large quantity of malt liquor is necessary
to support laborers of any description. After a certain moderate quantity is drank, it enervates the body
and stupefies the senses. A coalheaver who drinks
from twelve to sixteen pots of porter in the course of
a day, would receive more real nourishment, and perform his labor with more ease, and a greater portion
of athletic strength, if only one-third of the quantity
was consumed. He would also enjoy better health,
and be fitter for his labor the following day."

With the highly respectable classes—"our best
society"—wine is a *sine qua non ;* you scarcely enter
a mansion before you are asked to partake. And I
would not for a moment intimate that it is not offered
with the utmost innocence and good-will. There is
no thought that temptation is being put in one's way;
on the contrary, you are invited to drink as a mark
of friendship and respect, and in the most orderly and
pious families—even those of clergymen—wine is
prominent on all occasions; and I have scarcely
been able to make some of my religious acquaintances
believe that in the United States it is demanded in
the covenants of many of the churches that the members shall conform to principles of the strictest total
abstinence. The indifferent character of the London

drinking water is anything but favorable to the increase of cold water men. Such insipid, lifeless stuff, may you never have to depend on. I would not give one glass of pure crystal "Croton," or "Cochituate," for a hogshead of this miserable liquid. If there is any place under the sun where an indulgence in beer and similar drinks may be tolerated that place is London. The citizens are heartily ashamed of the poor water, and I am told that, at a comparatively insignificant expense, the city might be supplied with an unobjectionable article. Its introduction would, perhaps, do as much towards stopping intemperance as the eloquent appeals of Mr. Gough,* who seems like "Uncle Tom" to have literally taken England by storm. And indeed his mission is very timely, if we may accredit the startling facts and figures of the Rev. Newman Hall, who estimates the money spent in strong drink in Great Britian would every year support,

200,000 Missionaries (which would be about one to every 3,000
adult heathen) at ....each £200
2,000 Superannuated Missionary Laborers at .... " 100
100,000 Schoolmasters at .... " 100
Build 2,000 Churches and Chapels............................... " 2,000
Build 2,000 Schools at .... " 500

* If all the stories be true, the old Spanish maxim is scarcely applicable to London : viz., " Drinking water neither makes a man sick, nor in debt, nor his wife a widow."

Give to 50,000 Widows, ...each per week 5s.
Issue 50,000 Bibles every day at..................................... each 1s. 0d.
And 100,000 Tracts every day at .... per hundred 4s.
And present to 192,815 poor families £10 each on Christmas Day.

or it would in one year, supply each human being on the globe with a bible ; or it would, in one year, provide

200 Hospitals at .... each £200,000
12, 000Chapels at .... "   2,000
10,000 Schools at .... "   600
2,000 Mechanics' Institutions and Lecture Halls at.......... "   2,000
25,000 Almhouses at... "   600
1,000 Baths .... "   2,000
2,000 Libraries at .... "   500
200 Public Parks at .... "   5,000

Give 400,000 poor families £10 each, and present a new bible to each man, woman, and child in Great Britain.

So that the money spent in Great Britain alone, for strong drink, would, as far as outward ministry is concerned, evangelize the world—besides providing largely for temporal distress.

That illustrious character, Tony Weller, gave his son the best education in his power—he turned him into the street to shift for himself; and whether to their intellectual advantage or not, thousands of sons aud daughters appear to be literally turned into the streets of this metropolis to shift for themselves.

Men and women, boys and girls, all engage in street hawking. Apple stands (though apples are nowhere to be seen at present) are quite as much in

the way as in New-York. Cherries, strawberries and
oranges, are the chief articles on sale at these wayside markets. The cherries are not in the best condition this season, owing, it is said, to the continued
rains. They retail at about 12½c. per pound. You
get a very fair bunch, as many as you ought to devour
at once, for two cents. They are mostly of the
ox-heart species. Strawberries appear very plenty,
and are sold in "pottels"—baskets somewhat in the
shape of those used in the States, only much deeper.
They are sold at from 12½c. to 25c. each.

The berries grow to an enormous size, but very
seldom attain that perfection in color or shape peculiar
to the "Hovey" and other choice American seedlings.
I have seen some very excellent white strawberries.

The "British Queen," one of the best varieties of
the English strawberry, is often as large in diameter as
an American silver dollar, and generally of a trian-
gular shape, and should be cut in slices like a melon.
Stawberries are cried about the streets, being carried
in huge hampers on the heads of the pedlers; but, of
course, the extra choice ones are only to be found at
the confectioners. The strawberry beds about London are very extensive; I passed by one at or near
Hounslow, a few days since, which covered a number of acres. Still the delightful berry is not enjoyed
here as with you. It does not appear to be looked

upon as so great a luxury, and in truth it lacks that delicious flavor which characterizes it in America. Raspberries are plenty hereabouts, and they attain a size much greater than in the States. Their color is very rich, flavor good. Gooseberries are produced in abundance, and are held in high esteem. Everybody munches them, the same as cherries or plums. They too, grow to a wonderful size, and appear much more inviting than those cultivated in the States. Gooseberry pies and tarts, are very fashionable here at this season.

A novel and pretty feature of London custom, is the practice of selling roses in the streets, followed by large numbers of women and girls. They present to you a beautiful bunch of "opening buds," frequently of the most exquisite moss species. You may take your pick for a penny. Where these elegant flowers are obtained I do not know; but the button-holes of the coats of hundreds of merchants and clerks testify to the large number of customers daily met by the fair rose dealers.

The vegetables of the kingdom are generally excellent. Cabbage and salad are devoured by all. The latter eats beautifully, and I wonder it is not more popular with the Yankees. Immense dray-loads of this article are brought into the markets daily. It is piled up like cord-wood and readily sold. I have

not yet been fortunate enough to get a real good potato,
and my disappointment in this particular is great.
I had hoped that, with the good beef and mutton of
Old England I should be able to enjoy good mealy .
◆ potatoes—something better than the watery trash so
common in the New York markets.

Perhaps a brief allusion to the London markets
would be *apropos* at this point, particularly when I
tell you there are 20,000 persons engaged in killing
and selling animal food, and a greater number in
preparing and selling vegetables. I have not been
able to visit all the markets, but have been at Covent
Garden, Hungerford, Smithfield, and Leadenhall. The former is the great fruit and vegetable
depot, and is situated in one of the most noted portions
of the metropolis, viz., in the neighborhood of Drury
Lane theatre, and age has attached many interesting reminiscences to the market itself. The
vegetables are piled up all around the outside, and
beside the avenues through the market. The fruit is
chiefly exposed in the stalls. There is a centre walk
through the market-house, on each side of which are
small shops, occupied by the dealers in the choicer
fruit and berries, the windows of which are tastefully
decorated, and the fruit displayed in luscious order.
I have been in this market a number of times, and
always enjoyed a stroll through this avenue. Apri-

cots, nectarines, pine-apples, plums, and even a few rich-looking peaches are offered for sale, at anything but reasonable prices. Indeed, it would be folly to ask the price of a peach. I have heard shopkeepers on Cornhill and other streets, talk of 25 cents each, and the peaches are in no way equal to those raised in New Jersey. Hungerford market is mainly a fish market, and presents not much of interest. Leadenhall market is but a short way from Cornhill and the Royal Exchange. It is the principal poultry market of the city, and much live and dead poultry is sold there. The chickens and ducks are dressed more neatly than in Washington market. They are no cheaper, however. The coster-mongers, or small green-grocers assemble at the markets very early in the mornings, and cart away loads of produce to every section of the metropolis. Donkeys are their locomotives, and usually their main dependence. The coster-mongers are a race by themselves, a sturdy, quick-witted, laborious class of travelling shopkeepers, with many singular characteristics.

I was intensely interested in a visit to Smithfield market this morning. Monday is the great market-day, and going early in the morning, I had the opportunity of seeing business under full headway. Such a multitude of cows, oxen, sheep and pigs, I have seldom, if ever, seen together. The market is, in fact, the street, or several streets—an open area, containing five acres and three quarters, and surrounded by bone-houses, public-houses, and knackers'-yards. On Tuesday, Thursday, and Saturday, hay and straw are sold at this market. All the sales take place by commission. The city receives a toll upon every beast exposed for sale of one penny per head, and on sheep of twopence per score. The total produce to the corporation is from $25,000 to $30,000 per year. The sales are always for cash, and the salesmen estimate the weight of the cattle by the eye, and seldom make a mistake of even a few pounds. The average weekly sales of beasts is about 3,000, and of sheep 30,000, which is increased in Christmas week to 4,000 beasts and 47,000 sheep. There are some 5,000 butchers in the metropolis. I do not think you would be surprised at the enormous number of sheep sold, were you to see the shops for selling lamb and mutton: they line the streets, and, as I have heretofore intimated, everybody feasts on "chops."

Smithfield market is in the very heart of the city, and, as you may presume, such a collection of animals, brought together every few days, and kept kicking and bellowing, is not at all well suited to the comfort of the community. And then the driving of herds of cattle through the city, to and from the market. is neither safe nor pleasant. It is surprising that the people have not routed the butchers long ere this. In 1836 a good market was built in the outskirts of the city, but such was the prejudice in favor of " Old Smithfield," that the new locality had to be abandoned. It appears, however, that by act of parliament, the market can now only remain at Smithfield until the completion of a metropolitan market out of the city.

I cannot begin to describe the scenes afforded my eyes at Smithfield this morning. Indeed, I have seen no greater curiosity than this cattle market. Every stranger in London should make it his business to visit it. The cows and sheep were penned with temporary bars, put up all around the streets and were as closely packed as goods destined for Isthmus transportation. In an extract from McCulloch's " London in 1850–51," it is estimated, that in 1851 the annual consumption of butchers' meat amounted to 240,000 bullocks, 1,700,000 sheep, 28,000 calves, and 35,000 pigs, exclusive of vast quantities of bacon and ham. Is it any wonder that John Bull is a fat old fellow ?

There is much of sad history associated with this old market place. Of the two hundred and eighty holy men, who in different places in the kingdom, were led to the stake in the Marian persecution, besides those who perished of disease and famine in various

3*

prisons, not fewer than forty-six died at Smithfield,
all nobly confessing Christ and his truth.

The first on the list of these sufferers was John
Rogers, the editor of the first English translation of
the entire Bible. The date of his martyrdom is Feb.
4th, 1555. Others followed him in quick succession.
Before the expiration of the year, six more victims
were added to the list. In 1556, sixteen ; in 1557,
ten, and in 1558, the closing year of Mary's fearful
reign, thirteen martyrs were burned on the same spot.
Among these, Rogers, Cardmaker, Bradford, and
Philpot were distinguished by their position and
learning. Of the rest, who were chiefly from the
lower ranks of society, it may be said—

> " They lived unknown,
> Till persecution dragged them into fame,
> And chased them up to heaven."

The present* being the three hundreth year from
the date of this persecution, and, a favorable opportunity presenting itself in the removal of the cattle-
market from Smithfield, a desire has rapidly sprung
up thoughout the kingdom, and is extending itself to
America also, that a monument should be erected on
the site of these sufferings, as a perpetual memorial
of those who " counted not their lives dear unto
them," so that they might " testify the Gospel of the

* 1855.

grace of God." With a view of carrying this desire into effect, the Protestant Alliance earnestly invites the help of all who value Protestant truth. Their appeal is made to all sections of the Church, as having a common interest in these fathers of our Protestantism,

THE HOUSE OF COMMONS.

Introductory letters to the Hon. Arthur Kinnaird, M. P. for Perthshire, Scotland, and banker in Pall Mall, gave me an early acquaintance with that gentleman, and I was enabled to accept his invitation to visit Parliament. According to appointment, I met him at his office at 6 o'clock, P. M., and we went together to the session. On our way to the buildings, Mr. K., who is an exceedingly affable and democratic gentleman, pointed out to me many of the M. P.'s as they were jogging on to their labors. Several were on horse. At the members' entrance stood a row of policemen, and a number of anxious lookers on, evidently longing to get in among the law makers. It is no easy matter to gain an entrance. The members have the privilege of giving but two orders each per diem, and if a man has many friends, he usually has these orders promised for days in advance. The members have, however, the right to the personal introduc-

(60)

tion of one friend per day in addition to the two admitted by order.

We passed through a spacious hall, the largest I ever stood in, and thence through divers passage-ways, until we came to the hat-room, and a large apartment where the printed copies of the acts are kept, and the clerks have their quarters. The Parliament buildings are as convenient as elegant, and when fully completed will be unrivalled by any legislative halls in the world. The doors and seats of the House of Commons are of oak, and trimmed with brass. The hall is lighted from the roof. There are good seats for visitors, and on occasions when any important debate is looked for, the attendance of outsiders is very great.

We entered the hall without delay. Lord John Russell was on the floor. I recognized him instantly, having seen him on several occasions, of one of which I must tell you. A few weeks since he accepted her Majesty's appointment as president of her Cabinet, and it is necessary here for a member of Parliament thus promoted, to go to his constituents and procure a re-nomination or election to his old office. Well, Lord John, as he is invariably called here, had to ask his friends to stand by him. He represents the city of London; a most important district. While sufficiently popular to entertain no serious fears of a non-election, in order to assure his friends

of his political soundness, and silence any opposition
that might have arisen, he was to appear on a certain
day at the hustings, in the Guild, or City Hall, and
address the liverymen of London, as those who have
the right to vote are called. By good fortune more
than by arrangement, I was in the vicinity of the hall
just at the time of his lordship's arrival in a carriage,
accompanied by two ladies (said to be his wife and
daughter) and a little boy. A great crowd had assembled, and as he alighted a number of gruff English
cheers were given him. He smiled pleasantly, and
entered the hall. How shall I get in? thought I.
They were refusing admittance to any but liverymen,
but luckily a friend came up, and though not a voter,
contrived to assist me. Stopping a sturdy gentleman,
whom he said he knew to be a liveryman by his phiz,
he told him in as plain a manner as possible, that I
was an American, anxious to hear Lord John.
"Very well," said the good-natured liveryman;
"follow me:" and we passed the police, and I stood
among the London electors. At one end of a large
hall a stage had been erected; and upon it stood the
Lord Mayor, the Sheriff, and other officials of the city.
The hall was crowded, and there was much excitement. The Sheriff having read the call of the meeting, and legally explained its purposes, a well-known
banker, in an appropriate speech, nominated Lord

John for a re-election to Parliament. A gentleman seconded the nomination in flattering remarks. The Sheriff asked if any other nomination was to be made. No response was offered, and Lord John was declared duly elected amid cheers and excitement. It appears that when no opposing candidate is named, there is no poll held. Lord John was then loudly called for, and stepping on the rostrum, delivered a very good stump speech of thirty minutes' duration, in which he succinctly stated his views as to the leading topics of the day, but mainly as to the course to be adopted by the government in the present war crisis. He was interrupted several times by questions from his hearers, which he answered in an off-hand and independent style quite worthy of Tammany Hall. During his speech, the members of his family, to whom I have alluded, occupied a private box above the stage, and seemed much gratified at the proceedings.

As Lord John retired, amid much applause, one Urqhart, a violent political opponent, attempted to refute his sayings, but the audience would give no heed. This man is a most singular genius, and was at one time, if I mistake not, a member of Parliament. He affects to believe that her Majesty's government is " going to pot," that Lord John is a perfect desperado, and that the country can only be saved by his (Urqhart's) re-election to Parliament. He has been advertising his principles, and making speeches, for several weeks past ; but the fact that no one would come forward to put him in nomination, shows his ill success. I went to one of his electioneering meetings at the old London Tavern, a few evenings before the election day, and received a capital idea of London political manœuvres.

I have made too great a digression. Lord John Russell was calmly speaking as I entered the Chamber of Commons. He was merely offering an explanation concerning the war measures, and soon resumed his seat and hat. Lord John is not a brilliant or attractive orator. A man under the usual size, slender and care-worn, with sunken eye and sober expression : his head betokens no lack of brains, though *minus* a fair quantity of hair, time and hard legislation having flirted away the locks and left a portion quite bald. The portraits as frequently presented in *Punch*, give a good idea of the honorable gentleman's personal appearance. When he rises to speak, he generally manages to say something to the point, and his long and intimate connection with the British government and present position of high trust in the same, has been earned by effectual and severe labor, rather than maintained from party favoritism or political intrigue. He is no idler in the council chambers of the country. I can think of no Ameri-

can Congressman less pretending in his dress and
mien, and more free from aristocratic " airs " than
this celebrated statesman.

After Lord John, Sir James Grahan and other
prominent members spoke, but with no especial interest. The main discussion was upon a bill concerning
the interests of the Irish tenantry. Mr. Napier, one
of the Irish members, made a long and powerful defence of his position, which had been assailed by
other members. The arguments were highly personal,
and in an American assembly, would, I fear, have
led to serious results. The speakers were, none of
them, very eloquent. The members all sat with their
hats on, jerking them off, however, when rising to
speak. The Lord Chancellor sat upon the wool-sack,
appropriately wigged, and several of his attendants
wore wigs. The Sergeant-at-arms sat on a high seat
near the door, and wore a long cue, and had a sword
dangling by his side. From my seat in the visiter's
gallery, on the ground floor, I had an admirable
view of the whole hall. The members are, many of
them, young men, and their indifference to the proceedings, the running in and out, and the side-talk,
reminded me of other legislative bodies of which I
have some knowledge. Whenever a speaker would
say anything thought to be very good, the cries of
" Hear! hear!" became so numerous and loud as

to echo throughout the building. The sessions commence in the afternoon, and generally terminate at
two o'clock in the morning. The reporters have a
large gallery to themselves, just over the seat of the
Lord Chancellor. They work very hard, and are
completely exhausted at the close of the season. Their
wages are liberal, and they are mainly men of eminent attainments.

The members of the House of Commons, though
generally shrewd and able men, are by no means all
from the highest ranks of society. Many instances
have been brought to notice in which, from circumstances the most unfavorable, men have won high
parliamentary honors—and from all I can learn, it is
about as easy for one who has perseverance, political
sagacity, and a long purse, to secure a seat in the
Commons, as in America to obtain an election to Con-
gress. Marvellous stories are told, however, of the
costs in hotly-contested districts, and bribery and
corruption that would shame even New York, are, if
report be correct, sometimes resorted to, to secure
success.

There is however on the whole a healthy political
atmosphere, and few of the restraints to advancement
which I had expected to find. George the Third
frequently uttered the liberal axiom, "No British
subject is by necessity excluded from the peerage."

Consistently with this sentiment, he once checked a man of high rank who was lamenting that a very good speaker in the Court of Aldermen was of a mean trade. "What signifies a man's trade?" said the old monarch, "a man of any honest trade may make himself respectable if he will." And in the House of Lords, to which I was conducted from the Commons Chamber, there is pleasing proof of the truthfulness of the King's assurance. Several of the more prominent and influential peers of the realm sprang from untitled families, and hold their seats by virtue of their Sovereign's appreciation of honest worth and ability.

CHURCHES AND CHAPELS.

AFTER Westminster Abbey and St. Paul's, there are perhaps an hundred church buildings in London, each worthy a chapter of careful description—and I have notes of much of interest that I have found within the walls of those I have been able to visit, but must not attempt to incorporate them in this letter. Not a few of the older buildings have been remodelled, or "beautified," as it is here expressed, and often but little to their improvement. There is now a project on foot to take down several dozen of the structures in the city proper, inasmuch as the residents have, (like those of New York) gone further up-town ; but the old settlers, some of whom still cling to their old homes, protest, and it is likely nothing will be done yet awhile. The congregations in attendance at many of these city churches are very small, and not sufficient to warrant their support—but on the other hand the architectural richness of the buildings is too

(68)

great to be ruthlessly blotted out. Happily there is less vandalism here than in many American cities.

The chapels of the dissenters are every year becoming more elegant, and will soon be without the severe simplicity in their exterior and interior finish which has hitherto so much distinguished them from the churches. The difference will be rather in name than architecture, upholstery, or cost. There are many very wealthy dissenting congregations and there are few if any governmental obstacles to the rapid augmentation of chapels.

The pulpit orators of London, both among the Churchmen and Nonconformists, are in the main faithful, learned and eloquent men. I have been pleased with their manner of preaching. It is generally free from the rhetorical display so prevalent in America, and far better calculated to win souls.

On my first Sabbath here I started forth without any fixed determination as to what church or chapel I should attend—and strangely enough chanced to enter what proved to be St. Mary-le-Bow, Cheapside, which, next to St. Paul's, is better known in civic story, than any other church in London. It takes its name of Bow from having been one of the first built in England upon bows or arches. A romantic incident connected with this church is known to all the youth of England. The bells of Bow were those that

rung the prophecy in the ears of Richard Whittington
when he sat down disconsolate upon the milestone at
Highgate, the world and all its troubles before him,
and knew not where to go.

> " Turn again, Whittington,
> Lord Mayor of London !"

said the bells ; and he did turn, as all the little boys
and girls in Great Britain devoutly believe, and became indeed that high dignitary. The same bells, or
their worthy successors, still ring melodiously from
Bow steeple, and persons born within their sound are
as ever denominated " Cockneys," and made the butt
of much good-natured ridicule.

Rev. Mr. Vine, the rector of St. Mary-le-Bow, gave
an impressive discourse, and the singing by the charity children, whose prim gowns and bonnets enlivened
the galleries, added to the interest of the service. It
was difficult to tell the extent of the audience from
the extraordinary high backs to the pews—indeed
they completely shut the worshippers from each other's view.

In the evening I wound my way to John street
Chapel, to listen to the celebrated Hon. and Rev.
Baptist W. Noel, formerly of the Established Church,
and at one time Chaplain to the Queen—but who,
some two years since, joined the Baptists, and is now
considered one of the first dissenting ministers in

London. The John street Chapel is very plain, but the honest, intelligent look of the large and attentive audience assured me I had fallen in good company. The church numbers some six hundred members, and the Sunday schools are very large. There is nothing remarkable in Mr. Noel's style of preaching. He has a sweetly persuasive voice, and his *forte* seems to be calmness and kindness rather than novelty or boldness —and there is a delightful simplicity and sincerity in every word that falls from his ready lips. Those most hostile to his separation from the Establishment, where his name and talent would certainly have insured him great influence and honor, never for a moment question the conscientious integrity with which he entered his new ecclesiastical relations, and made a change involving a sacrifice of which an American can scarce form an adequate idea.

The Rev. Dr. Cumming, of the Scotch chapel near the Drury Lane Theatre, is very popular with the masses. He is a smooth, deep preacher. There is nothing startling in his manner, but much to delight. His chapel, rather an awkward building, is always full, and generally crowded to excess. Strangers happening in London over the Sabbath, make it a point to attend, and consequently the galleries contain mixed and strange audiences. I have been to hear the Doctor twice, and could secure a seat on neither occasion.

Dr. Cumming enjoys a high reputation as an author. His " Voices of the Day," " Voices of the Night," and " Apocalyptic Sketches," have had a wide sale, and withal he may be said to occupy the front rank in popularity among the metropolitan clergy. He is rather a comely man, with heavy bushy hair, and large, black whiskers, and is yet young in years, and apparently fitted for a long and energetic career.*

The Rev. William Brock is one of the ablest Baptist ministers in London. His chapel is on Bloomsbury-street, near Oxford-street—a very spacious and neat edifice. Mr. Brock is a regular John Bull in appearance and action. His sentiments are ejected with a sturdy emphasis, and one can but realize the preacher's devotion to his holy calling. He is a man of great talent, and enjoys the esteem of all denominations. Though differing in every respect from the Hon. and Rev. B. W. Noel, he has a reputation equally high; and together, these eminent divines

* Soon after Dr. Cumming was licensed to preach, he went to London, poor and unknown, taking with him a letter of introduction to a baker, whom he asked what he could do for him. The baker replied that they had a small church, but could not pay a minister ; but if he would stay a month with them he would board him. The young preacher assented, and said if they would give him the pew rents he would always be satisfied. " Why," said the baker, " they will not find salt for thy porridge." The bargain still remains, and it is said the popular preacher now receives £6,000, per annum.

give the Baptists a prominence and good standing in the metropolis, which they fail to have in many other portions of the kingdom.

The Rev. James Hamilton, D. D., F. L. S., the talented author of the "Royal Preacher," "Life in Earnest," and other justly popular religious works, is yet a young man. His preaching is of that plain and earnest style which at once impresses the hearer with its truthfulness. Dr. Hamilton holds a high position He is a Scotchman, and most of his church-members are from the "Land o' cakes." I had the pleasure of breakfasting with him a few days since, and found him as amiable in the domestic circle as in the pulpit.

The Rev. Thomas Binney is the "main stay" of the Congregationalists of London. He is a noble-looking man, and a forcible and popular preacher. I have met him on several occasions.

Having heard that Dr. McNeile was to preach in London, and having lost an opportunity of hearing him while at Liverpool, I was in attendance at the Rev. Mr. Nolan's Chapel, St. Johns, Bedford Row, where it had been announced that the eloquent preacher would appear. Long before the time of commencing, the sidewalk was thronged with persons anxious to get a hearing.

Rev. Hugh McNeile, D. D., of Liverpool, has long maintained an exalted reputation as a preacher of the

4

Gospel. He is about sixty years of age, some six feet in height, not very stout, and has as fine a head of silvered hair as you may meet in a day's walk. His voice is peculiarly fitted for attracting the attention—neither harsh nor faint, but melodious and most agreeably distinct. Standing in the pulpit, enrobed in the clerical gown of the Church of England, he presents at once a dignified and graceful appearance. He had no notes, but held a small Bible in his hand. Taking for his text the words recorded in the twelfth chapter and second verse of Hebrews, he discoursed for nearly an hour in a thoroughly practical and highly eloquent vein. His allusions to the war between England and Russia, and other exciting topics of the day, satisfied me that unlike many modern preachers, he sought to deal with his hearers as rational creatures, rather than as persons of fancy and fine spun theory. The large chapel was crowded to excess, every aisle and nook filled with eager listeners. Aged women officiated as sextons or pew-openers. The singing charmed me : "Old Hundred," sung with a will by the vast assembly, sounded more beautiful to my ears than the choicest opera ditty Maretzek ever imported.

Once or twice I have dropped in to listen to the "Golden Lectures," founded by a fund left many years since, and now delivered in St. Margaret's

Church, opposite the Bank of England, on successive Tuesday mornings, by the Rev. Henry Melville. These admirable discourses are listened to by hundreds of the principal citizens and merchants of London, and it would be difficult to speak too highly of their practical value.

Sheridan Knowles, once a popular actor and long noted as a dramatic writer of much ability, having lately entered the ministry (of the Baptist Church) I, with no little curiosity, embraced an opportunity to hear him in his new character and calling. His sermon or more properly lecture, given in one of the Islington chapels, was alike eloquent and powerful; and the rare talents so long directed merely to the entertainment of his fellows, are now fully consecrated to a higher and nobler end, that of their eternal well-being.

The City Road Chapel remains very much as in the days of the Wesleys, and is one of the modest lions of London. It is still in regular use, and is the home of a flourishing and influential congregation of that ever extending sect, for the etablishment of which the intrepid brothers learned :

"How sublime a thing it is
To suffer and be strong "

On the right of the chancel are plain tablets to the memory of John Wesley, Adam Clarke, Thomas

Coke, and Richard Watson, and on the left, are those
of Charles Wesley, John Fletcher and Joseph Ben-
son. In the yard just back of the chapel, and very
nearly in a line with the pulpit, is the grave of John
Wesley, around which thosuands of pilgrims from
all lands gather every year, to drop a silent tear in
memory of the great and good apostle. It has been
well said by a recent English writer: "The moral
state of that man is not to be desired who can enter
within the gates on the right of City Road Chapel,
and tread the narrow path which leads to the obelisk
tomb of the founder of Methodism, without solemn
thoughts and reflections, or throbs of deep emotion."
Close beside Wesley's honored grave, repose the remains of Dr. Adam Clarke, the wise and popular
commentator. Immediately opposite the City Road
Chapel is the small cemetery called "Bunhill Fields."
After the showy and costly sculptures of the Abbey
and St. Paul's, with their fulsome and oft unmerited
inscriptions, the plain grey gravestones here com-
pactly crowding one another, offer comparatively
little to attract the casual observer, but to him who
patiently treads its winding walks, and honors the
world's true heroes, "Bunhill Fields" discovers a
rare interest. Here is the tomb of that sweet singer,
Dr. Isaac Watts, whose beautiful songs range from
those taught us in our nursery days, and never forgot-

en, to the sublimest of our church hymns—and here also is the grave of Dr. Rippon, another eminent Christian psalmist. The chief attraction, however, amid the thousand monuments, is the unpretending slab, on which is written :

"MR. JOHN BUNYAN,
AUTHOR OF THE ' PILGRIM'S PROGRESS,'
Died August 31, 1688,
AGED 60."

From my earliest recollection, Bunyan and his immortal " Pilgrim's Progress " have occupied no small space in my affections, and to stand in the presence as it were, of the ashes of the "marvellous dreamer," was quite enough to stir the liveliest emotions of my nature. What writer has exerted a wider and happier influence than honest John Bunyan? What book has been so universally read and re-read, as his wonderful allegory ? Next to the Bible, and no book could more properly follow the divine word, it is every where cherished and admired. Even the poor Feejees (or Fijians) are soon to have it translated in their native tongue, and it will to them, as to the better civilized, prove a volume of the purest and most captivating interest. I wish I might enumerate the editions that have been printed in English alone. Every publisher has striven to give it a richer dress, every succeeding age claims for

it a higher value, and now, though the bust of the
Elstow tinker, who living had no friend at an earthly
court, has an honored place in the gallery of sculpture in the House of Commons, he lives far more
imperishably in the hearts of the brave and good of
every land. As, on the occasion of my visit to the
cemetery, several pretty children were lightly tripping through the narrow pathways, stopping here
and there to decipher the well worn inscriptions on
the moss-grown stones, and finally to silently gaze
upon the tomb of the stern old pilgrim, I was reminded of the never ceasing charm of his glorious
dream to the youthful mind, and its many lessons for
the young. Who may more appropriately linger in
" Bunhill Fields" than the children ?   Only the other
day, I was told of a sweet little boy, who, after reading the " Pilgrim's Progress," said to his grand-
mother : " Grandma, which of the characters do you
like best?" She replied, " Christian, of course, he is
the hero of the story." He responded, " I like
Christiana best, because when Christian set out on
his pilgrimage he went alone ; but when Christiana
started out she took the children with her." I wish
the little fellow was here that his tiny hands might
scatter flowers over the quiet grave of him who
counselled Christiana to take her four boys with her
to the celestial city !

WHEN I stood before the statue of Howard, in St. Paul's, I was reminded of his admirable prescription for shaking off trouble: "Set about doing good to somebody; put on your hat, and go and visit the poor, inquire into their wants, and administer unto them; seek out the desolate and oppressed, and tell them of the consolations of religion."

' I have often tried this," said the great philanthropist, "and found it the best medicine for a heavy heart," and many in all lands have fortunately had the same experience. Here even in this wilderness of trade and worldly gain, there are not a few who find their chief joy in doing good to their fellows, in feeding the hungry, clothing the naked, educating the ignorant, watching with the sick, and smoothing the pillow of the dying.

The English have good reason to think highly of their numerous and well directed charitable institutions and societies, especially those of a directly religious character. All classes of the well to do people, from the peer of the realm down, apparently have an intensely practical method of doing good, and few if any of their benevolent organizations fail to accomplish tangible and important results. Of late years a happy sympathy for the long neglected poor, and obdurate, so numerously existing in all the larger cities, has developed itself in many judicious and eminently praiseworthy efforts for their temporal and spiritual relief. Indeed it is necessary to look carefully to the former to insure success in the latter. "I have invariably found," says a keen observer of society, "that advice to a poor man goes best with a glass of beer, and *the beer first.*" The English philanthropists of the present day fortunately recognise the indisputable accuracy of this quaint observation and accordingly they now to a great degree feed, and clothe, and house the homeless and degraded before attempting to train them, in the things pertaining to morality and religion. I pass by the older and more pretentious charities, numerous and estimable as they are, to speak a word of the Ragged Schools now so generally and efficiently established in all the more destitute districts of London. What prodigious progress has been made in the provision for the children of the streets, since the days of John Pounds and

Jonas Hanway, the worthy founders of the Ragged School.

No organization of all the well managed philan-throphic enterprises of the day is more efficient than the " Ragged School Union." At its head is that sterling noble-man and Christian, the Earl of Shaftes-bury, who amid all the cares and perplexities of exalted public position and popularity,—has been neither too proud nor too busy to listen to the cry of the needy and suffering, nor in any wise to neglect the service of Him whose commands are infinitely above those of kings and princes. It is not in my power to enumerate all the excellent societies in which this truly remarkable and yet always humble man, is interested, and the interests of which he does much to advance. I have been told there is scarcely a day in the year that he does not give more or less time to earnest and often enthusiastic labor in their behalf. He is unquestionably the foremost philan-thropist of his age and country, and there can be no higher compliment than the world wide recognition of the fact.

It has been my privilege to enjoy several interviews with his lordship, and to find him an acute observer of men and things, a sagacious and persevering reformer, and a warm friend of America and the Americans. At the annual meeting of the " Protes-

tant Alliance" of which he is president, I was solicited
to speak for the new world in place of my absent and
venerated friend, Dr. Baird, and shall ever gratefully
remember the exceedingly cordial welcome and
introduction of his lordship.

Lord Shaftesbury is the son-in-law of Lord Palmerston, and was till within a few years past known as
Lord Ashley. His personal appearance is dignified
and noble. A pleasant smile ever glistens upon his
cheek. His voice is smooth and distinct, and though
not distinguished for oratorical perfection, he possesses
the happy faculty of being ready to speak, and to
speak to the point, at the shortest notice; but his
speeches are never protracted or tedious. In the
House of Lords his course has always been straight
forward, and fearless. While less brilliant in debate
than many of his associates, his amiable and sincere
disposition, his consistent and constant opposition to
the wrong, and his general good sense, have combined to secure him great influence and esteem. In
his religious views he is apparently above sectarian
prejudice, and mingles as freely with, and is as greatly esteemed by the dissenters, as the Churchmen. No
public man was ever more widely beloved, or more
worthily.

The Ragged School Union now embraces upwards
of an hundred efficient schools in operation in Lon-

don alone. Of these,* I have visited a large number, but shall refer to only one or two, and indeed they are characteristic of the whole. Perhaps the most prominent, certainly the most successful, is that in Field Lane, a by-street near Holborn-Hill, and a short walk from St. Paul's. This school has attached to it, as several other schools now have, a night refuge for the utterly destitute—a place where any poor outcast, old or young, black or white, may secure a night's lodging free of all expense, and to this important department I will first refer. For a long period it was a source of the deepest and most painful regret, that after dismissal from reading the Bible at Field Lane, many of the scholars—boys, youths, men— were turned back into the streets to sleep in dry arches, sheds, on door-steps, or wander shelterless about, a prey to hunger and uncurbed desperation. The knowledge also that a vast number of persons were daily released from the metropolitan prisons, who had expiated the violated laws of the country by limited imprisonment, for whom no provision was made—outcasts without character and without hope of finding food or shelter, except by the commission of some offence, through which they might be taken

* The total sum raised by the various Schools and Refuges in the year 1858 exceeded £28,000, and the whole income of the Union gives the sum of £33,240 raised for Ragged Schools during the year.

back to their prison home—induced the committee to cause these and similar facts to be brought under the notice of the Earl of Shaftesbury, when his lordship at once, through the munificence of a benevolent lady, caused the Refuge for the Destitute to be opened in May, 1851, and to be enlarged at the close of the same year, The Refuge can now sleep 100 hundred persons nightly—each person having a separate berth and warm rug: an excellent lavatory, together with hot and cold baths. A 6-oz loaf of bread is given to each inmate night and morning. A Christian master takes the superintendence, who does not leave his post after the inmates assemble, till their dismissal. The scriptures are read night and morning, to the practice of which very great importance is attached, it being believed that the word of God has a salutary influence upon the human soul, stifling the bad passions of men, awakening the recollection of that presence, under whose eye we live, amidst the struggles and casualties of chequered existence.

This Refuge has become a moral filtering machine for all the different Refuges of London, and receives many whom ALL the others reject. Regarded physically or morally, its introduction has proved a great blessing to a large class of miserable outcasts, who have far too long been neglected. The warmest expectations as to its utility have been abundantly realized.

It has proved a comfort and a real refuge to thousands who have sought its shelter. It is systematically opposed to vagrancy. Indoctrinated by the word of God, all the inmates are carefully taught to rely upon the faculties with which they have been endowed by a merciful Creator as responsible agents for their proper use. While sheltered from cold and exposure, no luxury is provided for the night beyond a boarded berth and a rug. A small loaf and water are not strong inducements to deter the idle from work. The periodical reading of the Bible, the regularity of prayer, the washing night and morning, the baths, the cleansing of the Refuge by the inmates, the strict discipline enforced, the necessity of attending the Bible and Secular Classes in order to keep their ticket—these things are not attractions for the lazy and the vagabond! but placed before the mind under the affectionate interest of the teachers of the Bible Classes, they are duly appreciated, and without this Christian influence the Refuge would have been a failure. In the majority of instances the Refuge has been a great boon in sheltering, rescuing, and assisting many really destitute fellow-creatures; it has been the means of distributing imperishable lessons of hope to hundreds, whose degradation had reduced them to despair.*

* At an Industrial Exhibition of the London Reformatory Institutions, held in June, 1856, the following were given as a few of the practical results of

A few extracts from the diary, most carefully kept by the Refuge Master, in which the history of the inmates is daguerreotyped, will serve to show that, in real life, "fact is much stranger than fiction :"—

"W. W., aged 28, whose father was a soldier, was brought up at the Duke of York's School. After he left it, he lived at a grocer's, a butcher's, and lastly at a cheesemonger's as porter. In this situation he amassed £15. Having this sum by him, he became proud and independent, and if told to do a job which did not suit him, he refused, and his employer discharged him in consequence. Reduced to extremities, he sought lodgings in Unions, etc. About four years ago two women were executed at Chelmsford, when he and a friend purchased a quantity of papers, purporting to contain their last dying speech and confession, which had been printed several days before. He then lived by the precarious trade of the mendicant. After being imprisoned at Kingston for begging, he was placed in the stocks in a village in Surrey for the same offence. On one occasion while in Winchester, being rendered desperate by cold and hunger, he with a companion entered a baker's shop and asked for a half-quartern loaf. He broke the loaf in two, giving half to his friend. The mistress said, ' You have not paid me.' To which he replied, ' We cannot.' A policeman was sent for, who said, ' Why did you take it?' ' Because we were hungry,' was the answer. ' But why did you not take a smaller one?' ' Because it would not fill us,' he replied. They were then marched out of the town. On reaching Salisbury, they determined to get into prison, and with that view each of them broke a lamp. As no one saw them do it, they gave information against themselves."

W. is now chief monitor ; and during the absence of the Refuge Master for two weeks, he, with two others, had charge of the Refuge, and effectually pre-served discipline during that period.

the Field Lane Refuge, from its opening to that date : " Strangers admitted since May, 1851, 5,261 ; admitted into the Refuge by ticket, 126,575 (average 71 per night since the opening) ; obtained imployment, 551 ; restored to friends, 117, emigrated, 14 ; enlisted, 46 ; admitted into permanent Reformatories, 256. Distributed 344,267 6-oz. loaves of bread.

The following is an amusing instance of perseverance :—

"E. W., aged 18. He went to the Union to get a night's lodging. He was refused admittance by the porter. Upon this he began knocking with all his might, using both knockers at the same time. The porter secured these, when he searched till he found a bell-handle, and made a tremendous ringing. The porter put an end to this nuisance by stuffing something into the bell. But as W. was not to be daunted, he took a large stone in each hand, with which he hammered so loud that the porter surrendered at discretion, saying, ' Come in, for I see you will let me have no peace all night.' "

Many grateful letters are yearly received from those who have enjoyed the benefits of the institution. Recently one came from a young man who had emigrated to New-York, in which he gives a graphic picture of the Five Points, the Field Lane of the American London. The Committee often encourage Emigration as being more likely to result in the future well being of the youths, especially where a career of crime has been embraced, and bad companions are known to watch for any tendency to relapse, the only possible safety consists in emigration. I may here remark that a peculiar characteristic of the Refuge is, that it provides a home for the outcast after he leaves its immediate privileges, and provides shelter, food, and education, industrial and religious, for several years, until a great process has been completed.

The day schools, the secular and religious evening

classes for both youths and adults, the industrial classes, the Bible Schools, and the Woman's Bible class, all work admirably under the patient and wise supervision of the honorary superintendent, Mr. Robert Mountstephen, and the honorary secretary, Mr. Samuel Tawell, to both of whom I am under many obligations for much courteous attention on all my visits to Field Lane. In the day schools, boys, girls, and infants are trained by experienced teachers, and as they are expressly intended for the children of destitute or profligate parents every precaution is taken to exclude others. By means of an active school missionary who is constantly on the alert, the superintendent is enabled to know the temporal condition of every applicant for admission. Hence it is that the offspring of scavengers, costermongers, sweeps, match-sellers, street minstrels and others whose callings none but the police could adequately describe, form the staple of the school. The number on the books is about 300 with an average attendance of 180. The classes for youths and adults on Monday and Thursday evenings, are devoted to the secular instruction of the inmates of the Refuge, and other lads and men, who are employed during the day. The average attendance is nearly an hundred. Of the industrial classes, the tailoring and shoe-making masters report the average attendance is about 65 boys and men.

A new feature of the institution is the "Ragged Church," established in the hope of securing the preaching of the gospel to many who would otherwise never be brought under its influence.

During the past year the service held on Lord's day morning, has been conducted with undiminished success. The average attendance for the first quarter of this year reached 341. On several occasions upwards of 400 persons have been present. At least one-half of the congregation consists of females; not a few of these are aged women; most of them are mothers; and the lives of too many supply painful evidence that sin is often judged by God even in this world.

Again it is pleasing to find that though the congregation continually changes, yet that upwards of one-third are regular attendants. This renewal in the elements of the congregation renders the service peculiarly solemn. It cannot be doubted that nearly 10,000 souls heard the Gospel proclaimed in this Ragged Church during the past year.

As a whole the Field Lane Ragged School with its many adjuncts is at once a remarkable and eminently useful institution. Little wonder that Lord Shaftesbury or any other enlightened statesman is ready to detect in its salutary influences much of hope for the uplifting of the illiterate and virtueless the bane of the metropolis. Little wonder that the press is ready to acknowledge their efficiency in reliev- ing the police and magistrates of much of their labor, and materially lessening the demoralization hitherto characterizing such neighborhoods as Field Lane.*

The average annual outlay for the carrying on of the Field Lane School is about £1,000, most of which is raised by donations and special appeals. The Teachers are ardently interested in their work and win many friends to it by their untiring zeal. I have attended several of their meetings and always to enjoy them. During the reading of the reports and discussions the ladies employ themselves in knitting, sewing or otherwise working for the benefit of the

---

* The *London Times* recently devoted a leader to this valuable institution. It appears that during the year (1859) 30,302 lodgings have been supplied to 6,786 men and boys, who have received 101,193 either six or eight ounce loaves of bread. At the same time 840 women have been admitted during the year, to whom have been supplied 10,028 lodgings, averaging eleven nights' shelter to each person, by whom 14,755 loaves have been consumed. The applicants in the winter months are admitted at five o'clock p.m., and in the summer months at seven o'clock. They obtain shelter for the night, a piece of bread, and a cup of coffee upon admission ; in the morning only bread and water. On the whole, 10,000 persons annually participate in the advantages of this Institution, and 1,222 of the most folorn and wretched creatures in London were last year taken from the streets and placed in a position where they might earn their own bread, and all this at the cost of 3s. 6d. per head per annum. Out of upwards of 7,000*l.* received in consequence of the *Times* appeal last year, the Committee have funded 5,500*l.* for the permanent relief of the homeless.

more destitute children, and each meeting is enlivened by the passing of tea and well spread bread. There is a sympathy and fellowship among all interested in the enterprise which does much to insure its success.

I have thus far omitted to speak of the appearance of the lads and adults attending the institution, for it is not confined to persons of any age. Those who are only present on Sunday are less forlorn in their appearance than those who frequent the night refuge. These latter are often indescribably wretched, indeed in some of the vacant faces it is hard to trace the lineaments of humanity. So near an approach to the brute creation is scarcely to be found among the lowest and vilest population of America. With a depraved and debauched ancestry for many generations, these unfortunate creatures have all the rudeness and ignorance of the savage, with far more of downright stupidity and inertia. Many of them appear to have received their first washing and combing in the lavatories of the refuge. And it is only by the severest discipline that when they first enter they are kept decently clean and in any approach to order. It requires a deal of patience and godliness to treat with such degraded objects, and yet they above all others demand our sympathy and care. It is matter for congratulation that already the agency of the London Ragged Schools and Refuges has accomplished so much for this large and literally abject class,* and undoubtedly much more may be accomplished for their improvement if the Committees, Superintendents, and teachers, continue to labor with the same self-denial and earnestness. Upon this latter characteristic of the teacher much depends. As Lord Shaftesbury has well observed : " He must have great zeal, very great zeal ; his heart must be in the work. The work must be his meat and drink, it must be almost his life's blood ; if he be not so, depend upon it he never does as he ought with the children."

In the various schools under the auspices of the Union, about two thousand voluntary teachers† give themselves to a most difficult task, which—in the outset at least, dealing with the wildest of both sexes— implies and involves great self-denial and moral courage.

Prizes are annually awarded to boys or girls over twelve and under seventeen years of age, who having been six months in a Ragged School, have since been

---

* At a recent annual meeting of one of the Refuges, Lord Shaftesbury said :

" Refuges and Ragged-schools had done more to humanize and civilize the people than any Institution that ever was invented, and if they persevered in developing their operations, he believed that in five years they would be the means of doing away with every vestige of vagrancy that demoralized and disgraced the metropolis at the present time."

† Now (1860) nearly three thousand.

in situations for twelve months with satisfaction to their employers. It is a proof of the value of this movement to note that the recipients of such prizes increase in number each year. In 1853, they were 144; in 1854, they were 327; in 1855, 366.*

Besides the Ragged and industrial Schools proper, there are various excellent institutions existing in all parts of London, for the bettering of the youth. Many of them are wholly supported by private munificence, and often by the members of a single wealthy family. An example worthy the emulation of the well-meaning millionaires of New York, many of whom if we may judge from their misplaced benevolence, have yet to learn,

"The use of riches in discretion lies."

One of these London charities, a model in its way, was lately established chiefly through the instrumentality of Messrs. Truman, Hanbury & Co., the eminent brewers of Spitalfields. This institution, located in Commercial Street, Whitechapel, in a neighborhood principally occupied by thieves and vagrants, is called "The Boys' Refuge," and is intended for the *prevention* of crime. The boys admitted are either *friendless orphans*, or the children of parents so depraved as to make it absolutely essential that they

* In 1859, they were 578.

should be removed from them. The mere fact of a boy having been convicted does not necessarily exclude him, for it is felt that many may have been led into crime, either from sheer starvation or from the baneful influence of bad example ; but *conviction* is not, as in other institutions, a *sine qua non*. On the contrary the fact of a boy having been in prison is a reason for investigating his history, in order to discover whether or not he has voluntarily adopted criminal courses and become thoroughly depraved ; in which case he is not admitted, other institutions providing for such cases. A few examples will serve to show the nature of the classes from amongst whom the boys already admitted have been taken. The narratives have in some instances been taken from their own lips ; in others they have been furnished by City Missionaries.

" S. G., aged 14, a native of Oxfordshire ; an orphan. Both his parents died about two years and a half ago, when he and his little brother were left entirely destitute. After trying unsuccessfully to get work in their native town, they walked up to London. On arriving there they lost each other, and never met again. S. has lived in the streets for upwards of two years, subsisting by begging, getting occasional employment at the markets, &c., sleeping in passages or wherever he could find shelter. He was often tempted to steal, ' but never had pluck enough to do it.' S. G. says his father was a drunkard ; but his mother was a good woman, very kind to him, and *who used to pray with him and his brother every evening before going to bed*. He wept bitterly when speaking of her and of his lost brother. So great had been his sufferings, that almost immediately on his being admitted into the 'Refuge' he was seized with fever and had to be removed to St. Thomas' Hospital, where he speedily gained the good opinion of the officials by his patience and good conduct."

J. W., aged 12 years ; father and mother both alive, and subsisting by begging. They are both drunkards, and grossly immoral. His two sisters, at the
almost incredibly early ages of 14 and 17, are living in sin. A Missionary,
who knew the family for several years, thus describes their present dwelling :—
' They were in a damp underground kitchen, to which I had to grope my way
in the dark ; and as there was a grating over the window, with articles of sale
put upon it for exposure, the light was so excluded that on first entering it
was impossible to discover the state of the room. There were in the room two
old broken chairs, a few broken plates, and some filthy rags in a corner on
which was lying a dog, but on which a dog of mine should not sleep ; and I
believe this constituted the whole of their household furniture. In this miserable den, however,' says the missionary, ' I was frequently assured that, after
nine o'clock in the evening, the family was usually feasting, not only upon
the best necessary food, but also upon positive luxuries.' No share of these
luxuries, however, fell to poor J.'s lot. He was left entirely to his own
resources, and was often reduced to starvation."

" W. B., aged 14 ; an orphan. His mother died when he was a child ; and
his father, who was very kind and used to take him to church regularly, married again. Stepmother married again after his father's death, and she and her
second husband both became drunkards. They used W. very harshly, and
ultimately deserted him. For about a month he slept under butchers' blocks ;
was taken into the employment of a Merry Andrew, but was dismissed because
he could not bend his back ; fell into the hands of a band of strolling gipsies
with whom he wandered about for nearly three months ; found his way into
Field Lane Refuge, and earned his living by holding horses, &c."

" W. G., aged 13. Mother dead, and father a drunkard. In consequence o
ill treatment, he left his father and earned his living in the streets ; sleeping
where he could find shelter. Slept for about six weeks in some wagons in
Shoreditch. About two years ago he was found guilty of stealing some horse-
hair, and imprisoned."

These extracts will sufficiently show that the class
of boys who are received into the Refuge are exposed
to influences of such a character that they cannot fail
to become criminal unless rescued from them ; and
the intention of the Institution is to afford an opportu-

nity of rising above their degraded condition to such as really have a desire to do so. In order to test the sincerity of applicants, and prevent depraved and corrupted boys from becoming inmates, those who apply are subjected to a probation. They are sent at first to a Dormitory in Colchester Street, established by the Rev. Mr. Champneys, Rector of Whitechapel, where they have to sleep on the boards. They come to the "Boys' Refuge" during the day, and while on probation are employed in scrubbing, chopping wood, or other household work. They are allowed breakfast and supper; but if they work steadily, they have dinner also, and are made to understand that the period of their probation depends entirely on their own conduct. This simple method is found to answer the purpose. The boys who are willing to do well, get through their probation with ease; while the lazy vagrant or criminal, commonly walk off in the course of a few days, of their own accord. So large a proportion as one-fourth of the entire number of applicants have already withdrawn themselves and returned to the streets. And here a question presents itself: Is it right that boys who have had the opportunity of doing well should be allowed thus to ruin themselves and become pests to society? Their doing so is very frequently the result of mere waywardness and impatience of control; and surely the law ought to interfere and compel them for their own good and the good of the country to remain steady.

As soon as a boy is admitted, he is put to a trade; the stouter boys being set to carpentering, while the lesser ones are made tailors or shoemakers. The industrial department has been placed upon a footing of considerable efficiency; none but first-class trades-men being employed, and only a small number of boys are placed under one man; and although the Institution is but of yesterday, already the advantages of the system are beginning to develope themselves. Thanks to the zealous endeavors of the excellent tradesmen who have been appointed, the boys are making such rapid proficiency in their several trades, that at no distant date every one of these branches seems likely to become self-supporting, or even remu-nerative. A part of every day is also devoted to the secular education of the boys; but while due care is taken to impart to them such an amount of knowledge as may fit them for taking their places as useful members of society, the greatest attention is paid to their moral training.

It would be indeed a grievous mistake to cultivate the hand and head, and neglect the heart. Now the true key to the human heart is kindness; but as this can be exercised by women better than by men,

5

female influence has been brought to bear upon the
inmates. While it is the special duty of the Gover-
nor to look after the moral well being of the boys, a
Matron has also been appointed, to assist him, and
to superintend the household affairs of the Institution.
The results have been of a very gratifying character.
The authority and influence of both have thus been
blended together; and through their united efforts
the rugged nature and rough habits of the boys are
gradually being moulded and softened, so that comparatively little difficulty has been experienced in
managing them.

But all this agency would be exerted in vain, and
the boys, although reduced to outward obedience,
might remain callous and indifferent to everything
that is good, without Divine aid. They, therefore,
have been placed under the ministry of the Rev.
Hugh Allen, of St. Jude's, Whitechapel, who kindly
visits the Institution regularly, to give them more
personal instruction; and constant endeavors are made
to impress their minds with a belief in the reality of
divine things.

Such is a brief outline of the character and operations of the "Boys' Refuge." The Institution commenced with two boys, and there are now upwards
of 30. That number have been removed from
wretchedness and degradation, and placed within the

influence of Christian kindness and comparative comfort. *If funds sufficient be obtained, more than four times the number may be received.* I can only imagine one answer to that question. I cannot conceive it possible that the London public, now that their attention has of late years been so fully drawn to the subject of juvenile delinquency and destitution, can allow an Institution like the "Boys' Refuge" to languish for want of support. The political economist, the philanthropist, the Christian, although differing perhaps on other subjects, may all unite in supporting it, for it meets the views of all. It appeals to the political economist, because it effects a saving of public money, *prevention* being cheaper than cure; to the philanthropist, inasmuch as it lessens the amount of human misery; and it appeals most powerfully to the Christian, because its main design is to bring the inmates to that blessed Saviour who said, "Suffer little children to come unto me, and forbid them not." Every consideration demands that we should be up and doing on behalf of our sunken population. Either we must elevate them or descend to their level; for it is impossible that a nation can flourish while vice is festering at the base of the social system. We might as well expect a plant to thrive with a worm at the root.

The Institution is open daily to the inspection of all those who feel an interest in its object.

TIME TABLE.

6 to 8 A. M.	....	Cleaning the Dormitories, &c.
8 " 8½ "	....	Breakfast.
8½ " 9 "	....	Prayer, Scripture Reading, and Singing.
9 " 11 "	....	Secular Instruction, Reading, Writing, &c.
11 " 1 · P. M.	....	Industrial Employment.
1 " 2 "	....	Dinner and Play.
2 " 4 "	....	Industrial Employment.
4 " 4½ "	....	Play.
4½ " 6 "	....	Industrial Employment.
6 " 6½ "	....	Supper.
6½ " 8½ "	....	Secular Instruction, Reading, Writing, &c
8½ " 9 "	....	Evening Worship.

On Sundays the boys attend divine service morning and evening, at St. Jude's Church: during the remainder of the day they receive religious instruction from voluntary teachers.

THE SHOE-BLACKS.

" Clean your honor's shoes ?" was for a long time
prior to the beginning of the present century, a
familiar cry in the streets of London, but about the
year 1820, with the improvement in the side walks
and street pavement, the shoe-blacks reluctantly
retired to private life, thinking undoubtedly that,
like Othello, they had utterly lost their occupation.
The " last of the Mohicans" is said to have been a
negro, who, under the new order of things murmur-
ingly retired to the work-house to end his poorly
requited days.   But with the high-noon of the century
and the Crystal Palace, came many wondrous things,
not the least in the long catalogue, the revival of the
shoe-blacks.   The credit of the restoration to society of
a class of humble artizans so eminently useful, even
in a cleanly city, belongs to my versatile and excellent friend John Macgregor, Esq., of the Temple, who
in his devotion to many of the important charities of

(101)

the metropolis, ranks as a second Shaftesbury, and
enjoys an enviable reputation, as a most intelligent
and untiring public benefactor.

It occurred to Mr. Macgregor, that on the opening
of the Hyde Park palace, (in the summer of 1851,)
London would be thronged with foreigners in attendance at the great exhibition, many of whom were
accustomed in their own countries to have their shoes
cleaned in the streets, (such has long been the practice in continental cities,) and would be pleased to
find such accommodation in London.   And some
London folks might like it, besides many poor boys
might earn an honest penny thereby.   But the project did not meet general favor, and but for Mr.
Macgregor's dauntless perseverance would probably
have been abandoned.   Five boys picked from the
ragged schools, and carefully instructed in the "art
of polishing," were sent out early in April to different
parts of the metropolis.   How the people stared at
the one that first appeared in Trafalgar Square, and
how they crowded around Mr. Macgregor when he
put his foot upon the box to give him a fair start;
but the shoe-blacks that very day obtained a footing
in London.   There were on an average about twenty-
five boys constantly employed during the Exhibition
season, and they cleaned 101,000 pairs of boots and
shoes, for which the public paid them over £500.

Kind nods of approbation were bestowed upon the
industrious and polite shoe-blacks, by all classes of
the people, and many a word of encouragement
spoken to cheer their hearts. Shop-keepers often
took a fancy to them, and gave them dinners. Ladies
feasted them in their houses, and called them to
their carriage windows to give them a sixpence, and
old gentlemen asked them many strange questions,
and told them they would all become Lord Mayors.
Boots and shoes were regularly brought out from
private houses to be cleaned, and sometimes large
establishments employed the boys; in one instance
several hundred pairs of shoes had to be cleaned in a
hurry, and a cab-load of the lads went to do the work.
A great deal of their success came from the knowledge of the good auspices under which they were sent
forth to their humble yet honorable employment, and
from the honest, courteous and industrious habits of
the lads themselves. Once a half-crown was given
by mistake for a penny, the regular fee, but the boy
quickly ran after the gentleman and returned it.
Once a sovereign accidentally slipped into a boy's
hands between two coppers, but the honest little fellow
after searching some hours discovered who had given it
him, and was rewarded for his trouble by a simple
" thank you."

The first company of shoe-blacks wore red-jackets,

and were mainly employed in the city proper, but
the business proved so encouraging that there are
now yellow and blue jacket brigades or societies, and
the well behaved lads are to be found in every quarter
of the metropolis; indeed they now have positions
regularly assigned them by the police authorities, and
are protected from interference by idlers and others
who have heretofore somewhat troubled them. Each
boy bears on his breast, two badges of cloth, on one of
which the words " Ragged School Shoe-Black Society," and on the other, his distinctive letter or number
are worked in white glass beads by the girls of one of
the Refuges. The box on which the foot of the
customer rests while his boot is receiving its polish,
and the mat on which the shoe-black kneels, are made
by the boys of the Grotto Passage Refuge—thus
the outcasts gathered in the refuges are being
taught to make themselves very useful.

I have frequently been in attendance at the office
of the red brigade, York place, Strand, at half after
six o'clock, the hour the lads return from their day's
toil. Each boy marches in with orderly step, deposits
his box, blacking, brushes and mat, puts his uniform
in a bag provided for the purpose, and counts his
receipts in presence of the superintendent. A daily
account is kept with each lad, and the money is
applied upon the following system: sixpence is

returned to the boy as his allowance : the remainder is divided into three equal parts; one third part is paid to the boy immediately, together with the sixpence ; one third part is retained by the Society to meet the salary of the superintendent, and other expenses, and the residuo (including odd money,) is paid to a fund which is reserved as a "bank" for the boy's own benefit.* The weather and the season of the year make a great difference in the receipts of the boys ; warm sunny days, after rain, are the most auspicious for them ; and, in general, fine weather is more profitable than wet. A public holiday always yields large returns. The largest sum yet earned by any boy in one day is about twelve shillings sterling, for which at the established fee of a penny per pair, he must of course have blacked *one hundred and forty four pairs* of boots or shoes—a pretty good day's work. The different stations occupied by the boys were soon found to bear very different values. Originally they were all occupied by all the boys in succession ; but subsequently the stations were divided into three classes. The boys were also classed in three divisions,

* In other words, each boy carries home as his day's wages, eightpence out of the first shilling which he earns, and fourpence out of every other shilling. Of the remainder twopence out of the first shilling, and fourpence out of every other is retained by the society ; and an equal sum, together with any odd pence not divisible by three, is paid unto the boys' bank. Some of the lads have £40 and £50 in bank.

corresponding to the divisions of the stations; and each boy is confined to the stations in his own division, which he occupies in rotation. When a boy enters the society he joins the third division, but he is quickly promoted to a higher rank if his conduct is good. When a boy rises to the second division he pays 2s. 6d. and when advanced to the first 5s. from his bank to the funds of the society. This tax was set on foot with a view to make the societies more self-supporting and is willingly submitted to by the boys, to whom promotion is an object of eager emulation.

The punishments for misconduct usually adopted are :—

1. *Fines** for late hours, absence, or other misbehaviour.

2. *Degradation* from one division to a lower, either permanently or for a limited period.

3. *Suspension* from work for a fixed time.

On the other hand, the rewards consist of prizes in money, medals, and promotions, for those whose monthly earnings are the largest.

Having rendered their accounts, the lads essay to the wash-room, where as may well be presumed, the scouring is long and vigorous ere they come forth suffi-

---

* The money received for fines is reserved as a relief fund for those who are ill.

ciently clean to be admitted to the supper department, where those who have no inviting homes to repair to are wont to refresh themselves. It would be hard to find a more hilarious or apparently happy company of youngsters than gather every evening around the well spread supper tables. Each lad pays for what he has, and with an air of amusing independence. On one or two evenings in the week the whole brigade is detained at the rooms for a series of lessons in reading, singing, etc., interspersed with addresses from the Committee and other friends.

I have on several occasions spoken to the lads, and always remarked their excellent attention. For the bringing up, or want of bringing up most of them have had, their deportment and intelligence is quite surprising. There can be little doubt that the instruction given them at the Ragged Schools from Sabbath to Sabbath, which they are obliged to regularly attend in order to retain their standing in the brigade, is of the happiest character, inculcating not only principles of honor, virtue and integrity, but a taste for general knowledge scarcely to be expected in a class hitherto so degraded and uncared for.

Many amusing incidents are told of the ready wit of the lads. An Irishman paying one of them with rudeness, the urchin drily said—" All the polish you have is on your boots, and I gave it to you." A gen-

tleman asked one of the boys, " How do the Committee know that you bring in all your earnings ?" " Oh
sir," he answered, " they always leave that *to our
honor.*"

The Committees directing the brigades are usually
composed of barristers, merchants and other gentlemen of means, who, while they employ the strictest discipline, devise every ingenious and liberal method to
please and benefit the lads. Out-of-town treats
are given every summer, and entertainments are not
unfrequently provided at the different city institutions. A few days since, Mr. Macgregor invited
me to accompany the " Red-Coats " to the Zoological
Gardens, Regent's Park, where they had been invited
by the Directors. I was glad to embrace the opportunity to see how a parcel of boys, picked up from
the lowest strata of London life, and heretofore entirely unacquainted with the Gardens, would conduct
themselves. The society marched from their rooms at
an early hour in the afternoon. Mr. Macgregor and
myself took a 'buss at a later hour, and found the
youngsters all in ecstasy amid the lions and tigers, the
monkeys and the orang-outangs. The behaviour of
the lads throughout was highly creditable, and the
interest manifested by many of them in the peculiarities of the animals, would have done honor to
more refined minds.

The distinguished hippopotamus, over which Mr. *Punch* has made so much sport, would not condescend to come out of his bath, notwithstanding the reiterated invitations of the keeper and swarms of visitors. The old fellow, who has grown to a gigantic size, would adroitly swim about, with his mouth just far enough above the water to catch every particle of biscuit or cake that might be thrown him. One of the shoe-blacks was put near, in hope that his red shirt might induce old hippo to come out; but it was in vain : he would not be persuaded.

The collection of animals of the deer species at the gardens is most superb. Specimens of almost every known variety of the light and graceful race may be found. The rhinoceros, the giraffes, the bears, are all of the choicest kind. The monkeys have a large mansion to themselves, and a curious crew they are. The room is kept warm, and as comfortable as a parlor. The birds and water-fowl are magnificent; the reptiles all that reptiles could be.

At four o'clock the lions were to be fed. For an hour before that time, every available spot near the lion cages was occupied by hundreds of men, women and children, waiting for the "feeding." The proprietors of the Gardens have actually erected a marble platform immediately opposite the dens, from which the "very best view" can be had. Anxious

to have a sight at the four-legged beef-eaters, I
wedged my way in at the appointed time. The
keeper soon made his appearance with a huge stick;
an assistant carried a tub of joints. For some cause or
other, the brutes did not appear so savage as usual, and
loud and long were the lamentations of the lookers
on, at the lack of growls, yells, and all those vocifer-
ations which lions are wont to indulge in when hungry and put into possession of liberal chunks of un-
cooked beef. I could hardly sympathize with those
who were so anxious to see the brutes display their
rudeness.

The shoe-blacks were permitted to take a ride on
the elephant, to their great delight. Their dashing
shirts gave them an odd appearance, as, mounted upon
the huge fellow, they rode through the shaded paths
of the gardens, and their visit was in every respect
eminently satisfactory.

" Once a shoe-black always a shoe-black," is by no
means the motto of the Committees. They desire
to make the occupation a stepping-stone to some
higher and permanent employ, and so soon as the
lads give evidence of established good habits, they
use their best endeavors to obtain positions for them,
in such trades or professions as they may desire.
Many of the lads go to the country, and many emi-
grate to America and Australia. The outfit of one

enterprising little fellow was lately provided at the expense of Charles Dickens, who has a practical sympathy with every movement for uplifting the lower classes ; but in most cases the boys have defrayed the whole, or the greater part of their outfit from their own earnings.

"Many a widowed mother," says Mr. Macgregor, "has been supported by her son, and the childish tears of a little sister wiped away by her brother's blacking brush." Taken in all their aspects, I consider the shoe-black societies among the most interesting and praiseworthy, reformatory and industrial organizations I have ever known,* and sincerely hope

* There are at present (1859), ten shoe-black societies for the employment of scholars from the Ragged Schools, in London, and its vicinity, based upon the same principles, and governed in the main, by the same rules as the original Society. All these societies comprising over 300 lads, met at a Winter treat at St. Martin's Hall, in February last, and had a grand time. A London paper says :

"They occupied the centre of the hall, and their varied uniforms, together with the flags and other insignia of the respective Institutions, formed a most picturesque and interesting scene. There was a large assemblage of noblemen, clergymen, and gentlemen, who had evidently come not only as witnesses, but with a view to welcome and encourage the boys.

"The arrival of the Earl of Shaftesbury was the signal for tremendous applause by the boys, and their cheering was renewed on several other occasions. The bringing in of the plum-cake, after they had partaken of the more ordinary accompaniments of tea, was one of the things which appeared to give them special pleasure. The instrumental band of the Yellow (South London) Brigade rendered essential service to the musical entertainments of the evening."

Lord Shaftesbury, who presided, congratulated the lads in a stirring address and those who had received medals during the year were presented to him, and

their success will lead all Americans visiting London
to rightly appreciate and generously patronise the
deserving lads who nobly prefer to gain an honest

received each a cordial shake of the hand, and an interesting book. A feature
of the evening was the singing by the lads of the American revival hymn,

" Say, brothers will you meet us?"

a copy of which had been procured by Mr. Macgregor during his recent tour
in the States.

The dates of the establishment of the various Societies and other particulars,
are shown in the following table :

	Date of Establishment.	No. of Boys.	Earnings during the Year.
Ragged School (Red Uniform).........1851		71	$1,785
East London (Blue)....................1854		82	934
South London (Yellow)............ 1854		40	625
North-West London (white)..........1857		20	135
West Kent (Green)....................1857		13	90
West London (Purple)...............,1857		21	196
Islington (Brown—Red Facings)......1857		25	235
Notting Hill (Blue—Red Facings) 1857		15	109
Kensington (Brown—Purple Facings).1857		14	119
Union Jack, Limehouse (Red—Blue Facings)................ 1858		16	80
		326	£4,308

Or about *twenty thousand dollars !*

An arrangement has been made between these Societies, by which each is
confined to its particular district, in order that no rivalry or jealousy may be
felt between those who are engaged in the same work.

There is, besides these, a Roman Catholic Society, which is not confined to
any particular district,' but occupies stations in all parts of London. This
Society employs about fifty boys : their badges are marked with the letters
" S. V. P."

The total number of boys employed in the original or Red Coat Society
since its establishment, April, 1851, is eight hundred and twenty-nine, and their
total earnings amount to £10,206.

livelihood by the most lowly vocation, rather than
grow up in idleness and crime.

The earnings of the boys in each year, and the mode of division, are shown
in the following table (in which shillings and pence are omitted) :—

	1852.	1853.	1854.	1855.	1856.	1857.	1858.	1859.
Average of boys employed	24	37	37	41	48	55	59	61
Earnings...........	£656	£760	£899	£1193	£1,432	£1,735	£1,785	£1,746
Boys' Wages	372	450	491	614	724	857	887	893
Boys' Banks........	142	148	205	289	355	843	454	432
Retained by Society	141	161	203	288	352	434	443	421

THE SUBURBS OF LONDON.

COWPER in his "Task," if I mistake not, sings of

> " The villas with which London stands begirt,
> Like a swarth Indian with his belt of beads,"

and these, and they have multiplied greatly since the sweet singer passed away, have seemed to me quite as worthy of consideration as many of the more grand and noted structures that crowd the business streets. The British are naturally fond of the country. Every man who can possibly do so, plants his residence amid trees and vines, and pure air; and for many miles around, may be found charming villages, built up almost entirely by merchants, tradesmen and mechanics, doing business in the metropolis.

London a hundred years ago was only winter quarters; when it went out of town (which it did in May and returned in October,) the fashionable world at first resorted to Islington " to drink the waters," to Hampstead, or to Chelsea. Swift, in his *Journal*

(114)

to Stella, repeatedly alludes to "Addison's country-house at Chelsea ;" and on taking lodgings there himself, talks of the beautiful scent of the new-made hay around, and says he gets quite sunburnt in his journeys to and fro, and whenever he stays late in London he congratulates himself on having no money, so that he cannot be robbed on his way home. The facilities for egress and ingress are so numerous, the fares so low, that one may live almost as conveniently at five or ten miles from his shop, or workhouse, as upon the next square. The railway arrangements are infinitely better suited for promoting out of town life, than those of New-York. One may go and come from almost any place within thirty miles of London every hour, and the accommodating railway which encircles the city, has a train every fifteen minutes, going to most of the villages, while the fares range from six-and-a-quarter to twelve-and-a-half cents. "Busses" also start from the Royal Exchange, and other central localities at frequent intervals, by which those who do not fancy the whirling cars, may be carried home with almost equal speed; for the jehus are given to rapid driving. The roads are kept in such admirable order that cabs may proceed as easily out of the city as within ; and as I have before stated, gas lamps are to be found for ten or twenty miles from the metropolis, lining the roads on either side,

and making them as passable and cheerful at night as
Fleet-street or Cheapside.

I have been, on several occasions, to Hampstead,
the most elevated village in the vicinity of London,
standing on a bold hill several hundred feet high.
From Hampstead heath one may get a better view of
the giant city, than from almost any other point.
The "busses" to Hampstead run every fifteen minutes; the fare is twelve-and-a-half cents, and the
distance about five miles from Oxford-street. On the
heath (sometimes used for horse-racing) there may
always be found a choice array of donkeys and their
carts, ready for hire. It is customary for children
and invalids to walk out here in the afternoon, to
snuff the clear air, and enjoy the pretty scenery, and
often to take a donkey conveyance for a ride in the
country. I wanted to reach Hendon, a few days
since. It is about three miles beyond the heath, and
as there was no "buss" going, to meet my engagement,
I thought it necessary to charter some means of conveyance. Winking my desire to secure the services
of a donkey and chaise, the crowd of youthful drivers
literally swarmed about me, and the vehement ejacu-
lations of praise they bestowed in rapid succession upon
their respective establishments, would have led a
blind man to suppose them all equal to the royal
carriages. I soon struck a bargain with a ragged

fellow, who repeatedly assured me his "donkey was a donkey as would go as fast as a pony." Indeed from his representation, I might honestly have taken the donkey to be a Lady Suffolk with lengthened ears. The chaise was a very poor one, and as I got in, the unpatronized drivers set up a vociferous cry in favor of their carriages, " which were fit for a gentleman to ride in." For the first five minutes our donkey moved sufficiently slow to render any one at all in haste, exceedingly uncomfortable. The jehu yelling and screeching at every step ; first jumping out and taking the beast by the head, then beating the poor specimen of stupidity with an enormous stick, which seemed to have no other effect than to knock it almost heels over head at every blow. Suffering a mile or so of this asinine conveyance, and provoked with the tediousness, as well as nearly deafened by the hooting of the excited driver, I ventured to tell him that, in my humble opinion, his donkey was far from being a fast one ; and, in fact, that I had never met a quick one in all my wanderings. There was no reply to this insinuation, but donkey got another terrible whack of the ox-gad, accompanied by a furious jerk of the lines ; which jerking, I may say, was kept up incessantly. Finding the place of my destination not far distant, I abandoned the intractable and deceiving donkey and driver, with a much

worse opinion of both, than when I bargained for my
ride, and would willingly have given a half crown to
have saved the time wasted in the vain attempt at
haste. Let me advise all travellers to have as little
to do with the Hampstead Heath donkeys as possible.
If you want to kill an hour or two, and pay twice as
much as you would to ride in a cab, employ one of
these absurd conveyances; otherwise avoid them as
you would any abominable nuisance.

Donkeys saddled for ladies and children are seen
all about the heath. They never run away with their
freight—the only consolation attending their use.
Hendon, or that portion to which I had made my
way under such trying circumstances, was purely the
country. I had gone to the farm of Tanqueray, one
of England's most extensive and celebrated cattle
breeders, whose stock of short horns is perhaps unsurpassed by any in the world. Meeting, as per arrangement, my good friend Strafford, the author of
the " Herd Book," and Mr. Tainter, a somewhat distinguished stock breeder of Connecticut, and having
the honor of a letter of introduction to Mr. Tanqueray
from Colonel Benjamin T. Johnson, of the New
York State Agricultural Society, I was heartily comfortable in my rambles in the company of the intelligent amateurs named. Mr. Tanqueray has a farm of
some three hundred acres of very choice land, all, or

nearly all of which is in grass, and used for pasture. About one hundred and forty head of cattle now make up his stock, and among the number are several of the finest specimens of the short-horn species the country has ever produced. The noble cow recently purchased by Mr. Becar, of New York, at the cost of seven hundred guineas, may be justly called the " Queen of cows." Drafts have repeatedly been made upon the Hendon herd by the principal amateurs or breeders, such as Col. Morris, Mr. Thorn and Mr. Becar.

The cows are all named, and cared for as carefully as canary birds. The long ranges of convenient and comfortable stables attest to the good judgment of the proprietor, whose experience in the rearing of choice stock has placed him in the front rank of European breeders. All the milk from the cows—some seventy-five, I should think—is given to the calves ; and taking into consideration the great expense continually incurred by Mr. Tanqueray, it seems absolutely ner cessary that he should now and then get an enormous price for an animal, to compensate for his great out lay. A six hundred and fifty guinea bull was shown me, (the Duke of Gloucester.) He is a valiant fellow, and now the property of a distinguished American.— Judges pronounce him superior to any bull ever imported into the States. " Why don't some of you

Yankee dealers buy me out entirely?" said Mr. Tanqueray, good-naturedly, as we walked through the sheds; "they are constantly making inroads upon my stock—let them take it all." It is undoubtedly the fact that Mr. Tanqueray's best customers are Americans, enterprising gentlemen who have done much to improve American stock; and the time is not far distant when we may find as extensive and valuable a variety of thorough-bred cattle at our great shows, as at any of the English or Scotch fairs.

To give some idea of the value of land at Hendon, say eight miles from London, I may state that Mr. Tanqueray informed me he had been offered two hundred and fifty pounds per acre for his farm, (three hundred acres,) by a cemetery company, and that he could readily get three hundred pounds per acre, The land is well situated for building purposes.

The other day I had another enjoyable time at Hendon. I accompanied my friend P. and his agreeable family to the annual commencement of the "Mill Hill School" at that place. This school was instituted in the year 1807, with the view of giving an education equal to that furnished by the leading public schools of the country, but free from those conditions which restrict their advantages to the members of one religious body. It was founded by religious men, for the sake of extending the means of religious education : and the manner in which this design has been carried out is attested by the confidence it has secured from all bodies of evangelical dissenters, as well as from many members of the established church. The estimable Dr. John Harris, author of "Pre-Adamite Earth," and other valued works, was once the head-master of this school. The Rev. Philip Smith, B. A. now occupies this responsible position. The com-mencement exercises were attended by many friends of the pupils, and passed over very creditably; one lad recited Longfellow's Excelsior with good effect. At the close the visitors were invited to a sumptuous dinner, at which after diligent eating and drinking, many toasts were offered and responses made. The lads then joined their parents and friends and started for their summer vacation, but not without an affec-tionate parting with their teachers. "Dotheboys Hall" has no counterpart in Mill Hill School, where there would seem to be constant good living and the best feeling between teachers and pupils.

The school building is on an elevation command-ing a most beautiful prospect. Near at hand is the village of Harrow-on-the-Hill where Lanfranc built a church, Thomas a Becket resided, and Wolsey was rector, but better known for its school founded in 1592 by a substantial yeoman named John Lyon, and ever since a celebrated educational establishment.

6

The scholars are chiefly the sons of noblemen and wealthy gentlemen. Among the eminent Harrow-vians are Sir William Jones, the Oriental Scholar: the Rev. Dr. Parr; Lord Rodney, Lord Palmerston, Lord Elgin, Lord Shaftesbury, Lord Byron, Sir Robert Peel, and the distinguished American the Hon. John A. King.

In the chapel, the church, and the school, there is no distinction of seats for the sons of noblemen, and it is said that it was for this reason that Rufus King when American Ambassador to London sent his sons to Harrow, as the only school where no distinction was shown to rank.

Hackney is one of the prettiest surburban villages of London. It wears a deligtful rural aspect, and is easily approached by " buss" or rail at all times, and is but three or four miles from the heart of the great city. I need hardly remind you that the term " Hackney," as applied to coaches, was derived from this village. In former times, before London had expanded so greatly, it was a good drive to Hackney, and many coaches were employed in carrying pleas-ure parties, to enjoy the pleasant scenery of the place; hence the term now so general.

Hounslow, upon the South-western railway, twelve miles from the Waterloo Station, is a quiet retreat. I have been there on two occasions to visit a friend.

By "buss" it may be reached in two hours from the Strand, London, (fare twenty-five cents) passing by Hyde Park, and Kensington Gardens. A beautiful route.

I sailed up the Thames as far as Chelsea a few days since, in one of the little black racers—for the insignificent little steamers move along at a furious pace. The sides of the river, even so far up, are thickly built upon.—There are several docks where the boat stops, one near Lambeth (above the Houses of Parliament and on the opposite side of the river,) where the Archbishop of Canterbury resides.—It is a dreary looking old place, set up more like a State than a Church establishment. The Houses of Parliament are seen to the best advantage from one of the ferry boats.

"Can you go to Woolwich and Greenwich on Thursday ?" said my friend M., as I sat in the great chair at his elbow, in his quiet chambers, near the dusty Temple Bar, that famous relic of ancient London.

"At your service," I replied, with no little satisfaction ; and so, when Thursday came, we took to one of the dingy Thames steamers, paid our sixpence, and started for Woolwich and Greenwich, some six or eight miles down the river from St. Paul's. The day was a genuine English day—dark, and suggestive of rain. The sky looked black, and the atmosphere was fairly dense with fog. But we had our umbrellas, and, as usual, it did *not* rain, although the sun failed to get his bright face clearly out of the gloomful clouds during the whole day.

Woolwich is of great note for being the oldest military and naval arsenal in England, and for its royal dockyard, where men-of-war were built as early as the reign of Henry the Eighth. The Thames is here so deep that the largest ships may at all times ride with safety. Having made a hasty survey of the extensive artillery barracks, and the royal military academy, we soon reached the gateway to the great dock-yards. It was the dinner hour, and as the men were all away, we could not get immediate admission. The renowned Woolwich common was but a little farther, and to that we turned our steps. Conceive of a beautiful plot of ground, as nature made it, a parallel for our justly prized Boston Common, and you will have a clever daguerreotype of this, the chief of John Bull's training schools. Here many a fresh recruit has first appreciated the science of war. Here many a time-worn soldier has returned, to show his scars to a grateful country. We could not gain admittance to the dockyard after all. A curious dilemma presented itself. It was against the rules to admit foreigners, without a permit from the Admiralty Office. The register called for my residence, as well as name, and when I honestly wrote "New York," the polite official "was sorry to say" I could not be allowed to enter. M. became highly excited, and demanded to see the Commander-in-Chief. "Certainly," said he at the gate, "I'll send a guard with you." So a tall, orderly policeman went with us, and heartily did he laugh at the idea of calling any one a foreigner who spoke the English language so well. M. saw the Commodore, was kindly received, but it was of no avail. "It would cause great difficulty to infringe upon the rules; was very sorry," etc.; so we took the boat for Greenwich, and an inspection of its celebrated hospital.

Greenwich is a fine, quiet old place, closely tied to London by railway, coach and steamer. The hospital buildings are numerous and imposing, built of dark grey stone, and in a massive style. The extensive and elegant grounds are admirably kept. Troops of veteran mariners were strolling about in cocked hats and blue coats. Some were lame, others blind, and not a few had one leg less than nature originally provided them. We entered the painted hall, or picture gallery—sixpence was the fee. A lofty room is hung with a variety of superb oil paintings, chiefly representing distinguished naval commanders and noted naval engagements. The brave Nelson's victories are

appropriately commemorated. Our attention was
called to a neat case containing the identical coat and
vest worn by the daring hero when he fell mortally
wounded on the deck of the *Victory*. The English
sailors all delight to talk of Nelson. He is the Washington of their imagination. Surely he was a man
whose memory will be preserved to the latest generation. Many beautiful incidents of his affectionate
and endearing manner, both in public and private
life, live in the warm hearts of his admiring countrymen. "I have seen him," says the poet Rogers,
"spin a tetotum with his *one* hand a whole evening,
for the amusement of some children." His universal
kindness to those under his command was a notable
feature of his excellent character ; when forced to see
men whipped upon his ship, he ascended to the deck,
read rapidly and in an agitated voice the rules of the
service, and then cried : "Boatswain, do your duty .
Admiral, pardon !" He would then look around upon
his officers, and all keeping silence, would say,—
"What ! not one of you, gentlemen, not one of you
has pity upon that man in his sufferings? Untie the
man ! My brave fellow, on the day of battle remember me." It was very seldom that the sailor thus addressed by his commander did not distinguish himself
in the hour of conflict. It is related that one, John
Sykes, saved his (Nelson's) life twice by parrying the

blows aimed at him, and on one occasion actually interposed his head, receiving a severe cut intended for
the admiral.

The Greenwich hospital is not, like our American
hospitals, merely an abode for the sick. It is the
grand retreat of all the old and homeless members of
the ~~Royal~~ family, and a comfortable place it is. In
one of the buildings we walked through a long corridor, and saw the snug little rooms where the venerable tenants have their quiet homes. In nearly every
one there was some memento of Nelson—a splinter
from one of his ships, a picture of one of his memorable battles, or a wood-cut, lithograph, or steel engrav-
ing of the great victor himself—and not a few of the
old men seemed to envy the good fortune of the daring John Sykes. You will remember how some of
these veterans who were at the hero's burial at St.
Paul's seized the tattered flag that was to have been
placed by his side in the grave, and moved by one
impulse, rent it in pieces, keeping each a fragment.

The Greenwich fair is a relic of old English customs, which has thus far escaped the devastating
hand of progress. It is held annually, continues for
several days, and brings together a vast concourse of
the scum of the London populace. It was, in fact,
a day after the fair, but the oddly mingled attractions
had not all been removed, and a few fast boys and

rude girls were amusing themselves with the various
games which the ingenuity of a regiment of showmen
had devised, to fill their pockets with coppers. Punch
and Judy were busy as usual, and their grotesque
antics met the satisfaction of the idle throngs. An old
and curious custom always in vogue at this fair, is
that of the " scratchers." Both men and women, boys
and girls, large and small, provide themselves with
what Yankee urchins denominate " crickets." With
these they not only keep up an incessant clatter, but
it is considered highly proper to scratch them over
your back, when your eyes are not on the watch. A
large one will do serious damage to a coat. Fortunately, the majority of these amiable performers had
left the fair grounds before our arrival, and we
escaped a scratching.

Donkey races are always popular at Greenwich
fair. A certain sum, ten shillings or upwards, is put
up as sweepstakes, and the donkey rider going
over the course and arriving at the judges' stand first,
merits the money. It matters not whether the pace
be a trot, canter or gallop. As may be presumed
these popular races afford a vast fund of amusement.

The world-renowned Greenwich observatory, built
by Charles II., on the summit of a hill, called Flam-
stead Hill, from the great astronomer of that name,
who was here the first astronomer royal, is a small

building. The spires of London may be plainly seen from it on a clear day—so my friend said, as we walked across the broad Greenwich Common, and caught the omnibus for Charing· Cross and our city lodgings.

*   *   *   *   *   *   *

I was at Aylesbury a few days since, forty miles from London. The fare to go and return, second class, was $2 16. Taking the London and North-western rail from Euston Square to Chadington Junction, from whence by single rail there is a train to Aylesbury, a perfect sample of an English inland town; old and secluded, a place where one might live undisturbed by the din of progress; a capital home for superannuated parsons or politicians, or even a congenial retreat for mercantile fogies. The agricultural district around about is extremely rich and fertile. Indeed, the vale of Aylesbury is thought to be second to no section of England in the produce of good crops. I happened to enter the town while the annual wool fair was being held. Large bales of wool were piled in the market and town square. I mingled among the farmer salesmen, and, if they did not pull the wool over my eyes, (they had no cause to, knowing I was not trying to speculate,) the prices obtained were in advance of those of any recent sales. The market is a building well suited to the town.

6*

Beneath the clock, upon the tower, the words, "The hour is at hand," are painted in large letters, and can but be observed by every passer-by. A singular position for such an intimation, and yet what should be kept in mind more constantly by those who engage in the uncertain business of earth?

The fame of the Aylesbury duck is world-wide. Over $100,000 has been returned to the town during the past year, from the sale of ducks! Think of it; and think better of the poultry trade than you ever have before! I visited the duck breeders, or several of them. One has had as many as 2,500 at once. They are mainly devoured by the London epicures.

Having indulged in an agreeable dinner at the White Hart Hotel, on the day of my arrival in Aylesbury, I had the good fortune to make the acquaintance of the amiable host, Mr. Fowler, to whom I am greatly indebted for interesting information relating to the town and surrounding country, the crops, stock, and many other matters. The antiquities of his hotel, one of the oldest buildings in the south of England, (long kept by his father, and considered one of the best public houses in the country,) merit notice. Let me speak particularly of the large room of the house—the ball, or dining room. It is, according to mine host, some thirty-nine feet long by twenty-three wide. It is paneled from top to bottom, -

and has recesses formed for the reception of paintings. It has the " egg and tongue" ornament carved around the cornice, richly gilt; and the fire-place is handsomely carved with scroll work, and gilded in like manner. The upper part of the paneling is arranged alternately with groups of fruits and flowers, and warlike trophies. The ceiling is divided into nine compartments, with gilt bosses at the intersection of the beams. The centre compartment is filled with a painting on canvas of two figures, representing Peace and Concord, holding palm branches and cherubim flying from behind clouds ; two of the jolly urchins are bearing a crown and the initials C. R., above the principal figures, where two others are below, bearing a scroll with this legend :—

" Let Peace and Concord sit and singe,
And subjects yield obedience to their Kinge."

A motto meeting a much wider response now than when it was painted upon this scroll.

The sides of the room were undoubtedly meant to represent a statue and picture gallery. They are lined with well-painted figures, such as Diana, Juno, Venus, and Mercury. Over the fire-place is a picture of " Thomyris," queen of the Scythians, receiving the head of the great Cyrus, first king of the Persians, after she had defeated him, and uttering the memorable words, " *Satiate sanguine quem semper sitisti*" —"Satiate thyself with that blood which thou hast always thirsted for." The huge grate in this curious room was from Nell Gwynne's house London.

Mr. Fowler, besides being a popular landlord, is a skilful and extensive farmer. A walk through his wide fields proved he was no novice in the science of agriculture. "Step with me," said he, "into this wheat field. 'Tis acknowledged to be the best in the vale of Aylesbury." The stalks measured over six feet ; we were as much hidden from view after wandering through them a few yards, as we should have been in a dense forest. Passing further on, he pointed to the circle taken by the steeple-chase riders, meeting at Aylesbury, annually. Various ditches and hurdles were designated as having been the scenes of severe accidents to both horses and riders. Near by we inspected a half-dozen two-year old colts—mammoth fellows—brought from Belgium by Mr. Fowler, where, he informed me, he secured them at a price very far below that for which such animals could be purchased in England. They were much like the large dray-horses, and I doubt not the investment will prove a profitable one to him. Mr. Fowler also took me to see his sheep and poultry, and in fact, treated me with rare kindness, and when I left his establishment, gave me a most pressing invitation to visit him again at my earliest convenience, not as a traveler' but as his welcome private guest. Such is a good specimen of English hospitality.

WINDSOR CASTLE AND FARMS.

I HAVE made two trips to Windsor. On the first occasion, it was not my privilege to enter the castle, owing to the presence of the, Royal family. But on my last visit, thanks to the Royal absence, I had the pleasure of going all over the stone mansion and fortress, having secured an order from Messrs. Ackerman, the long-established dealers in Artists' materials on the Strand, who are empowered to issue gratuitous tickets of admission.

The distance to Windsor is twenty-six miles, per South-western railway, from Waterloo Station. The train puts you down adjoining the castle, an imposing sight of which is had long before nearing the village. It looms up in the dim distance like a mighty mountain of art, and is indeed a truly massive and imposing structure, in every way fulfilling my boyish ideas of a regal stronghold of the olden time.

The first part of the Royal establishment at Wind-
(133)

sor to which attention is called, is the mews or stables.
Entering the office of the "keeper of the horse," you
are provided with a pass, and a guide, who, without
fee, conducts you throughout the magnificent and
extensive stables and carriage-houses. Over a hundred of the most superb horses were standing in the
stables. Several white Arabian ponies, presented to
the Queen by his Imperial Highness, Omar Pasha,
struck me as being unusually pretty. There were
whole ranges of saddle-horses; some for the use of
Her Majesty, others for the Prince, and many for the
sporting juniors of the crown family. The stalls are
all of the most spacious area, and the name of each
horse is placed over his head. One in particular, is
honored with the strange title, "Arsenic;" and another showy animal, often driven by her Majesty,
bears the real rustic name of "Phœbe." The posting,
or road horses, large bays, were almost as elegant as
the noble animals of the American Express Companies. In each department the grooms were busily at
work, all in the Royal livery. The carriage-houses
are stocked with every species of vehicle : carriages
for State occasions, carriages for pleasure riding about
the farms ; light carriages, with India-rubber cover-
ings upon the tires of the wheels, for riding through
the garden paths ; carriages for posting long journeys; carriages for shooting ; carriages for the ser-

vants to go to the races, and carriages for the ladies-in-waiting upon the Queen. Most of these vehicles are painted black, and striped with red, and are less clumsy than many English conveyances. One old and rusty-looking green coach, the guide said, was used by the Queen when she wished to go anywhere *in cog.* On such occasions she has no outriders, and the carriage would be generally supposed to belong to an humble farmer's wife. Under one roof, I was shown a parade of the " coaches of other days," including one in which George the Third was wont to travel, and several used by other defunct kings. There are also many carriages which have been presented to the Queen—several really elegant ones from the Emperor Nicholas; also, two sledges from his highness. These were used last winter. The stables and horses, the carriages and sets of harness belonging to the royal establishment, are all kept in a manner worthy their magnificence. The various rich kinds of harness, and scores of saddles and bridles, would make a wholesale saddlery wareman think his stock insignificant.

Passing from the mews, I entered the Castle, and with a party of like strangers, under the attendance of a polite guard, had a full and minute inspection of the celebrated and interesting premises. The historic associations of the time-honored building are among

the most exciting in British annals. The royal, or
state apartments, the all-attractive portions of the
Castle, are unoccupied during much of the time.
Her Majesty having the Buckingham Palace, the
Osborne House, Isle of Wight, the Highland home, at
Balmoral, and several other mansions, it is expected
that but a few months of the year will be devoted to
Windsor, though the connection of the royal farms,
etc., makes it by far the most pleasant place, I should
presume. The state apartments comprise some half
dozen spacious rooms. We were first shown into the
Audience Chamber, a pleasant room, well lined with
paintings, and, if my memory serves me, some fine
specimens of Gobelin tapestry. Next came a large
hall, in which we were pointed to many paintings
from the pencil of Van Dyke, and other eminent
masters. One or two small but elegantly furnished
rooms being examined, the attendant ushered the
delighted party into the grand ball-room, which far
outvies anything of the kind I remember to have
seen. The ceiling, some forty feet in height, is
gorgeously decorated with gold, while the walls of
the room are illustrated in superb style. At the
end toward Eton College, is the famous window,
from which the prospect is surpassingly sublime. I
fancied myself in fairy land, as I looked above,

around, and on all the splendor, both natural and artistic.

We were conducted into the immense dining-room, which is two hundred feet long, and proportionally wide. The shields of the knights of the kingdom are displayed on the walls, and at one end of the room is a beautiful throne of oak, on which her Majesty may preside at great festivals. Passing out of the room at a door opposite to the throne, we came to the Armory, where there is an endless variety of weapons, arranged in beautiful order, forming stars, crowns, etc. A piece of the ship "Victory," surmounted by a superbly wrought marble bust of the immortal Nelson; several captured cannon, and a host of other trophies of war and naval and military accoutrements, fill up the room. I dare not attempt to enumerate half of the articles, though scarcely one of them is devoid of great historic interest.

The living apartments of her Majesty are not shown. Very properly so, for the scores of visitors would soon sadly interfere with their neatness.

The scenery adjoining the Castle is chaste, elegant, and truly English. The large parks, the rows of trees, especially those beside the "Long Walk,"—a road leading directly from the front of the palace to the end of Windsor Park—are grand beyond description. The walk alluded to is, I think, the most

enchanting I have ever strolled through. A considerable improvement has been made to the palace and
grounds during a few years past, and, with the exception of one or two dilapidated sections, there is nothing
to lead you to believe it of so long standing. Windsor Castle is thought by many to be the most noble
and extensive building of its order now remaining in
the kingdom. Its size is immense. The view from
the Castle terrace, out upon Windsor and Eton, the
College and the shallow Thames, is picturesque in the
extreme, and the whole vicinity has, you know, been
honored with the criticism and admiration of Pope,
and others of those whose names are immortal.

To see the stables and the palace, is generally the
sum total of the ambition of the visitors (unless the
Queen should be "at home," when they would be
anxious to peep at her.) But I had no thought of
returning to London without making myself somewhat familiar with the manner of Royal farming. A
letter from a good friend in the metropolis to Mr.
Wilson, her Majesty's head agriculturist, gave me
access through the fields. There are two or three
very large farms connected with the Castle. One is
known as the "Shaw Farm," and one as "Prince
Albert's Model Farm;" for His Royal Highness
pretends to be a practical farmer. Indeed, I believe
his love is much stronger for plowshares and pruning·

hooks, than for swords or battle-axes. Not a bad feature, this, in his otherwise admirable character.

I had to walk several miles to the farm entrance-gates, and was first directed to the gardens, where were large supplies of vegetables, fruits and flowers, and the evidence of skilful attention. Several veteran gardeners were lounging about.

From thence I stepped into the poultry-yards, and had a pleasant welcome from the royal crowers and cacklers, and an agreeable conversation with the poultry-keeper. Two independent-looking roosters were pointed out as the pets of the young princes. Her Majesty's collection of poultry is not so good as I anticipated, nor is it at all in keeping with the perfection of her stock of cows and pigs. But who could expect Victoria to pay much attention to chicken-breeding? By-the-by, I saw a few half-feathered relics of the choice lot of " Gray Shanghais," presented her Majesty by a Yankee amateur, a year or two since. He would scarcely recognize them in their English condition. They seem to thrive sadly, (pardon the bull) upon anti-republican care.

'Twas but a short distance from the poultry-yard to the dairy buildings. I had to pass through the milk room to find the royal butter makers. An odd old brace of souls have charge of the dairy operations. No " up country" village could produce a more rustic-

looking couple. They were indulging in a quiet meal
in a side room of their cozy cottage. ' I waited a few
minutes for the completion of the repast, when the
good dame set earnestly to work informing me on
the important duties of her office. I was first
marched through a long room filled with pans flowing
with the richest milk, not inferior even to "pure
Orange County." The pans or dishes were all of
porcelain, pure white, and oval shaped, and the old
lady descanted merrily over their many good qualities.
Acknowledging them the most convenient and tasteful articles of the kind I had ever seen, and expressing intense satisfaction at the looks of the milk, I was
conducted to several mysteriously covered wooden
platters, and before I could give a thought as to their
contents, the covers were jerked off, and my eyes
feasted upon a great array of table rolls of rich-looking new-made butter.

"And where are these consumed ?" said I. "Oh !
at Buckingham Palace," replied the proud mistress of
the rolls ; " we send them away every morning at two
o'clock, and they are on her Majesty's table at breakfast time." On examination, I found that each roll
bore the stamp of the sovereign, V. R., and a crown.
"These are also sent to Buckingham every day," said
my guide, pointing to several portly cans of *bona fide*
cream. "Why, what can they do with it all at the

Palace?" I asked, " Oh! use it for coffee and tea,
fruits and the like." I concluded that there was at
least one place in the world where strawberries and
cream could be enjoyed in perfection. Re-assuring the
obliging old lady of my profound gratification at the
condition of the dairy, I was shown by her husband,
a much less enthusiastic spirit, into the barns and cat·
tle yards. Fifty cows are kept, and many of them are
famous milkers. The short horns compose the principal part of the herd. They were quietly chewing
the cud in the yard, and one or two men were
engaged in milking. An elegant stone edifice, with
high clock tower in the centre, is so divided and
arranged as to give the most ample and queenly
accomodation to all the royal stock. The building is
conceived in beautiful taste, and designed, as all such
erections should be, to afford complete comfort to the
useful occupants, and prove an ornament to the farm.

The royal pigs deserve more than a casual notice.
The " Prince Albert Suffolk" is a deservedly popular
species. His Royal Highness has given considerable
attention to the improvement of the breed, and has
been a successful competitor at many of the recent
important shows of stock in different parts of England.
On the whole I was well satisfied with the reward
attending my honest curiosity in the investigation of
her Majesty's plantations. One visitor in a thousand

would not care to roam beyond the Castle walls. I found much more of interest in the farms, than in all the venerated rooms of the old building.

The well-known fact that both the Queen and the Prince take much personal interest and pride in their farms and farming, has elevated them in my regard more than all the political prowess they have ever displayed. 'Tis in the communion with nature that refinement and worth of character are revealed far more than in the study of courts and parliaments.

SHEFFIELD AND CHATSWORTH.

One might easily anticipate a dingy town from the appearance of the outskirts of Sheffield. For miles we passed through avenues of factories and furnaces. The thick, black smoke rising from a regiment of dignified chimneys, the throngs of strong-armed men, the clatter of a hundred trip-hammers, the whirl of a thousand grindstones, the puffing and snorting of a host of steam-engines, combine to assure the new-comer that Sheffield is truly the seat of industry. Cabs attend the station, as in all English towns and cities, and for a sterling shilling I was carried, bag and baggage, to a convenient hotel.

Architecture has scarcely dawned upon Sheffield. With one or two exceptions, there is not an edifice worthy of note. The streets are many of them narrow,* and the houses universally plain and dreary

* One of the main thoroughfares is called " Washington Road." There is a " Washington Street" in Glasgow

—mostly built of brick. He who can draw satisfaction from an acquaintance with the progress of mechanism, may, however, at almost every step, discover something to delight his fancy. It has been my fortune to visit many of the extensive manufactories. The Sheafe Works, long widely known, were, until recently, carried on by the Messrs. Greaves. They are now conducted by other parties. Although rather after hours this afternoon, I was kindly permitted to go through the premises. About a thousand men are employed, and the buildings are most extensive, lying on both sides the canal. Cart and coach springs, chisels and files, are the principal articles manufactured.

Ródgers & Sons, the world-renowned cutlers "to her Majesty," have their works in Norfolk Street, and have for many years carried on a most extensive business in the manufacture of knives, scissors, razors, etc. Their show-rooms are well worthy of examination.

·I went into an establishment for making silver and Britannia dishes, covers, etc. The process is both curious and interesting. Most of the articles are stamped, but the most expensive are hammered out by hand. The stock of stamps astounded me, as well as the rapidity with which the dishes are completed. Powerful hammers stamp the handles and ornaments at a single blow. A number of persons follow this business, and I noticed, as in all English manufactories, that most of the journeymen were men advanced in years. Such able and experienced workmen are seldom found doing journey work in the States.

Dixon & Sons, makers of plated wares, are among the largest manufacturers in Sheffield, employing nearly, if not full, a thousand workmen. But I must not attempt to even give the names of the enterprising firms. Sheffield manufacturers have a world-wide fame, and their city is strongly bound to America by commercial ties—more strongly, perhaps, than any other English city. "If it were not for the American trade, I don't know what would become of us," said a manufacturer to me yesterday. Everything pertaining to America is eagerly listened to. I have seen several public notices concerning "our land." The following which I copied this morning from a large poster, may amuse you, as it has me :—

AMERICA AND THE BIBLE.

MR. J—— B——

Will lecture in the Adelphi Theatre on Sunday, Monday, and Tuesday, August 6, 7, and 8. Three Lectures on America, as follows :—

SUNDAY, AUGUST 6TH.

America—its Soil and Climate ; its Government and Institutions and Laws · its Botanical and Zoological Productions, etc. Game and Vermin.

7

MONDAY, AUGUST 7TH.

America—its Reforms and Reformers, Political, Civil, Legal, and Moral,
including the Anti-Slavery, Woman's Rights, Temperance, and Maine Law,
Land and Labor Reform, Bible and Religious Movements.

TUESDAY, AUGUST 8TH.

America—the Customs and Manners of the People ; Education, Music and
Songs, with specimens of Negro and other popular Melodies ; Prospects of
Emigrants, Labor, Wages, and Prices of Provisions ; Difficulties and Dangers
of Emigration ; Spirit Rapping, Clairvoyance, &c.

Questions may be put at the end of each Lecture, or one hour's discussion·
Ten minutes being allowed to each speaker.

Prices of admission, 3d, 2d, and 1d.

I would give much to attend this promising course
of lectures, but cannot stop long enough. The lec-
turer will have his hands full, if he does justice
to all of the topics enumerated, and many strange
questions will be put to him, if his hearers are as
inquisitive as most Englishmen.

I also find attractive advertisements announcing
that " The great American Doctors have arrived !"

*   *   *   *   *   *   *   *   *

Sheffield has long been justly proud of her Montgomery, and it is but a few months since he was
called to exchange worlds. A Christian warrior, ripe
in years, hoary in the service of his Master, he was
not dismayed at the summons from time to eter-
nity. .Those familiar with his beautiful poems,
have not failed to admire their devotional spirit.

Seldom has a writer of such rare genius and earthly fame evinced so much of religious feeling and faith. With a desire to visit the spot where the good man had so long lived, I found my way to his mansion on "The Mount," a very pretty elevation, just in the outskirts of Sheffield ; a location fit for the abode of a lover of the picturesque, and retired. Just across the road are the popular Botanical Gardens. Having taken the precaution to procure an order from a proprietor, I readily secured admission. Every proprietor has a right to give cards of free admission to persons living over seven miles from Sheffield, and I had little difficulty in proving I lived at a greater distance. Almost every shopkeeper in Sheffield is a proprietor, and strangers find no trouble in getting tickets at any time. The gardens are tasteful and extensive, well sustaining the repute in which they are held by the people of Sheffield. They abound in pretty plants and shrubbery, long secluded walks, and shaded avenues. A large green-house contains the choicest flowers. There are several ponds of water, and various hills and dales, setting off the grounds very nicely. I am not surprised at their popularity as a place of resort. Such an oasis is especially to be prized in a closely-built manufacturing city

Montgomery took much pride in these gardens,

visiting them very often. Near the main entrance
are several thrifty evergreens, planted by him. Long
may they keep his memory green. The dust of the
poet was deposited in the new Sheffield cemetery ; a
few moments' walk from the gardens brought me to
the grave. A new and imposing stone chapel has
just been completed on the most elevated portion of
the grounds. Immediately in front of this chapel is
a large circular plot, directly in the centre of which
lies all that remains of the Sheffield poet. The grass
has scarcely grown over the mound. "He was much
esteemed," said I to an Irish laborer engaged in
raking the dry leaves off the adjoining pathway.
"Indeed he was, sir: no man in Sheffield ever had so
great a burial."*

An elegant monument will be placed over the
grave. The cemetery promises to vie with Green-
wood in beauty, and its precincts will ever be
hallowed by the memory of the honored poet whose
sainted spirit is far from the gloomy shades of earth,

---

* Somebody once robbed Montgomery of an inkstand, presented to him by
the ladies of Sheffield. The public execration was so loud, that the thief
restored the booty with the following note :

" BIRMINGHAM, March, 1812.

Honored Sir—When we robbed your house, we did not know that you wrote
such beautiful verses as you do. I remember my mother told some of them to
me when I was a boy. I found what house we robbed by the writing on the
inkstand. Honored sir, I send it back. It was my share of the booty, and I
hope you and God will forgive me."

for now he rests in the happy land he so well described :

> ' Where chilling winds and poisonous breath
> Ne'er reach the healthful shore,
> Where sickness, sorrow, pain and death,
> Are felt and known no more."

A monument, or statue, to further commemorate his memory, will be immediately erected in a prominent place in Sheffield.

* * * * * * *

It was my original plan to reach Chatsworth from another place than Sheffield; but good friends here having satisfied me that I could find no more convenient point of approach, I concluded to make an excursion there on the day after my arrival.

The scenery immediately around Sheffield is highly picturesque, and most refreshing to the eye after a sojourn amidst the noise and smoke of the manufacturing town. The houses in the suburbs are built of stone similar to that used in the erection of the Houses of Parliament, for the quarries are near here. The coachmen pointed out the residences of many of the princely manufacturers. I don't wonder they prefer living several miles from the town. Our road then passed through the moors—desolate looking enough. Here the late Sir Robert Peel came regularly to shoot. He is said to have been an excellent shot, often bagging forty brace of birds in a day. His sporting house where he lived in good style when at the moors, may still be seen. Game-keepers' lodges are placed at appropriate distances over this sporting territory. Portions of the scenery farther on were compared to that of Wales, by two fellow-travelers who had just been rambling in that country. We met scarcely a vehicle upon the road. A halt of a few moments at the "Peacock," a half-way, road-side inn, gave our coachman and the anti-teetotal share of our passengers a good opportunity to "whet their whistles." It is strange to notice how much a man will drink when traveling. Many travelers never pass an inn without taking a glass of something more potent than Adam's ale.

Chatsworth, the seat of the Duke of Devonshire, and a fine specimen of a well preserved and extensive ducal estate, the magnificence of which John Bull never wearies in extolling, is in the county of Derbyshire, near Buxton, a celebrated watering-place, and thirteen miles from Sheffield. The nearest approach by railroad is to Rowsley, distant six miles, where 'busses and coaches are at all times in readiness for Chatsworth. Visitors usually adopt this route.

Having prevailed on two gentlemen who had been my coach companions to tarry and visit the palace with me, and meeting two other Sheffield gentlemen just about to start from the "Wheatsheaf," where we had left the coach, we all put off together. A mile across the fields brought us to the kitchen gardens. Passing a chaste and spacious house, which we found to be Sir Joseph Paxton's new mansion, we came upon the gardens. A gentlemanly fellow appeared as our guide, and forthwith we entered upon our examinations.

Sir Joseph Paxton has been in the Duke of Devonshire's employ for twenty-eight years, and was first engaged, I believe, as an ordinary gardener. He stays here but a small portion of his time. Our guide said that he had been employed on the premises for six months, and had never yet seen Paxton! We were not allowed to approach very near to his mansion on account of the presence of Lady Paxton. One of my companions was trying to decipher the following enigma, viz.: If visitors are not allowed to come within gun-shot of the Duke of Devonshire's gardener's lodge, when the gardener's wife happens to be at home, how near may they be allowed to approach to the Duke's palace when his lordship is on the premises!

The pine-apple house, and the houses for all foreign plants, are crowded with elegant specimens. In one green-house we were shown a very large peach-tree, said to be forty years old, and the largest in England.

It has borne as many as ninety dozen peaches in one season. The conservatories are of the most approved construction. Tan bark is used to protect the vines and increase the heat; water is constantly kept on top the furnace flues, to render the air moist. There are three ranges of hot-houses, each eighty-five yards long, and several extensive peach-houses; also a mushroom-house. About one hundred and forty men are constantly employed. In the room devoted to the rare East India plants, the thermometer stood at 85 degrees. The Victoria Regia Mansion (for such it deserves to be called) next attracted our admiration. The famous plant only flowers at 8 o'clock at night, or on a very dull day. At first opening the flower is of a delicate French white. It usually closes at 6 o'clock the next morning, and on the following morning is quite dead and withered.

" We bloom to-day ; to-morrow die."

Paxton was the first to flower this fine plant.

We visited the vineries. There are three ranges, two hundred and forty-nine feet in length. But we must proceed to the palace. We saw several groups of from twenty to fifty deer quietly grazing upon the lawn, and were informed that the Duke's stock consisted of two thousand head. The graceful creatures were, many of them, of a rich mottled color, and all so tame as to permit of our close approach. ,The distance from the vegetable gardens to the palace is nearly a mile. The pathway, through the middle of a retired vale, forms an attractive walk. We met a number of ladies and gentlemen enjoying it, and soon came to the "bower of Mary, Queen of Scots," a small tower shaded with trees, encompassed by a moat, and 'approached by a flight of stairs. It is said, that in the garden which formerly occupied its sum· mit, that beautiful princess passed many of the tedious hours of her confinement, and the communion with nature's lovely handiwork on every side, must have gone far to relieve the sadness of her unfortunate lot.

As we neared the palace, its noble dimensions loomed up in all their grandeur. There is not very much of regularity in the buildings, additions having been made from time to time, without regard to a likeness in their architecture. We were admitted at a grand gateway, and were soon gazing upon the internal grandeur of the mansion. The great stairway and reception hall amaze everybody. But we are already among the pictures.

A picture of several of the children of one of the former lords of Devonshire, painted by the immortal Hogarth, amusingly illustrates his genius. In one room we found a most extensive collection of etchings, by the most illustrious of the old masters. Our

guide intimated that we were fortunate beyond most
visitors, in gaining access to this department, as
it was seldom opened. The elegance of the picture-
galleries, and their extent, I cannot attempt to describe. I have seen nothing to approach them in
any private residence, nor, indeed, do many of the
public collections at all equal them.

The present Duke of Devonshire, unlike most of
the English noblemen, is no sportsman; but that one
of the old dukes had a love for the turf, is evident
from the annexed certificate, the original of which I
found attached to a large and unartistic picture (in
one of the halls of Chatsworth House) of that world-
renowned steed, " Flying Childers."

Sept. 28, 1719.—This is to certify that the bay horse, his Grace the Duke of
Devonshire has this day bought of me, was bred by me, and was five years old
last Grass, and no more.

Witness my hand.

GEO. CHILDERS.

The red velvet room, or billiard room, is conveniently located. This room was used as a sitting-
room by Queen Victoria, on her last visit to Chatsworth. It is tastefully ornamented. One of the
most attractive pictures found on its walls is that
called the " Spartan Isadas," representing a noble
youth who, by his intrepid valor, saved Sparta from
plunder by the Theban soldiery, and was awarded a

crown of honor for his distinguished services. This masterly and energetic composition is by Eastlake, the Royal Academician. In this room I also feasted my eyes on Sir Edwin Landseer's original and elegant picture representing "Bolton Abbey in the olden time." The painting is one of rare perfection, and has given much honor to the painter, who is considered one of the first artists in the land. In this room there is also a superb likeness of the Hon. Mrs. Norton, whose exquisite poems are popular the world over.

Throughout the house there are numerous presents from the "Autocrat of all the Russias," who only a few years since, spent a long time at Chatsworth, as the intimate and esteemed friend of the duke. The splendid portraits of the Emperor and Empress hang over the main stairway, and the lady-like guide told me, in reply to my inquiry, that the duke would allow none of the emperor's gifts to be put aside because of the present antagonism of the countries, having received them as a private friend, and not as tokens of political regard.

There is no stated charge for inspecting Chatsworth House and grounds, but the servants expect a fee for their attention. One of the gentlemen in our party had been over the premises repeatedly. Thinking he could manage the ropes to our advantage, we appointed him purser. He reckoned our outlay at about three shillings each. The visitors cannot feel any repugnance at paying, for the liberality of the duke in allowing his private mansion to be shown, is quite condescension enough, without expecting him to pay a regiment to exhibit it to the throngs that annually visit it.

Visitors are admitted only between the hours of 11 A. M., and 5 P. M. Our guide gave us the most minute description of every one of the wonders. She was a young lady, more refined, attentive, and graceful than the generality of females occupying similar positions.

Leaving the statuary hall, we passed into the gardens, having exchanged our fair attendant for one of the rougher sex. Leisurely tripping it over the grass, and through the secluded avenues, we first came to the waterfall, where, by an ingenious machinery, a flood of water from the surrounding hills is so turned as to show a young Niagara, at the will of the master of the fall. Huge steps have been placed up the side of a steep hill, and the sight of the foaming flood leaping over them is very pretty in a country where natural waterfalls are few and far between. Then we came to the "Spouting Tree"—a dead tree filled with water pipes, and so perforated in its trunk and branches as to throw water in every direction, like rain—a very cute affair—quite worthy a Yankee's inventive genius. We next came to Sir Joseph's artificial mountains, and so closely do they imitate the genuine article, that it is hard to discover the counterfeit. Great rocks are seldom put together so skilfully and naturally. A huge, swinging stone gate surprises us, and in a few moments the magnificent Crystal Palace bursts upon our view.

This building, erected ten years since by Sir Joseph Paxton, then plain Mr. Paxton, suggested the famous Hyde Park wonder, which gained the Chatsworth gardener his honorary title, and a reputation for taste and architectural skill, second to that enjoyed by no man in Great Britain. It is a most symmetrical and spacious building, two hundred and seventy-seven feet long. Of the expense incurred in keeping it properly warmed, you may attain a conception from the well-authenticated statement of our guide, that the furnaces devoured five hundred tons of coal per annum! Trees, shrubs, and plants of the choicest tropical species, fill this extensive palace, and all seem in luxurious growth. The cocoa-nut and bread-fruit trees are of a size far beyond any in Europe, if I am correctly informed. The fountains were next shown us; one of them will throw a jet two hundred and sixty-seven feet high. It is called the emperor's

jet, having been first used during the presence of the
Emperor of Russia.

Another half hour devoted to a careless wandering
about the front of the premises, the examination of
several distinguished trees, or trees planted by distinguished persons, (the Queen, Prince Albert, and others,) and we made our way back to the hotel.

We were prepared for a hearty dinner, and such we
enjoyed. A cosy parlor had been set aside for our
use, and everything was neat and good. A well-
roasted duck, a brace of stewed pigeons, a dish of
freshly caught trout, joints of different kinds of meat,
and a dessert of delectable tarts, made up the " bill of
fare." Expense about three shillings sterling each,
minus the wines, in which my English friends indulged freely. The luxury of the ample repast was
materially heightened by the graceful attention
shown us by the pretty waiting-maid. Just such a
rosy cheeked modest creature as a fellow having a
heart at all tender, would find it difficult to resist
falling in love with, after the dishes were removed.

My companions were deeply interested in America.
One of them, an extensive manufacturer, has an
agency in New York. They toasted the stars and
stripes, and cheered to the long endurance of the
kindly feeling now existing between the old kingdom
and the young republic. I was to return by coach,

but my kind friends insisted on my accepting a seat in their carriage, and so, the dinner comfortably finished, we rattled over the smooth road at a rapid rate, and were in the dingy city to an early tea.

In the long day's conversation with my intelligent companions I could but observe as I had in London, and everywhere else in England, the marked peculiarities in the everyday language of the people. To many words in ordinary use, there is quite a different meaning attached, from that which we would think them to convey. For instance, if you say a man is a "smart man," you are supposed to intimate that he is foppish, rather than that he is intelligent; and again, if you call a man "clever," it is understood that he is witty, original, or cute, instead of merely sociable. To say that you are "well posted up" on a subject, will always make an Englishman laugh; or to make use of that Yankee-ism, "I guess," or worse, "I reckon," has the same effect. An Englishman most always commences a question with "I say:" thus, "I say, Cabbie, do you want a fare?" We would say, "Halloo, driver, what will you take me to so and so for?" When I want to appear a true Briton, I invariably prefix to my interrogatories the "I say." It acts like a charm!

OLD YORK.

In all England there is no city more rich in historic associations, and, certainly, none more inviting to the American tourist, than York on the Ouse. Its hoary age and ivied quiet are in striking contrast with the vaunting youth and bustling progress of our republican metropolis. Like the veteran of many wars, the one rests, laureled and honored, while the other, though ardent and sanguine, has yet scarcely experienced the first skirmish with time, the common enemy.

Like most of the old cathedral cities of England, York never possessed an especial fame for either commercial or manufacturing enterprise. Shell combs and kid gloves have, however, been produced, in considerable quantities, for a long period. The Archbishop of York has the title of Primate of England, with the privilege of crowning the queen-consort, and ecclesiastical authority over the province of

(160)

York, comprising the Sees of York, Durham, Carlisle, Chester, Ripon, and Sodor and Man.

Vestiges of the old Roman road from York to Scotland are still visible, and, throughout the city, relics of the Roman occupancy may frequently be found. After three years' residence, the Emperor Severus died at York, in the year 210, and was succeeded by his sons, Caracalla and Geta. The former soon murdered the latter and made his escape to Rome. Carausius landed in Britain a hundred years after, and was proclaimed Emperor of Rome at York. In the year 272 Constantine the Great was born, and in 307 his father died at York. It was the Eboracum of the Romans—at that time the first city in Britain—and continued in great power till the time of William the First, by whom it was destroyed, after having surrendered to him through famine.

The " Black Swan " is one of the oldest inns in this part of England, and has always been widely known. In coaching times it was the grand depot of the London coaches. The following quaint announcement is copied from the well-preserved original, now hanging in the coffee-room. It is a curious relic :

"YORK in Four Days.

"STAGE COACH

"Begins on Friday the 17th of April 1706—

" All that are desirous to pass from *London* to *York*, or from *York* to *London*, or to any other place on the road, Let them repair to the *Black Swan* on Holbourn

In *London* or to the *Black Swan* in Coney street in *York*, At both which places
they may be received in a Stage Coach every Monday, Wednesday and Friday,
which performs the whole journey in four days (*if God permits*) And sets forth
at five in the morning. And returns from *York* to *Stamford* in two days,
and from Stamford by *Huntington* to *London* in two days more. And the like
stages on their return.

"Allowing each passenger 14l. weight, and all above 3d. a pound.

"Performed by $\left\{\begin{array}{l} BENJAMIN\ KINGMAN, \\ HENRY\ HARRISON, \\ WALTER\ BAYNES. \end{array}\right.$

"Also this gives notice that the Newcastle Stage Coach sets out from York
every Monday and Friday, and from Newcastle every Monday and Friday."

How changed the times! Oh, steam, thou great
invader!

The churches, and they are numerous, form the
main attraction of the city. Connected with many
of them are extensive burial-grounds, ivied and
grim—

"Where many a tomb is graved to stand unseen,
And waste its record on the heedless throng."

In one of these church-yards were interred the
remains of Richard Turpin, the notorious highway-
man, who was tried for horse-stealing at the York-
shire Assizes, and executed April 7, 1739. The
inhabitants of the neighborhood still point out his
grave, and tradition asserts that, early on the morning
after the execution, the body was stolen for the purpose of dissection, but a mob having assembled
on the occasion, it was traced by them to a garden,
whence it was borne in triumph through the streets

on men's shoulders, and replaced in the same grave, and a quantity of slaked lime deposited around the body.

In all the churches are tablets to commemorate the virtues and services of the distinguished dead. Indeed, these well-wrought mementoes are now the chief interest of the venerable buildings; for, whatever may have been their architectural magnificence, time, the great destroyer, has sadly disfigured it.

The old gateways under the city walls are, many of them, still preserved, and massive affairs they are. The city extends beyond the walls for a goodly distance. The streets are narrow, and many of the houses have the projecting upper stories, so that you might almost jump from one to another. How such top-heavy buildings have been kept from tumbling over, one cannot imagine. There are many fine shops, and the railway station is a magnificent affair— better than any in *New* York, with all its boasted thrift and enterprise. Trains, for all parts of the kingdom, start almost every hour during the day and night.*

The walls surrounding the city merit more than a passing notice. These mighty and impassible bulwarks in the sieges and battles of yore, are in most

* At present we fly from York to London by the light of a single winter's day.—*Macaulay*.

excellent preservation. Their ancient builders knew well the honorable art of masonry. The top of these noble barriers forms a delightful promenade. Far and near, the dainty landscape offers a picture of unbroken and unrivalled beauty.

The river Ouse winds its peaceful way through the heart of the city. It is a much better-looking stream than the Thames, though not so wide. The water is quite clean and clear, and boats of two or three hundred tons may come up to the wharves. Steamers ply regularly between York and Hull. Opposite the city the Ouse is sixteen feet deep. Beautiful walks extend along the banks of the river for several miles, huge trees shading them on either side. It was in the Ouse near Bedford, that John Bunyan fell when a young man, and very narrowly escaped drowning.

The far-famed Minster, or cathedral, is the absorbing wonder of York, and to the examination of its gigantic proportions visitors invariably devote their first hours. It is considerably larger, and, internally, in a much better state of preservation than the Lincoln minster, and it is of much easier access, being almost in the centre of the city, and on a level with the leading streets, as well as very near to the hotels. It is a massive and superb structure, well worthy the study of all who delight in architectural grandeur. Near to the door which opens into the interior, is a

Latin inscription, in Saxon characters, which reads
thus :

"Ut Rosa flos florum
Sic est Domus ista Domorum."

It has been thus rendered :

"This is the chief of Houses
As the Rose is the chief of Flowers."

This is said to have been a compliment paid to the
building by a Hollander, who had travelled the world
over.

In the words of another: "How individual is every
cathedral. York is not like Westminster, nor like
Strasbourg, nor Cologne, any more than Shakspeare
is like Milton, or Milton like Homer. The cathedral
of York has a severe grandeur peculiar to itself."
The entire structure covers some six acres. The
stained glass windows, elaborate carvings, and superb
statuary, surprise the beholder. Magnificence on
a scale so extensive is scarcely dreamed of in this
modern age of gold and extravagance.

From the north transept a vestibule leads to the
chapter-house; this is an octagonal building, sixty-
three feet in diameter, and sixty-seven feet ten inches
in height, supported on the outside by eight massive
buttresses. "The more minutely," says Rickman,[*]

* Gothic Architect, p. 265.

"this magnificent edifice is examined, the more will its great value appear. The simplicity and boldness, and, at the same time, the great richness of the nave, and the very great chastity of design and harmony of composition of the choir and great tower, render the building more completely one whole than any of our mixed cathedrals; while the exquisite beauty of the early character of the chapter-house and its approach, forms a valuable link to unite the early English transepts and the decorated nave. This chapter-house is by far the finest polygonal room without a central pier in the kingdom; and the delicacy and variety of its details are nearly unequalled. Too much praise cannot be given the dean and chapter for their careful restoration of every decayed portion. By this restoration, the whole of the west front may be considered in as good a state as when first erected."

Many rare relics are shown by the aged guides. A chair in the chapel is designated as the one in which those amiable kings, Richard III. and James VI., were crowned. A good idea of the impressive grandeur of the Minster is conveyed in the following incident related by Mr. Catlin, the well-known painter and friend of the Indians. That gentleman says: "I took a party of American Indians into the building—you know they never express surprise—and yet, when they entered, all instantly lifted up their hands in awful astonishment, breathing a low-whispered hush, as if fearful that their deep-struck imagination might break out into words ! On coming out, they said to me : ' We never thought anything of the white man's religion before !' "

York Cathedral stands on the foundations of the old Norman church, built in 626, by Edwin, the Saxon king of Northumberland. It was fired, and a portion of it very seriously burned, some years since. A man concealed himself in the building on a Sabbath afternoon, and soon after the service carried out his infamous design. He escaped by an ingenious contrivance placed at one of the side windows (the window was particularly shown us), but was finally captured, tried, pronounced insane, and confined during the remainder of his days in a lunatic asylum. The wood-work of the towers, etc., injured by the fire, was all speedily repaired. The new roof is wholly constructed of teak, presented by the government, and is covered with lead procured from the mines of the Greenwich Hospital estates. It is stated by Gent, that Cromwell granted permission to a person to pull down one of the handsomest portions of the building, and build a stable with the materials. The statement is quite too gross to be credited.

Remaining in York over the Sabbath, I of course

attended service at the Minster. The Dean of York was present—a very aged man. The exercises were conducted by several younger clergymen, one of whom delivered a sermon. The music was at times grand beyond description ; one of the pieces in the afternoon being the most exquisite that I ever listened to, and the voices of several of the singers remarkably clear and bold. When the organ-pipes opened to their fullest extent, and the singers " did their loudest," we could compare the noise to nothing but that of a thunder-storm, and the lowering clouds having overshadowed the Minster with darkness, all that was wanting to make the simile perfect was a few vivid flashes of lightning. When, at the end of a bar, the instrument and voices would suddenly pause, the echo of notes rang through the building like the sound of distant artillery.

As the audience retired I noticed it numbered many of the aged and humble, as well as many representatives of wealth and nobility—and not a few dashing fellows, and extravagantly dressed belles, whose appearance did not at all chime with the ancient and solemn edifice.

At York Castle, and Mary's Abbey—the latter one of the most interesting ruins in Britain—the traveler always finds much worthy of his attention. The castle is still used as a prison. Within its walls the poet Montgomery was once confined for publishing a patriotic song on the destruction of the Bastile ; and here in 1795, he wrote his " Prison Amusements."

8

"MINE OWN ROMANTIC TOWN."

SUCH was the fond appellation given the proud capital of Scotland, by Sir Walter Scott, who, born within its precincts, never failed to extol its indisputable merits with the warmest enthusiasm, while Coleridge, critical Coleridge, named it first, of the five finest things in Scotland.

Such laudatory mention by two lettered worthies, if nothing more, should lead the tourist to a scrupulous inspection of its varied wonders, and he will not regret his painstaking. After the dull, rusty towns of North England, its bright busy streets and clean faced buildings, wear an air of freshness and life altogether pleasing. I refer especially to what is known as the new city, for the old part of Edinburgh is crooked and time-worn beyond measure. Indeed the two great divisions of the city, the old and the new, are as different as possible, and stand in striking contrast, fit exemplars of the past and present.

I naturally wandered over the old city first, and
(170)

much there is within its confines to attract the obser
vant eye. What a world of ancient lore concentrates
in its every street and close. What visions of by-gone
days, and church history loom up, in the old awkward house in the crowded Canon-gate which our
guide proudly announces as the home of John Knox,
that staunch servant of the Lord, who, through long
years of persecution poured forth the truths of the
gospel with marvellous eloquence and effect.

I entered the venerable pile with much reverence,
for the name of Knox has from boyhood been honored
on my lips. The identical room in which the great
reformer studied, and where it is safe to presume
many long hours were spent in silent and solemn
communion with the divine source from whence his
strength was drawn, is still shown in its original condition or with little alteration. Within this room is
the pulpit which was used for his street preaching,
and the communion table around which his devout
followers were wont to unite, and from time to time,
re-affirm their faith and renew their zeal in the holy
service to which they had pledged their hands and
hearts. These relics carry one back to the every
day life of the Scotch reformers, and you almost look
for the modest figure of their valiant leader, he who
" never feared the face of man," at every opening of
the ponderous door.

It was from a comparatively small window in this
room, that the eager crowds in the street were often
addressed by Knox, and even his hard-hearted perse-
cutors were more than once made to weep by his
searching eloquence. One of Queen Mary's worst
charges against him, was, that he caused her to weep
by his plain and pointed conversation.

The stout timbers, low ceilings, and massive walls
all denote the great age of the building, and the
protestant world has reason to rejoice that it is to be
carefully preserved, and that the receipts from its
exhibition, a small fee being required of each visitor,
are to be given to the preaching of that word which
the fearless reformer so faithfully and successfully
dispensed. Within a few years past a neat and commodious building, called the "Knox Chapel" has
been erected on a lot immediately adjoining the
house, and as it is in a densely populated part of the
city it is not found difficult to secure large audiences.
I once attended service at this chapel, and was much
impressed with the solemnity of the occasion.

Not far from the "Knox Chapel" is the old palace
of Holy-rood, the only Royal palace of Scotland that
has not fallen into ruins. The chapel exhibits some
curious features in the enriched pointed style of
architecture, and in many of the rooms the antiquated
furniture is admirably preserved. In one of the

towers are the Presence Chambers in which Queen
Mary had the well-known interview with Knox, the
Dressing-Room, and the small apartment adjoining it,
which has a secret stair case leading from the chapel
to the palace, by which Darnley and his associates
entered and murdered Rizzio ; and the Bed-Chamber
in which is still the Queen's bed and bedding, with
some other relics of those days. This is by far the
most interesting portion of the palace, and will ever
remain so, from its associations with the unfortunate
Mary. Rizzio's blood (despite Sir Walter Scott's
whimsical episode of the Brummagen Bagman and
his "scouring drops" in the introduction to "The
Chronicles of the Canon-gate,") is still shown at the
head of the stairs leading to the Queen's apartments :
his body was pierced with fifty-six wounds.

What are now known as the Royal apartments, or
those used by Her Majesty Victoria, and the members of the Royal family when in Edinburgh, were
recently re-decorated and contrast strangely enough
with the other portions of the superannuated building.
Her Majesty not unfrequently tarries here on her
way to and from the Highlands.

After Sir Walter Scott I will not presume to speak
of the Canon-gate with its historic associations, and
present interest, save to say that I have in many
strolls through its still bustling limits, found it diffi-

cult to realize its former glory. Where are the crowds that gathered anon to applaud, and then to insult the heroic Knox, himself the same alike in prosperity and adversity, in sunshine and in storm? Where are the actors of whom Scott's chronicles preserve so vivid a picture? Where is the amiable Sir Walter himself, whose footsteps so often pressed the rough pavement of the historic neighborhood, and whose genius revelled in its legendary lore?

Like a vigilant sentinel, the castle of Edinburgh frowns from its lofty height, alike upon the plebian hordes of the Canon-gate and the lordly throngs of Princess-street. From every point in the consolidated city it is impressively prominent. I can compare it to no fortified building I have seen, excepting Stirling Castle, to which it bears a close resemblance. From 1707 to 1818, a long and eventful century, the massive regalia of Scotland slumbered within one of its inner chambers, its whereabouts unknown even to the citizens of Edinburgh, and only discovered by a fortuitous circumstance. The royal baubles are now shown with evident pride, and constitute the chief interior attraction of the fortress. From the lofty parapets of the outer-walls the survey of Edinburgh and all the country round is such as to well repay the tedious ascent of the castle hill, and the united cities are remarkably fortunate in possessing many admir-

able points for viewing their rare beauty of locality.

It is Miss Martineau in her " Retrospect of Western
Travel," if I remember correctly, who says, " it would
be wise in travelers to make it their first business in a
foreign city to climb the loftiest point they can reach,
so as to have the scene they have to explore laid out
as in a living map beneath them. It is scarcely cred-
ible how much time is saved, and confusion of ideas
obviated by this means." Most heartily subscribing
to the doctrine, I had been in Edinburgh but a few
hours, ere I mounted the ramparts of the Castle, the
Calton Hill, the footpath on Salisbury Crags, and sat
composedly in Arthur's seat, whence in the felicitous
words of the guide book, " the old and new town are
seen in beautiful contrast to one another, the former
looking like some ancient mother of a numerous and
thriving progeny, placed in the chair of precedence,
and surrounded by her gay and youthful family."
So grand is the survey from either of these eminences
that one is never content with a single view, but cannot resist the temptation to frequently clamber to
their peering heights, and is always abundantly
rewarded for his labor. Though a clever companion
is scarce ever an intruder, I am of the opinion that
one best enjoys the striking and romantic views from
these lofty galleries, when solitary and alone. The

mind and eye want no interruption, not even that of a friend alive to all the grandeur of the panoramic scene.

How indissolubly connected with the great relig- ious and philanthropic interests of Scotland, is the revered name of Chalmers. How precious his mem- ory to all good men. His mortal remains mingle with their mother dust, in the "Southern Cemetery" opened but a few weeks prior to his death and situated at the grange, a singularly beautiful spot, near the old town, surrounded on all sides by green fields, and on the South and West by lines of well-grown forest trees, that must have seen at least their century, while in front it commands one of the finest views of the city. Never in the memory of man did Scotland witness such a funeral as that of Chalmers. "Great- ness of the mere extrinsic type," says his devoted friend Hugh Miller, " can always command a showy pageant; but mere extrinsic greatness never yet succeeded in purchasing the tears of a people; and the spectacle of yesterday (June 4th, 1847,) in which the trappings of grief, worn not as idle signs, but as the representatives of real sorrow, were borne by well nigh half the population of the metropolis, and black- ened the public way for furlong after furlong, and mile after mile,—was such as Scotland has rarely witnessed, and which mere rank or wealth, when at the highest or the fullest, were never yet able to buy. It was a solemn tribute, spontaneously paid to departed goodness and greatness by the public mind."

The same good authority estimates the number of spectators at the funeral of the "mighty dead" at rather over than under an hundred thousand persons. There were few indeed, even among those who differed widely from many of his views, who did not feel the deepest emotion at the remembrance of his great and eminent merit. His actions, his efforts, and his written works, have all too deeply impressed the public mind to ever be forgotten.

I was glad to gain an interview with his son-in-law, the Rev. Dr. Hanna, now a prominent minister of the Free Church in Edinburgh, and by whose advice I am going to study the comparatively unknown but really wonderful mountain scenery of the Isle of Skye—which he thinks will in a few short years, or so soon as rightly appreciated, be one of the most popular summer resorts on the coast of Scotland.

Many of the more noted ecclesiastical structures are in the old town. Here, on High Street, is the High Church or Cathedral of St. Giles, the tutelary Saint of Edinburgh. In the reign of James II., Preston of Gorton got possession of the arm-bone of the saint, which he bequeathed to this cathedral, where it was kept among the treasures of the church until the

8*

Reformation, when with a deal more superstitious trumpery it was thrown to the four winds. The building contains three places of worship. The division called the High Church has a gallery with a throne and canopy for the Sovereign, which is used by the Lord High Commissioner to the General Assembly when attending divine service during the sitting of that body. Right and left of the throne are pews appropriated to the magistrates of the city, who appear there on Sabbath in their robes, and the Judges of the Courts of Session and Exchequer, also in their robes. The musical bells of the cathedral are rung every day from one to two o'clock P. M., the ringer being paid from a fund left for the purpose by a generous resident of the city..

In the ground between the church and the court-houses were interred the remains of John Knox, and within the cathedral repose the bodies of Regent Murray, who was shot at Linlithgow in 1570, and the great Marquis of Montrose, who was beheaded in 1650. On the outer wall facing the High Street, is a mural tablet, pointing out the family burying-ground of Napier of Merchistan, the celebrated inventor of the logarithms. The Parliament House is hard by, and full of interest; and far down the street is the " Tron Church " where Chalmers preached.

On Sabbath I went to hear the Rev. Thomas

Guthrie, D.D., whose writings are not unknown in America, and who is here esteemed as one of the leading preachers of the Free Church. His chapel, called " St. John's," is very near Victoria Hall, a building erected for the meetings of the General Assembly, or Convocation of the Church of Scotland, and the spire of which is two hundred and forty-one feet high, and esteemed the most symmetrical of its kind, excepting (says the guide-book) that of Grace Church, New York.

Dr. Guthrie reminded me not a little of Dr. Duff, whose visit to America will ever be remembered. He is the same order of man—physically, if not mentally. His practical discourse was made the more impressive by the strange gestures of his long swinging arms, and a broad dialect more forcible than mellifluous. But while eminent as a minister and theological writer, he is quite as well known for his long and assiduous labors in behalf the destitute children and youth of Edinburgh. " Dr. Guthrie's original Ragged Industrial School " in Ramsay Lane, (so called from the house of Allen Ramsey the poet, adjoining) is one of the most interesting and useful institutions in all Scotland. It has been (1854) nearly eight years in operation, and every year the Directors, in reporting on their progress, have done so with increasing satisfaction. I have visited the establishment, and would that it had a counterpart in every destitute section of this and all other great cities. It is in some respects superior to any of the industrial schools in London, and in its every department reflects the highest credit upon its patriotic founder and intelligent management. The children appear in excellent health and spirits, and there is a cheering air of industry, comfort and happiness* throughout the building. From the Seventh Annual Report, lately issued, and kindly handed me by the Superintendent, I glean a few suggestive statistics :

One of the best evidences of the discipline of a school is the average daily attendance. In the present instance, the average numbers on the roll being 304, the average daily attendance was 250. The average number of absentees was 74 ; but of these 24 were absent on account of sickness, leaving 30 as the number which represent the daily amount of truantage whether forced or voluntary. It is worthy of remark that in calculating the average attendance, the Sundays are included, on which days the attendance is always somewhat smaller than on the other days

* It is no less interesting than instructive to know that the Cholera, which committed such ravages among the poor in Newcastle, did not attack one of the children at the Ragged Industrial School of that town. The only means of prevention were—wholesome food, cleanliness, warm clothing, and well-venti lated school-rooms.

of the week. The difference in the average being as 230 on the Sundays to 260 on the week-days.

The most serious difficulties to be contended with, in securing regular attendance, are twofold; 1st, The utter indifference, or worse, of many of the parents in reference to this matter; and, 2d, The strong errant propensity which the majority of the children exhibit on their first admission, and especially those children who are sent to school by the magistrate, and over whom there is, at present, no legal power of detention. In the majority of cases, no doubt, the moral power exerted in the school regimen ultimately prevails; but were the legal power referred to possessed by the School officials, it is confidently believed that the regular attendance of all these unfortunates would be secured. The subject of the treatment of destitute and delinquent children has been recently investigated by a Select Committee of the House of Commons, and the Directors are glad to think that there is a high probability that the want of power referred to will be supplied during the next Session of Parliament.

The following table exhibits the educational work that has been done in the school during the year:

BOYS' SCHOOL.

Number at present on the Roll, 110.	When Admitted.	Present Date.
Unable to read	60	5
Could read a little.............................	20	14
Could read tolerably.................	20	28
Could read well......................................	10	63
Total............................	110	110
Unable to write	102	55
Could write a little............................	6	4
Could write tolerably....	2	20
Could write well.................................... ..	..	31
Total.................................	110	110
Could do nothing in arithmetic................... ..	104	61
Could do a little..........	6	36
Proficient in elementary rules......................	..	13
Total.......................	110	110

GIRLS' SCHOOL.

Number at present on the Roll, 91.	When Admitted.	Present Date.
Unable to read	73	18
Could read a little....................................	16	10
Could read tolerably	2	27
Could read well	..	36
Total...	91	91
Unable to write	88	50
Could write a little...................................	3	13
Could write tolerably.................................	..	14
Could write well......................................	14	14
Total...	91	91
Could do nothing in arithmetic......................	91	51
Could do a little......................................	..	40
Proficient in elementary rules......................	..	..
Total...	91	91

Of the Industrial training the following table is
given :

Number of Boys employed in tailor's shop..........................	10
" " " in shoemaker's do.........................	5
" " " in carpenter's do.........................	4
" " " in boxmaker's do.........................	30
" " " in bracemaker's do......................	12
Younger boys employed in hair-teasing and other simple work.......	49
Total...............	110
Number of Girls learning to knit...................................	62
" " to sew...............................	91
Number of Girls who take their turn in washing	30
" " who have regularly done kitchen work	36
" " who take their turn in cleaning the school-rooms...	60
Number of Girls employed daily in assisting in the Kitchen..........	3
" " in washing the rooms three times a week..	24
" " in washing their own and the boys' clothes	
once a week..................................	20

Another Table exhibits the amount and the finan-
cial value of the work done in the School during the
bygone year. It appears as if several of the depart-
ments had been self-supporting, and in one sense they
have been so, for they have paid their own expenses.
But in another sense, they have not been self-supporting; for the profits realised from them are fractions
when compared with the sum paid for the education
and support of those from whose labor they were
derived. The difference between these profits and
the whole sum paid for the management and support
of the school is the price of the education and train-

ing which the children have received; and viewing the matter financially, all that can be said of it is that the Industrial Department of the Boys' School, after paying its own expenses, aided to the extent of £20 in meeting the general expenditure of the Institution. In doing this it has done much.

The moral training of the scholars is carefully looked to, the Bible being the daily text book.

Some £1,400 have lately been subscribed toward purchasing an Industrial Farm for the school, which will greatly add to its usefulness. Many touching incidents of the gratitude of the poor little ones already rescued from want and misery by its kindly instrumentalities are recorded on the reports, and pleasant recollections of my visit to Ramsey Lane and its noble charity will be ever associated with my sojourn in the Scottish capital.

On the same Sabbath that I listened to the fervent Guthrie, I heard Dr. Candlish, another noted Free church pastor. At precisely the announced hour the Doctor and precentor entered the chapel, preceded by a sexton carrying the pulpit bible and hymn book. Both the Doctor and precentor were dressed in large loose black gowns, such as are worn by the Episcopal clergy. The worship was initiated by the singing of a psalm to the tune of "Brook Street:" the psalm having been first read, and the tune announced by the Doctor. The clerk who sat immediately beneath the pulpit was an agreeable looking young man, and started the tunes in good style, and stood during the whole singing. The audience, which was large and highly intelligent though very plain, joined in the singing with hearty good will, and I thought the music superior to much of a more artistic cast to which I had listened in the English Churches.

Dr. Candlish is a nervous, powerful preacher, somewhat singular, but certainly very impressive in his manner. He has been prominent in the history of the Free church movement and is classed among the foremost of its many able and eloquent defenders.

Outside the walls of church or chapel, I have attended a very curious religious meeting. It was held in one of the large public halls, and was convened to listen to a debate or controversy on Romanism *vs.* Protestantism. Neither of the disputants were educated men, or men of much note, yet they were well informed on the various cardinal points at issue, and the emphatic manner in which they expressed themselves, seemed to vastly delight the auditory, which was composed of very plain people about equally divided in their sympathies, as they clamorously evinced by their vociferous applause at the more palpable hits of their favorite disputant. At one time the excitement ran so high that a riot appeared

imminent, but no blows were exchanged, and at a
late hour with an agreement to meet again at an
early date, the champions and their friends retired in
comparative order. These popular discussions are
very common here, and throughout Great Britain.
They are often had in the open air, indeed the street
preachers of London spend much of their time in con-
troverting the fallacies of Rome, and a fierce and
unrelenting war is waged against the Pope. Whether
this course is calculated to make converts to protestantism is a question to which, for one, I am by no
means ready to give an affirmative response, though
many prudent men believe it quite effectual.

The rooms of the Royal Highland Agricultural
Society well repay examination. There is a growing
taste for enlightened agriculture throughout Scotland.
The modest Ayrshire ploughman would hardly know
how to wield the improved implements now in vogue.
At the Annual Fair of the Royal Highland Society,
held at Berwick upon Tweed, a few days since, there
were as intelligent farmers, choice cattle, fine grain'
and other products as at the English Fair at Lincoln,
which I lately attended.

Referring to the ploughman of Ayrshire, it would
perhaps be inexcusable to leave Edinburgh without
allusion to the enthusiasm in which his memory is
still held by all classes of the people. As has been

gracefully said : "Every man's and boy's, and girl's head carries snatches of Burn's songs, and can say them by heart, and, what is strangest of all, never learned them from a book, but from mouth to mouth."

The Burns monument near the High School is not so elegant as that near the Doon in Ayrshire, and is quite surpassed by that to Scott on Princess-street, which displays much architectural taste, and rightly commemorates his immense genius and literary achievements. It forms an appropriate centre to the united city, while Scott alone rivals Burns in the hearts of the people of Edinburgh.

From the gardens surrounding the Scott monument the new city with its regular and well built streets presents a most inviting appearance. With less of historic interest than the old city it yet boasts no insignificant claim to a first rank among the great cities of Great Britain.

There is indeed a classic air about the very streets, and one instinctively feels himself in contact with a scholarly and refined people. A visit to the art galleries and other institutions materially adds to the favorable impression.

A place of decided interest is the spacious bookstore of the Messrs. Blackwood, whose venerable magazine is equally a favorite on both sides the Atlantic, and has for more than a generation past enlisted the best literary talent, of all lands.

Of the many extensive and elegant stores and shops, I have been most taken with those where the Highland plaids, tartans, and tweeds are sold. You know each Scottish clan has its peculiar tartan and adheres to it with great tenacity. The tartans are of Saxony wool and spun silk, and are often very rich and costly. They are not however worn on all occasions except by a few who will listen to no innovation in dress. There are also shops expressly for the sale of what is termed Highland jewellery, which appears to include snuff-boxes, segar cases, and an hundred other articles of every day use, all tastefully manufactured in wood colored in keeping with the various tartans.

AN EVENING WITH HUGH MILLER.*

HAVING found from several attempts that it was quite impracticable to secure an interview with Mr. Miller (who of all living Scotchmen, I most desired to know), at the office of the *Witness*, I accepted a kind invitation to spend the evening at his surburban residence, " Shrubmount," some five or six miles from the city. Starting just at sun down the ride by coach in the cool of the evening over an excellent road and 'mid scenery the most picturesque, was exceedingly pleasant. My open air companions, for I had taken an outside seat, were chiefly tradesmen and clerks, who, unlike their more fortunate professional and mercantile brethren, had been unable to escape

"The heartless city, with its forms, and dull routine,"

until the close of the day. They were however in much good humor, and to the timely courtesy of one

* It may add to the interest of this sketch to state that the interview it recounts was had but a short time prior to Mr. Miller's melancholy death.

(189)

or two who sat nearest me, I was indebted for a gratifying description of the various points of interest in
the charming region through which our ambitious
team whirled us with surprising speed. As we passed
beyond the Calton Hill with its imposing monuments,
and 'neath the ever awing shadow of Arthur's Seat,
the busy marine towns of Leith and Portobello opened
to our view, and beyond their forests of masts, lay the
broad, deep sea,

" The blue, the fresh, the ever free !"

as placid as Lomond or Katrine in an August day.
On either side the smooth roadway, fine mansions and
tasteful gardens attracted my envious admiration, and
indeed I had scarce enumerated the teeming beauties
of the unrivalled panoramic view from the coach-top,
ere the heavy vehicle rattled through the rough steeets
of Portobello, and the obliging driver delivered me
at the very gate of Shrubmount, the comfortable yet
altogether unostentatious home of the distinguished
man who, with certainly far more of genuine respect
than idle curiosity, I so longed to meet.

A gentle tap at the bell soon brought a smiling
lassie by whom I was ushered into the presence of
Mrs. Miller, a lady in every way worthy her estimable husband, and whose face, though long years have
past, retains not a little of that "waxen clearness of

complexion" which the Cromaty poet so admired when like "a fair child rather than a grown woman" she "came hurriedly tripping down the garden-walk." All the romance of the curious courtship which ultimately made her Mrs. Miller came to my mind, as announcing my name and place of residence, I was given a true Highland welcome, such as Burns irreverently commemorates:

> "When death's dark stream I ferry o'er,
> A time that surely shall come ;
> In heaven itself I ask no more,
> Than just a Highland welcome."

Mrs. Miller, herself an accomplished writer and scholar, was quite ready to converse intelligently upon American affairs, and I had a delightful chat ere Mr. Miller came in from the Museum building in process of erec ion within the Shrubmount grounds. To this structure he was giving much devoted attention in the expectation of securing a place of safe keeping for the many rare and valuable geological specimens accumulated in his passionate fondness of the noble science which, while yet a boy, he so successfully studied among the pebbles of the Cromarty shore.*

Shrubmount is within the precincts of Portobello,

---

* I afterwards found some of Mr. Miller's first collected specimens in an unpretending museum at Stromness in the Orkneys.

a favorite sea-side resort of the citizens of Edinburgh, and Mrs. Miller told me her good husband had secured the place, which is quite aside from the bathing grounds, purely for its seclusion and amplitude of land. There is certainly much space, and room for the most extended improvements, and Mr. Miller undoubtedly has it in view to here establish a home stead worthy his illustrious name and fame.

Mr. Miller's entrance was with an apology for having detained me, and a hope that "Lydia" (Mrs. Miller) had given me a hearty welcome to Shrubmount, "where from his close application in Edinburgh, he was only able to receive his friends, and then sometimes too fatigued to rightly entertain them."

After hastily reading my letters of introduction from several of his American acquaintances, he sat himself close beside me, and began an earnest and minute inquiry regarding the geological peculiarities of the United States, and especially of the State of New York. "Pray how far are you from the great forests of which I have heard so much?" asked he with a broad Scotch accent, and ere I could reply, with boyish eagerness he exclaimed, "Ah! how I should like to see your great rivers and mountains."

And then with almost breathless attention he listened for many minutes to my humble description of some of the more marked geographical features of the different States of the Union.

"Your great country has many geological wonders," he remarked, as I paused for any comment he might offer. "Ah!" he continued, "I do indeed wish I might study them, and your enterprising people." "Will you not come then," I replied, "the journey is now made comparatively short and safe, and all America would gladly welcome you; indeed," I added, (as was the fact,) "I have now with me an invitation for you to give a series of your instructive geological lectures under the auspices of an association in New York—come, and we will give you large audiences, and practical proof of our admiration of 'The old Red-sand stone,' and your other works, as well known throughout the new world as here in your native Scotland." "But," he naively answered, "I am too busy here,—Edinburgh gives me editorial work enough—to say nothing of my attention to geology—I can't go to America, it's of no use to think of it—I have not the time." "But you really need relaxation, and as you have well said, we have many geological wonders that would delight you."

Here Mrs. Miller interposed and made several suspicious inquiries regarding the streets of New York. She had heard marvellous stories of their filth, and wondered if they were true and the city healthy. It was no easy task to conscientiously evade a direct reply, which must certainly have been derogatory to the sanitary regulations of the American metropolis. Mrs. Miller also expressed a doubt as to the comforts of a sea voyage, and in this was joined by her husband, who jokingly thought " he was too cumbersome for ocean travel." They both, however, evinced no little admiration of our broad republic, its free institutions and happy people, but the evening's conversation was mainly upon its geological formations, and fossiliferous remains. Nearly every query put to me by Mr. Miller was expressive of his favorite science, although he is equally at home upon other scientific subjects, and upon the great political, religious, philanthropic, and educational questions of the day, and everywhere honored as the defender of revealed truth, and the champion of the church of his fathers.

When the ever memorable contest in the church of Scotland had come to a close by the decision of the House of Lords in the Auchterader case, Mr. Miller's celebrated letter to Lord Brougham attracted the particular attention of the party which was about to leave the Establishment, and he was selected as the most competent person to conduct the *Witness*, the principal metropolitan organ of the Free Church. The great success which this journal has met is owing doubtless, to the fine articles, political, ecclesiastical, and geological which Mr. Miller has written for it.*

If, as in his own words, he was " but a slim, loose-jointed boy, fond of the pretty intangibilities of romance, and of dreaming when broad awake, " he is now a stout wide-shouldered man, of fine physical presence, though of far from ruddy health. When recently lecturing in Exeter Hall he was obliged to keep his chair during the evening, and it is painfully true that toilsome devotion to the various duties resting upon him, apart from his intense application to geological study has seriously undermined his sturdy Highland constitution. It was with much of sincere regret at this too obvious fact, that I left Shrub-mount and bade adieu to him, who to say nothing of his other masterly achievements, has by his own unaided energies, and while yet in the prime of life, rendered himself, "first among his countrymen in an interesting and important department of Natural Science, to which there is no aristocratic or royal road."

* Prof. Agassiz' Memoir.

THE BIRTHPLACE OF THOMSON.

Though I have been to the "land o' Burns," and studied the manifold attractions of Abbottsford, I pass them by to give you some account of a visit to Ednam, the birth-place of Thomson, immortal as the author of "The Seasons," the "Castle of Indolence," and · "Liberty," for the reason that while every tourist in Scotland writes elaborately of Burns and Scott, comparatively few make allusion to their illustrious compeer whose name should be equally precious to all lovers of true poetry. The glowing admiration in which he was held by Burns is perpetuated in the manly and graceful poetic tribute beginning with the stanza:

> " When virgin Spring, by Eden's flood,
> Unfolds her tender mantle green,
> Or pranks the sod in frolic mood,
> Or turns Æolian strains between."

The train took me from Edinburgh to Kelso on the Tweed, or at the junction of the Tweed and Teviot, in a fine fertile plain, and near to the tract of country called the "Merse." Nothing can exceed the beauty of this neighborhood, which abounds with wood and water, and is adorned with all that wealth, taste and industry can bestow. The venerable structure of "Kelso Abbey" one of the oldest in Scotland, is a fine specimen of the purest Saxon, and well worthy the attention of the artist and antiquarian. The only son of King David I. and many other illustrious persons are interred within the walls of the Abbey, and it was here that Henry III. of England and his Queen, met Alexander III. of Scotland and his Queen, on which occasion history tells us, that great pomp and splendor were displayed. In 1460, James III. was crowned in Kelso Abbey. It frequently suffered from the hostile incursions of the English, and was demolished in 1569, at the time of the Reformation. At which period it passed, by grant, with all its possessions, to the Duke of Roxburgh.

The environs of Kelso are happily painted in Leyden's "Scenes of Infancy :"

> " Bosom'd in wood where mighty rivers run,
> Kelso's fair vale expands before the sun,
> Its rising downs in vernal beauty swell,
> And fringed with hazel, winds each flowery dell,
> Green spangled plains to dimpling lawns succeed,
> And Tempe rises on the banks of Tweed ;
> Blue o'er the river Kelso's shadow flies,
> And copse-clad isles amid the waters rise."

In 1787 Burns made a tour on horseback through this country,* which strongly interested his fancy. His journal contains frequent reference to the "enchanting views and prospects on both sides of the Tweed."

Two-and-a-half miles to the north-east of Kelso, and three miles from the border, is Ednam, one of the most retired and humble villages in Southern Scotland. Aside from the great thoroughfares, and far from the smoke and confusion of the manufacturing districts, it presents a picture of exquisite rural quiet, to whose honest and peaceful denizens,

> " Contentment gives a crown,
> Where fortune hath denied it."

I found the wayside cottagers mainly ignorant of Thomson or his works, and it is remarkable that while Burns and Scott o'ershadow the whole country, and their poems are household words alike in palace and cabin, the gifted author of the "Seasons," whose works are equally well-known and admired in America, is scarcely remembered in many parts of his native land. It is true he spent much of his time in England, yet this is no good reason why he should be forgotten in the "land o' cakes."

The walk to Ednam, for on such excursions I

---

* Called by Beattie " the Arcadian ground of Scotland."

usually prefer to depend upon my perambulatory powers—was through a winding pleasant country road,
environed by flowery meadows and thrifty gardens, the
varied beauty of which was much enhanced by the mellow summer sun and exceeding stillness on every side.
More than once I felt the aptness of the poet's own
exclamation :

> " These are the haunts of meditation, these
> The scenes where ancient bards, the inspiring breath
> Extatic felt."

Just fairly out of Kelso village I passed a park
over the superb stone gate-way to which is inscribed :

> " Erected by the inhabitants of Kelso in testimony of their respect for Mrs.
> Robertson of Ednam House, and of their gratitude for her munificent gift."

I had not time to enter its tempting precincts, but
pressed forward, and soon on a graceful slope to my
right saw what I presumed must be the monument
to Thomson, and on my left the scattering cottages
composing the village of his birth. The vale of
Ednam is distinguished for its quiet beauty, and as I
crossed the tiny river Eden, which Burns with poetic
license calls " Eden's flood," I paused before entering
the village, to admire the singular loveliness of the
peaceful scene—a scene I can never forget.

The one long street of which the village of Ednam
is composed, is lined with thatched cottages of the
humblest order: indeed, I noticed but one or two

pretentious houses. There is the usual village school-
house, and as if to make the scene complete, a smoky
shop, where the blacksmith

> " Bares his sinewy arm,
> And early strokes the sounding anvil warm."

I had no difficulty in finding the manse, and Mr.
Lamb, the rector, to whom I had been directed as the
proper person to give me all the information I sought,
received me with the warmth of an old friend. I
was instantly at home in his comfortable library, and
lost no time in broaching the object of my visit. He
was quite as enthusiastic in Thomson's memory as I
could desire. After assuring me the house in which
the poet was born had been torn down, and the
school-house erected upon its site, he pointed to the
new church, upon the spot where stood the venerable
kirk of which the Rev. Thomas Thomson, the poet's
father, was long the faithful pastor. The new building is as uncouth a specimen of church architecture
as I have seen in all Scotland, a fact to be regretted
the more for the interesting associations by which its
locality is surrounded

Mr. Lamb kindly produced for my inspection, the
old church records, which were commenced as early
as 1666. This entry remains in a clear bold hand :

> 1693, September 9th. This day, Mr. Thomas Thomson, minister of Ednam,
> and Beatrix Trotter, in the parish of Kelso, gave up their names for proclama-
> tion in order to marriage."

In 1697 there is mention of the baptism of a son (Alexander), the result of this marriage, and in 1699 (January 4) of a daughter called Isabel ;* but by far the most interesting is the following :

"1700. Mr. Thomas Thomson's son JAMES, baptized September 15th."

By this it appears that the future poet was baptized when but four days old, having been born on the 11th of the same month. He was educated at Jedburgh school, then kept in the aisle of Jedburgh Church, and went from there, in March, 1715, to the University of Edinburgh, being intended for the church. An essay on "Country Life," written by him while at the University, shows how early the love of rural scenery and pursuits took possession of his mind.

When in 1725 he sailed from Leith to try his fortune in London, Dr. Johnson says: "His first want was a pair of shoes;" and adds, that "he had many letters of introduction; but having tied them up in a handkerchief, they were stolen from him—an accident sufficiently disastrous to a young stranger in the metropolis, to explain his condition." But with all his hard fortune, the early death of his father, his want of means and other sore troubles, he sang so sweetly that his name soon became familiar to cultivated ears, and the world, while he yet trod its mazy

* There were nine children in all.

9*

paths, began to shower upon him the honors his memory now so universally enjoys. His life was on the whole much less chequered and sorrowful than that of Burns or even Scott.

There are many quaint entries in the old church records at Ednam. The following, which Mr. Lamb kindly allowed me to transcribe, speaks well for the church discipline:

" September ye 6, 1685.

This day after prayer Roger Dickson being summoned and cited, composed and said that he had called John Dickson's wife and Marion Dedds witch-birds, but would not be convinced that it was a fault, being removed ye Elders now consulted what their censure should do : which was unanimously ordered that he should stand during ye whole of ye sermon at ye pillar. And after sermon to confess his fault. And to beg God and the people's pardon. And particularly the persons offended ; he refusing from ye sentence is referred to the judge."

This reminds me of a passage in the records of the parish of Cortachy, in the county of Forfar, which runs thus :

" No sermon at Cortachy this day, the minister being at Clova, at the trial of a witch."

On the 7th of January, 1853, a person called on Mr. Lamb, and stated that he wished to have the parish register searched with a view to ascertaining whether the birth or baptism of one James Cook was recorded therein; or in other words, he wanted evidence that the Parish of Ednam was the birth-place of the father of the renowned Captain Cook, the hero of our school-boy days. The person's name was Cook, and he claimed relationship to the intrepid voyager, and assured Mr. Lamb it had always been the belief of the family that the said James Cook came from this part of the country, and on leaving it had taken up his residence at Ayton in Berwickshire, and subsequently at Martin, Cleveland, where the future captain was born. Mr. Lamb was not a little surprised to find in the records the following entry fully confirming the accuracy of the family tradition :

"1693. Dec. 24. John Cooke in this parish and Jean Duncane in the parish of Simaillhume, gave up their names for proclamation in order to marriage. A certificate was produced of her good behaviour.

"John Cooke and Jane Duncane were married Jan. 16, 1694."

Mr. Lamb also subsequently ascertained that John Cooke, the father of James Cooke and grandfather of the Captain, was an elder in Ednam parish in 1692. Rev. Thomas Thomson, being then the parish minister.

As I admired the rich landscape view from the windows of the manse, Mr. Lamb directed my attention to an aged elm in a garden hard by, such an one as Hood sung of :

"A goodly elm of noble girth,
That, thrice the human span—
While on their variegated course
The constant seasons ran—
Through gale, and hail, and fiery bolt,
Has stood erect as man."

This noble tree is in girth at the ground 23 feet, and at the height of 10 feet where the first large branch springs, 10 feet, and at the height of nearly 25 feet where the second large branch springs, 9 feet. It is nearly 60 feet in height, and its branches spread over some 25 yards in circumference. The trunk is sculptured with ridges like a cork tree, and orna- mented with some fine tufts of *polypones sqiremosus.* It is safe to presume that beneath the leafy canopy of this old hereditary tree the gentle poet of Ednam passed many of the innocent hours of his infancy, though at a very early age he removed to Ancrum, and here too perhaps, the pious ancestor of the famous ocean navigator may have found a grateful shelter from the sultry sun of refulgent summer.

Reluctantly leaving the time honored manse of Ednam, and the truly Christian courtesy of its intelli- gent rector, I silently retraced my steps toward Kelso. Crossing the musical Eden on the dry stones, above the water mark, I soon came in sight of the Thomson monument, and could not resist a closer inspection of it, than was to be had from the road side, though at the risk of being seized as a poacher upon the highly cultivated field through which I forced my way to its modest inclosure. The tall waving grain was quite as high as my head, and white for the harvest. I found the monument a plain affair, not to be compared with those to Burns and Scott, and the enclosure over-run with shrubbery less choice than luxuriant, and evidently sadly neglected. A very little care would make the spot far more neat and creditable.

On one side of the cenotaph, which is a four sided cone thirty feet high, of drab stone, is this inscription :

ERECTED

IN MEMORY OF

J A M E S   T H O M S O N ,

AUTHOR   OF   THE   SEASONS,

BORN AT EDNAM,

11TH SEPTEMBER, A. D. 1700.

Thomson died at Richmond, near London, on the 27th of August, 1748, having within a few days completed his forty-eighth year. He was buried in Richmond Church, where there is a small brass tablet with the following inscription, no word of which can be said to exaggerate his merits :

In the earth below this tablet
are the remains of
JAMES THOMSON,
Author of the beautiful poems entitled,
" The Seasons" the " Castle of Indolence," etc.,
who died at Richmond
on the 27th of August
and was buried
On the 29th O. S. 1748.
The Earl of Bucham
unwilling that
So good a Man and so sweet a Poet,
Should be without a memorial,
has denoted the place of his interment,
for the satisfaction of his Admirers,
in the year of our Lord,
MDCCXCII.

Beneath this inscription his lordship added this striking passage from " Winter :"

" Father of Light and Life I thou God Supreme I
O teach me what is good I teach me thyself I
Save me from folly, vanity, and vice,
From every low pursuit I and feed my soul
With knowledge, conscious peace, and virtue pure ;
Sacred, substantial, never fading bliss I"

There is also a monument to Thomson in Westminster Abbey, between those of Shakespeare and Nicholas Rowe, poet laureate under George the First.*

* Thomson appears sitting, leaning his left arm upon a pedestal, and holding a book with the cap of liberty in his right hand. Upon the pedestal is carved a bas-relief of " The Seasons," to which a boy points, offering him a laurel crown as the reward of his genius. At the feet of the figure is a tragic mask and ancient harp. The whole is supported by a projecting pedestal : and on a

But except to rebuke the shameless indifference of some who have the honor to reside where he first saw the light, there is little need of a marble pile to perpetuate his exquisite works, and keep his memory green :

"Nature for him assumes herself the task,
'THE SEASONS' are his monuments of fame
With them to flourish, as from them it came."

Returning to Kelso I embraced the opportunity of an hour's leisure before the departure of the train for Edinburgh, to visit the St. James' Fair, held at Kelso annually on the fifth of August. Crossing the Tweed a short walk brought me to the grounds, which were spacious and thoroughly occupied. All sorts of cattle and horses were on sale, and though there were few specimens of ingenious handi-work, or fine fruits or flowers, as common at the American fairs, there was all the bustle of busy tradesmen, of boisterous drovers, of roystering horse-jockeys, of minstrels, puppet-shows and drinking booths, requisite to make up a successful fair, according to the old country estimate of such an institution. I walked carefully through

panel is inscribed his name, age, and the date of his death, with the following lines from his " Summer :"

"Tutored by thee, sweet poetry exalts
Her voice to ages ; and informs the page
With music, image, sentiment, and thoughts,
Never to die !"

the long avenues of busy traffickers, and was urgently
besought to buy everything, from a dray horse to one
of gingerbread, from a score of sheep to a mug
of beer. Great exuberance of spirits marked the
assembled crowds, and the occasion was only marred
by the number of intoxicated men literally lying all
over the grounds. I never saw one tithe of the
drunkenness at any fair in the States, and felt indeed
proud that the rum-fiend had no such undisputed
sway in the new world.

The locality of the fair grounds was beautiful
beyond description. From a rugged range of wooded
hills they ran across a lovely plain embracing perhaps
an hundred acres, to the very edge of the Tweed,
while just across the swift-running stream, in the
centre of a broad and magnificent lawn, stood "Fleurs
Palace," the seat of the Duke of Roxburgh, a stately
structure well preserved by its noble owner. As far
as the eye could span the fertile banks of the gentle
river, they were attired in nature's richest garb, and I
turned to the cars exclaiming, with the enamored
poet:

" What beauties does Flora disclose ;
How sweet are her smiles upon Tweed !"

PARIS AND THE EMPEROR.

TWICE have I tarried in Paris, and many were the novelties presented to my observation on each occasion. I shall never forget my first stroll up and down the beautiful streets, and through the gardens adjacent to the royal palace of the Louvre. The grandeur of every thing around me, the gaiety of the chatting multitude, the whirl of the vehicles, the steady pace of the *gens d'arms*, and a thousand other things made an indelible impression upon my mind.

Paris has never been too highly praised as a gay, gorgeous metropolis. Its architectural triumphs are among the choicest in the world and afford food for prolonged and careful study. Its historic associations render it intensely interesting to the student of the wonderful in the world's transmutations. One fancies he can almost see the blood in the streets, lingering from the fearful revolutions so memorable among the sanguinary conflicts of civil excitement.

(209)

The bayonet has been fearfully used all about that great palace of the Louvre, and no one knows how soon it may again glisten in open revolution against the singularist now claiming the French throne, and holding it by might rather than right.

But let us hope for peace, so long as no greater injustice is done to the people. They can endure the Napoleon of to-day, vile as he may be politically, for there are some good traits in his nature, and not the least, a constant regard for the employment of the working classes. This has led him to the demolition of whole rows of old rookeries, the building up of magnificent structures, the cutting through of new and spacious avenues, and other significant improvements, all adding vastly to the glory of the metropolis it is true, but obviously conceived to keep laboring Paris in a state of quiet, or in other words to spike the guns of rebellion with bread and cheese, and thus save the crown to the cunning " nephew of his uncle."

There is every variety of condition and life in Paris, and the representatives of all classes nowhere mingle so freely as in the parks. Turning into the Tuilleries gardens or Champs Elysee of a sunny afternoon a new world reveals itself to the observant eye. There range the children laughing, chatting, singing. There patrols the stiff laced guardsman. There comes the witching flirt as naive as a Yankee belle, and twice as polite! There lounge the beaux, prim and haughty, see how they wink at yon black eyed maiden, the confectioner's daughter of the Rue Vivienne!

Then we meet the men and women of toil, off for an hour's diversion, and as usual in the best possible humor. Indeed Paris is a grand smile, a broad grin, and scarce ever sad.

Qn the Champs Elysee, let the afternoon be fine, and whole troops of horsemen, fashionable and cheerful, fill the shaded avenues, while coach loads of ladies give richer grace to the scene.

"There is no policy like politeness," says Bulwer, and the shop-keepers of Paris practice it to a nicety. One is apt to purchase innumerable articles by force of their irresistible gentleness. Shopping is made a positive luxury. In several days spent in making various purchases, I have not seen an impatient or ill-humored salesman or woman, and I am sure I have been a tedious, if not troublesome customer. When will our American tradespeople learn the value of such courteous manners? When they do they may be sure of quick sales and large profits.

And yet withal, Paris is a soulless place. Amid all the sunshine and fashion and even courtesy, nobody seems to really care for you, and instinctively you seem to care for nobody, while you loiter within its gaudy precincts. It is a well authenticated fact that one out of every three thousand Parisians commits suicide. London with all its fog—its saturating mist —its narrow endless lanes—its cobwebs and soot, suits me infinitely better than the glittering French capital, and the sturdy, gruff Englishman with his round cheek, lion voice, great heart, and marvellous self-esteem, is extremely difficult to beat in all that pertains to the noblest style of man.

Paris has few homes and no Sabbath ; and a city or country without these seems to me like a great desert, a barren waste, quite destitute of a relieving oasis. Man wants one quiet day in the week to rest, to collect his thoughts, to indulge in a reverie, to say nothing of a prayer. Paris gives six days to business, and the seventh to the devil—little time left for home and the service of the Almighty.

I saw the Emperor and Empress this afternoon. They ride out every fair day. Passing by the Seine side of the Tuilleries, an irregular gathering of people in the vicinity of the great gates attracted my attention, and upon inquiry I found the Royal pair were expected " out " in a few minutes. Quite ready to see the show, if I could do so by waiting a short time, I fell into the ranks. Soon the police stopped all vehicles from passing, and just as we all strained our eyes for the imperial *cortege*, imagine our chagrin to find that it had gone out by the gate upon the Rue de Rivoli. A portion of the crowd ran pell-mell across the gardens, a quarter of a mile, to get a glimpse at the illustrious party. I have learned better than to damage my boots either for an Emperor or Empress. Concluding, without much hesitation, that it was a court trick to avoid the outsiders, I was for the moment rather out of humor, and turned off for a walk along the Seine, over the bridges, and away toward the gloomy Notre Dame. Having completed my stroll, I turned toward my hotel by the Tuilleries, when, nearing the gates, I saw some dozen people loitering about. Presuming it was about time for the third Napoleon and his lady to return from their drive, I inquired of a cocked hat if the Emperor was expected to enter by that gate upon his return. He replied in the affirmative ; so I sat cosily down upon one of the stout stone seats, on the edge of the broad sidewalk. In a moment or two the royal carriages came dashing on ; the golden dress of the outriders and drivers, the prancing of the spirited horses, enlivened the scene. The Emperor and Empress rode in a beautiful open barouche, drawn by four bay horses, richly caparisoned. A second barouche, of nearly equal elegance, contained an elderly gentleman and some ladies, whose position I did not ascertain. The Emperor sat at the left of the Empress. He appeared careworn and tired. His mammoth moustache and

goatee seemed quite out of place on a face so pale
and haggard.   He was dressed in a plain citizen's
dress of black cloth, and wore a black hat.

The Empress was richly dressed, and her prominent
and somewhat pretty features gave her an attractive
and handsome appearance. She is generally admired
both for her beauty and gentle disposition, and is probably quite as much of a lady as an Empress can be.

Not more than two or three dozen people were near.
As the carriages entered the gate, several bowed to
the Emperor, who raised his hat in return, but there
was no cheering, no shouts of " *Vive le Empereur*,"
no enthusiasm of any stripe.

A DAY IN GENEVA.

It was after nightfall when we reached the outskirts of the Swiss capital, and the long rows of glittering lights lining the roads, and here and there suspended across them in the singular continental fashion,
looked cheerful and inviting. A moment's halt at the
guard-house, an exchange of our well-worn passports
for the more portable "cards of leave," serviceable
during the continuance of our visit in the city, and on
we rattle over the hard smooth pavement, at a rate
positively startling to the reposing denizens. The
Diligence office is soon reached, and a busy scene
ensues. Boisterous porters, clerks and obtrusive beggars, crowd around our heavy laden conveyance, the
great black trunks are removed from their traveling
quarters, we stretch our wearied limbs, fairly stiffened
from the long confinement in the uneasy *coupe*, and
soon bargain with a stout fellow commanding a cumberous wheel-barrow to take our luggage to the

(215)

"Hotel des Berges," whither we turn our steps, carefully following the beautiful bridge across the "arrowy Rhone," halting for an instant to admire the placid countenance of the silvery lake, and the splendor of its mountain frame-work, and then enjoying the easy chairs of the spacious reception room of our resting place. Few hotels present better accommodations, more careful attendants, or greater comfort and quiet: while from every window the land and waterscape looms up with impressive magnificence. Tall, rugged Alpine steeps cluster in gorgeous profusion, and the white-capped pinnacle of Mont Blanc, the glorious old mountain monarch o'ershadows every thing with royal dignity and grandeur. The sun, as though proud of the privilege of gilding such imperial scenery, shines with a double brilliancy, while the azure and richly tinted clouds fairly smile on the sublime panoramic picture.

Geneva may justly prize its sightly location. The explored world has few combinations of natural and exquisite scenery equal to that in the very heart of which it has its "local habitation," and I make no wonder that tourists of every clime unite in its unqualified laudation.

We slept sweetly after our long journey from Paris, our hours of quick railway travel, and tiresome Diligence experience. There were two parlors, each with a pleasant fire-place, and sharp crackling wood, and our rooms opened out into cosily furnished corners, all plain, but delightfully neat and clean.

I have an instinctive liking for morning explorations, and before breakfast had an experimental and highly satisfactory experience with the chief streets and places of the honest old capital. The market-women with hearty, smiling cheeks, furrowed by time and toil, but fresh with rural health and trading earnestness, were out in great numerical strength, and very polite. I bought pears and grapes, yellow and white, ripe, rich and delicious, for a sum so trifling that my companions would scarce believe my report. We had a fruit breakfast, a fruit dinner, and munched mellow pears and juicy grapes, as we rode all day in our cushioned *cabriolet ;* for we could command but little time before turning toward Turin, and it must be well improved to do justice to our contemplated sight-seeing.

The situation of Geneva, saving the lake and Alpine scenery, is much like that of Edinburgh— indeed there are two distinct cities, divided by the Rhone, as its blue waters sweep toward the valleys of France. They are not so widely different as the old and new Edinburgh, and the march of improvement is noticeable in many new buildings in progress of erection. It seems to me one of the most desirable

10

places of residence in Europe. The people appear peaceful, cleanly, and industrious. We saw many women of the poorer classes vigorously washing at the washing houses on the river banks. These do not extend, however, to the lake shore where there are fine streets, and a beautiful park has recently been laid out.

Judging from the signs and shops, a large proportion of the residents are directly or indirectly interested in the manufacture of watches. We went into several of the larger establishments and saw the ingenious artisans at work. The reputation of Geneva watches is world-wide, and immense numbers are annually sold. America is one of the most steady and remunerative markets, and there is the same deep interest among the manufacturing classes in our national prosperity that I remarked in Sheffield and other English cities. Nor is this interest solely with an eye to sordid gain.

We had, as I have intimated, but a single day for Geneva and its wonders, and therefore took a *cabriolet* soon after breakfast, first for a ride about the city and a glance at the more noted public buildings, and afterward to call on various friends to whom we bore letters of introduction. Just in the suburbs is the sequestered residence of Dr. Cæsar Malan, a patriarch whose white locks and radiant face few Protestant travellers are willing to 'miss seeing. As an earnest evangelical pastor and writer, he is widely known.

A mile or more from the business districts, on the lake shore road, in commanding view of the city and the Jura mountains, is the cottage home of Dr. Merle D'Aubigne, literally encompassed with flowering shrubbery and luxuriant vines. Over the door-way, in accordance with an old-established custom among the Swiss Christians, is the motto, "Tempe Breve," and we deeply felt its too oft forgotten truth, as we entered to present our introductions to the eminent and honored historian of the Reformation. It was said of Burke, that no one could stand under the same gateway with him during a shower of rain without discovering that he was an extraordinary man, and the first sight of Dr. D'Aubigne is sufficient to satisfy the most skeptical of his indisputable claim to celebrity. I think Dr. Cheever, who has spent much time in Geneva, compares his personal appearance to that of the late Daniel Webster, and the simile is very striking.* He is tall, erect in carriage, and has just such a lofty brow, penetrating eye and dark shaggy eye-brows, as had the lamented sage of Marshfield. We were heartily welcomed to his study, and there had an unrestrained and delightful conversation on

* Others have compared it to that of President Wayland, of Brown University.

Genevese and American topics. The Doctor was
curious to know all about the "American party" now
creating such a furore in the States, and gave us
much interesting information regarding the religious
and political aspects of Switzerland. He spoke indig-
nantly of a recent governmental insult to the Protestant populace of Geneva, in ordering that the annual
election should be held upon the Sabbath and in
a Roman Catholic Church, and is evidently apprehensive of the inroads constantly being made upon the
established customs of the fathers, who in their day
"made Rome tremble at the name of Geneva."

From the historian's flowery nest we returned to
the city, and had a brief interview with the celebrated
Madiai family, "sufferers for righteousness' sake," for
whom so much sympathy has been shown in America.
Both Monsieur and Madame are in improved health
after their long season of trial in Tuscany. The fresh
air of Switzerland, and the kind attention of devoted
friends, have served to cheer their troubled spirits,
and renew their physical strength, while, like all true
martyrs, their enthusiasm is in no wise abated:

> "The good are better made by ill,
> As odors crushed are sweeter still!"

They speak warmly of the affection of their American friends, but in answer to my inquiry as to
whether they would visit the States, Madame

replied that she feared she should never enjoy the
privilege. The husband was in the new world several years since, and has a great admiration for it.*

In the afternoon R. and I drove some miles out of
the city to call upon Colonel Tronchan, a prominent
benefactor of the Waldenses. His mansion is just
under the shadow of Mont Blanc, and an evidence of
his philanthropy and well spent wealth, is shown in
the recent erection on a portion of his lands, and
entirely at his own expense, of a commodious and
well appointed hospital, to which I believe all worthy
Protestant sufferers are admitted free of charge. The
Colonel told us much of the Italian evangelical
churches, and appeared a man of clear intellect and
fine heart. We were over-persuaded by his courtesy
to remain to dinner, and were throughout most generously entertained.

I must not forget that in the city we were carried'
back to the stern days of the Reformation, by a visit
to the house in the Rue de Chanoines long occupied
by Calvin, and now by a happy coincidence the home
of the Young Men's Christian Association of Geneva,
one of the most efficient institutions of its class in all

* To-day (1860) the Duke of Tuscany is a fugitive from his kingdom, and the
Madiai are busily engaged in circulating the Scriptures, the Provisional Government of Tuscany having proclaimed freedom of conscience and full religious
liberty.

Europe. The cathedral of St. Peters, where Calvin preached, also remains and is still in possession of the established church, the portico of the pulpit is daily pointed out as a portion of the desk from whence he nobly and fearlessly proclaimed the truths of the gospel. His grave is said to have no distinguishing mark, save the initials J. C. on a plain slab—nevertheless it is a Mecca to which hundreds of reverent pilgrims from all quarters of the Christian world, annually pay their heartfelt homage.

What an example was Calvin's to the labor-saving ministry of the nineteenth century. Some have reckoned his yearly lectures to be an hundred and eighty six, and his yearly sermons two hundred and eighty-six, besides other labors incalculably numerous and burdensome. Even in his dying illness, when his friends endeavored to persuade him to rest, he replied, "What! shall my Lord come and find me idle?"

CROSSING THE ALPS.

AFTER a delicious sleep, we left Geneva at nine o'clock in the morning, the weather being agreeably clear and cool, for Turin, via Chambery and Mount Cenis. Very beautiful are the environs of Geneva, with their snowy Alpine and Jura framework. We were loth to proceed from the splendrous mountain pictures unfolded to our gaze at each advancing mile, and found no language competent to give expression to our admiration of their exquisite and imposing grandeur. For one I am quite ready to accept the poetic theory:

> " Who first beholds the Alps—that mighty chain
> Of mountains, stretching on from east to west,
> So massive, yet so shadowy, so ethereal,
> As to belong rather to heaven than earth—
> But instantly receives into his soul
> A sense, a feeling that he loses not—
> A something that informs him 'tis a moment
> Whence he may date henceforward and forever."

What constitutes an exceedingly impressive feature

of the Alps, is their imposing continuity, and their
striking contrast with the mellow, sunny, fruitful
plains at their feet. One is constantly surprised at
the proximity of winter and summer, the bleak and
the mild, the gentle and the austere. The Alps in
Labrador would be robbed of half their charms.

But despite the sublime scenery, the diligence carried us through many poverty stricken towns, and we
were beleaguered by pertinaceous beggars, from the
infant to the grandsire, at every turn in the circuitous
road.   Our passengers, excepting our own party,
were all natives of the continental countries and very
companionable travelers : seldom out of patience, but
by no means communicative. I was so fortunate
however as to excite the conversational powers of a
Sardinian soldier who sat beside me much of the time.
When he discovered I was an American he grew rap-
turous, and filling from a convenient bottle, a cocoa-
nut cup of toothsome wine, pressed it upon me, at the
same time himself drinking with great gusto to the
prosperity of " *des etats unis.*" Throughout Europe,
especially among the lower classes of the people, I
have found an admiration often amounting to an irrepressible enthusiasm for our great republic, and its
free institutions. We passed Aix les Baines, a popular watering place, amid the most romantic natural
surroundings, in the afternoon, and, after several hours

of driving through a region of vineyards, broad fields of Indian corn and buckwheat, and scenery even more magnificent than that of the morning, just at dusk descended the long steep hill to the historic town of Chambery the capital of Savoy, and were soon at dinner in the "Hotel D' Europe." Fair rooms were supplied us, and fire proved very comfortable. The dinner would not have pleased John Bull, but for the less fastidious and hearty Yankee, its soups, veal, poultry, pears, grapes and maccaroni, to say nothing of very palateable wines, were quite sufficient. After its deliberate discussion we walked through the town, but saving a few fine old buildings, some odd stores, and a curious fountain in which the water gushes from the trunks of several huge Elephants of bronze, found little to admire in its narrow and poorly lighted streets. It was in Chambery that our roving countryman, Joel Barlow, wrote the "Hasty Pudding," the most popular of his poems. In the morning we took to the diligence at an early hour, and better realized the extremely picturesque situation of Chambery. The day proved worthy its predecessor. An uninterrupted view of surpassing mountain scenery, of luxuriant vineyards and prolific orchards feasted our delighted and unwearying eyes. The diligence, though less comfortable, presents many of the advantages of the English stage coach, and is vastly prefer-

10*

able to the railway where one desires to study the
country through which he is passing. The cumberous
vehicle is not unfrequently propelled by mules and
even horned cattle, whose speed is a guaranty that no
point of interest will be lost to the anxious eye by
any undue haste.

It was nearly forty-eight hours after we left Chambery when we descended from the crowded coupe,* at
four o'clock in the morning, and entered the venerable hotel in the sleeping village of Lanselebourg. A
little mummy-like old man, with an exceedingly insignificant head, enveloped in an exceedingly insignificant night-cap, came groping out, an antiquated
lantern in his right hand, and a suspicious looking ladder in his left. Placing the latter against the
vehicle, and mounting up, as a boy would to look
over a fence, he stuck his nose into our compartment,
and asked if we would not like a cup of coffee before
proceeding to cross the snowy mountains. We accepted his curious French invitation to dismount, and
so did our English friend in the "interior," and our
Italian companions in the "parquet."

All the continental country hotels have enormous
kitchens, and they are put just where you would
expect to find the drawing-rooms, viz., upon the front

---

* Name of the division of the *Diligence*,

of the first floor. Why this arrangement is so tenaciously adhered to, I cannot divine, unless it be with
the supposition that marching all the visitors through
the cooking. department may tend to impress them
with the dignity of the establishment. To do this
effectually, the dishes, the floors, tables, and servants
should be kept in better order than they are. We
tumbled in, half asleep and half awake, as merry as
circumstances would allow. Servants were flying
round the kitchen in genuine French confusion, and
a number of inquisitive villagers, who should have
been in bed, stood ready to stare at us. The kitchen
walls were profusely decorated with huge frying-
pans, mammoth kettles, spits, griddles, and an endless
variety of copper dishes—for nearly all the French
cooking utensils are of copper. On a mammoth
stove in the centre of the room, stood a famous pot of
scalding water, and the servants were soon busy in
preparing the coffee. A long, rough table was filled
with large blue cups and saucers, good-sized pitchers
of milk, and huge loaves of black bread. Our companions, particularly the Italians, poured down the
scalding coffee at a rapid rate. I enjoyed the survey
of the apartment, the manœuvres of the servants, and
the jollity of the travellers far more than the coffee,
clear and refreshing as it was. The greatest good-
humor prevailed. The hot liquid had opened every

one's throat, and all were gaily jabbering. Our conductor—a remarkably clever fellow and good-looking
withal—amused himself by toasting broad slices of
brown bread in the ashes, and vigorously courting a
good-natured French lassie, the prettiest servant in
the kitchen.. Her coquettish smiles seemed to make
a deep impression upon his open heart, and very loth
was he to leave her pleasant society.

Luxuriating in a half-hour's lounge, and warming
ourselves well by the blazing fire, we responded to
the cry of "Montez!" and took our seats. We were
to commence our new post with no less than twelve
animals to pull us—our eight sturdy horses and four
gigantic mules. The blue-shirted drivers crack their
tremendous whips; conductor cries "All right;" and
on we move. A few rods and the cattle stop. The
yells of the drivers and furious strokes of their lashes
soon start us again; but the hill proving very steep,
we conclude to get out and stretch ourselves. What
an odd appearance we make, struggling up the steep
ascent beside the trundling omnibus. It is as cold as
mid-winter; the thermometer loiters at twenty-five
degrees. H. vows he'll freeze, but we are in good
humor, and that is half the battle. Closely wrapped
in our overcoats and plaids, we walk on. Our lady
friends grow enthusiastic as we proceed; one gay
Italian girl sings merrily, and with her classic beauty

gains the attention of all the young men. Soon the broad crystal daylight brought out the towering mountains' height in bold relief. Rising in all their stateliness toward heaven, their stalactical peaks looked more grand than anything imagination could portray : and when, in a short time, the morning sun burst forth in unusual brilliance, and added a golden tint to the pure, snowy landscape, we united in pronouncing the effect the most sublime we had ever witnessed. Certainly, nothing in this world could appear more magnificent, and had we not been satisfied, from the earth at our feet, that we remained on *terra firma*, we should have been slow to allow that our pathway was not supercelestial. Our raptures increased at every step, as we wound round and round the ascending roadway. Napoleon would have had just claim to immortal fame if he had accomplished no other achievement than the construction of this important and astonishing pass. None but a mighty mind could have conceived so noble a work ; none but a mind of extraordinary perseverance could have perfected it. The pass is 6,700 feet high !—and though the pass of the Simplon, also constructed by Napoleon, is generally considered the more remarkable, it cannot possibly exceed the grandeur of this wonderful road.

After winding our way for an hour or two after

sunrise, we were surprised to find the village of Lanselebourg lying just at our feet. So crooked is the
way, that, though we were many miles from the
village, by the road, we were comparatively near, in
a bee-line. The higher we reached, the more lively
our party, and particularly the romping Italian belle.
At times we were far ahead of the diligence, which
the dozen sturdy animals appeared to find difficult to
move, though emptied of its cargo. Some were
roving across the hills, others running over the frozen
road, and it was hard work for the most active to
keep comfortably warm. At last we reached the
perpetual snow—the hills, the road, all covered except
the track, and that frozen with Greenlandish solidity.
Here we saw the first of the four and twenty houses
erected as places of residence for the keepers of the
road, (those who keep the track clear,) and also as
refuges for fatigued or storm-stayed travellers. These
houses are one story high, built of stone, the windows
all protected with massive iron bars. I determined
to gratify my curiosity by entering the first one. On
the side, in large Roman letters, were the words,
"*Regia Cassa di ricovero*, (*No. XXIIII.*)" The
inscription is prominent on all of them. I found two
rooms carpetless, but decently clean and comfortable;
one appeared to be used as the sleeping apartment,
while the other served as a reception and cooking-

room, saloon, or what you may choose to call it. A good-sized stove, placed in the middle of the latter room, gave forth a glowing heat, of which I was glad to avail my pinching fingers and toes, even for a moment. One corner of the apartment was filled with fire-wood; a dining-table occupied another part, while on the side, a rack attached to the wall was covered with bottles of wine (and something stronger), plates, cups, saucers, tumblers, etc., enough to serve a small regiment. The lady of the refuge, a tall, polite Italian, was dealing out miniature glasses of a mixture, which the drivers of our cattle, who had left their duty for a moment, appeared to swallow with famous gusto. She gave me a chair by the stove, stirring up the fire, and I enjoyed my visit greatly. I went into several more of the retreats, and was well received. The men were all off at work. We had met many of them, muffled in a world of cloaks and mittens, with their great snow-shovels on their backs. They seemed more stern and industrious than any laborers we encountered.

As we neared the summit, the atmosphere became intensely cold. Having exercised to our satisfaction, we took to our seats, and found it difficult to keep from freezing, even under our extra heavy Scotch plaids. The snow here appeared frozen upon the surface, so that we could walk upon it as upon ice,

without leaving an impression. We passed a number
of store-houses and abandoned refuges. They wore
an air of the most dire desolation, blocked up in the
snow-drifts, without a shrub or a tree to relieve
the cold cheerless monotony. At last the top
came—or we came to the top—at about half-past
eight—over four hours after we commenced the
ascent. Here we made a brief halt, and entered
a curious little building nicknamed a "hotel." In one
of its dingy rooms was an old chap surrounded with
account-books. Our conductor obtained a slip of
paper from him, which I think was a receipt for toll.
From this post to Lanslebourg the peasants use sledges,
in the winter, when the snow has filled up the
ravines, and by this means they descend the mountain in about ten minutes.

Unhitching our mules and horses excepting the
two at the wheels—sending our extra drivers back
with them to Lanslebourg—the whip was furiously
cracked, and we were rapidly making the descent.
We did not escape the snow for several miles, and
saw two or three tightly frozen lakes—capital skating
ponds. At one point, we passed a mass of dilapidated government buildings, a fortification which a
boarding-school military corps might readily over-
throw. All the way along we saw the houses of
refuge: at the top of the mountain they are very near

together. If we were surprised at the ingenuity displayed in the construction of the ascending portion of the pass, we were more than surprised at the difficulties overcome in the descent. Such masterly engineering and masonry would do credit to any nation or age. The road became more winding than ever— in fact, twisted like a jack-screw, and more than once we were in fear of being thrown from the diligence, which our driver whirled about the acute corners as recklessly as he did his long whip-lash about the heads of our faithful horses. At many places the road is cut directly through the solid rock, while at others it is built up of heavy masonwork. It is, perhaps, sixty feet wide. We were not at all crowded by the numerous carts conveying goods across to Switzerland. A stout stone and wooden railing protects the outer edge of the road for many miles. The telegraph poles which we had for grim companions through the snow still kept by our side, and accompanied us all the way to Turin.

Two hours more of rapid riding, and we reached the village of Susa, each one voting himself a regular Napoleon, having fairly crossed the Alps ! For miles before arriving at Susa, that place appeared within a stone's-throw ; the long turns in the road were innumerable. On the descent we had many magnificent views, and were ever and anon upon the very verge of startling precipices. Susa looked pretty in the distance, and so did the entire valley through which our peering eyes could almost discern the distant and elegant city of Turin. We were glad to wash and brush up, get our breakfast and easy chairs, though the accommodations were rather shabby and we were not in very good condition for eating. The poets are not always reliable and my experience goes to prove him quite the contrary who coolly sings :

> " Travel all night
> Till broad daylght,
> *You'll breakfast well in the morning.*"

Susa proved hot and unattractive, an old-fashioned dirty town, with the usual Italian variations of revolting beggary and indolence, surprising architectural remains, and melancholy quiet.

The thermometer paced up to 75°, a sensible change from our morning temperature, and after two hours of pleasant rest, we took the luxurious cars for Turin, the transalpine Paris. As we whirled rapidly through an uninterupted and enchanting chain of orange and mulberry groves, richly interspersed with blooming gardens, and vineyards clustering with ripening grapes, the receding mountains with their white-capped peaks kissing the silvery clouds and shadowing the surrounding landscape, the eager eye found " nothing vile but man."

TURIN.

Our first surprise was at the freshness and regularity on every side. The streets straight, clean and well paved, the houses tall, even and elegant, peering to a height even surpassing that of the loftiest Parisian palaces, and adorned with exterior and interior finish and decoration alike tasteful and elaborate.

An omnibus carried us to the diligence office, from whence our trunks were taken on a hand-cart to the "Hotel de Grand Britaigne," which we reached after a brief walk. Fronting the broad piazza on which the Royal palace and state buildings are erected, we were well located for sight-seeing, and certain to have the benefit of the daily military parade of the royal guard. The manœuvres were usually very creditable, but we were better pleased with the soul-stirring music of the bands. The Sardinian army is one of the best in Central or Southern Europe, and with the zealous and intelligent supervision of the King is likely to improve with every year.

(235)

We made an early visit to the Royal palace and were kindly shown its many elegant apartments, not excepting the living rooms of the royal family, a privilege extended us no where else. The furniture is very rich and only inferior to that of Buckingham and the Tuilleries. Many trophies are preserved in one of the large halls and shown with pardonable pride. We saw neither the King or Queen during the few days we remained in Turin, they having gone on a brief visit to one of their rural palaces. It is a note-worthy fact that all the soverigns of Europe have country resorts of which they are apparently very fond, and to which they hie at every available opportunity, evidently but too glad to escape

"The public burden of the nation's care."

Looking either way from the rectangular streets of Turin the eye feasts upon natural scenery the most rare and enchanting : here upon the coruscant snow wreaths of the Alps, whose rivulets of crystal water generously wash the pavements of the city : here upon the perspicuous face of the "wandering Po," and here upon the blooming olive and orange groves, and fruitful vineyards of the elysian valley through which we came from Susa.

Few European potentates have more loyal, contented or prosperous subjects than the brave Victor

Emanuel. His throne depends for its security rather upon the affections and graitude of an intelligent and hopeful people than upon the bayonets of a standing and mercenary army. You will remember it was at the hands of his magnanimous though unfortunate father, the late Charles Albert, that the people of Sardinia, in 1848, were granted a constitution, of which religious liberty was a bright feature, and which both Victor Emanuel and his parliament have manifested a surprising firmness in upholding, and it has received the cordial support of two eminent prime ministers, first, the all-accomplished Marquis d'Azeglio, and now that truly enlightened and able statesman, the Count Cavour. Though restricted until within a few year, that historic and interesting people the Waldenses, are now allowed all the privileges enjoyed by other inhabitants of the kingdom— and throughout its length and breadth the country wears an air of wholesome life and activity surpassed by none other upon the continent, not excepting France. Railroads and telegraph lines, admirably managed, traverse every section. The press is quite untrammelled ; some thirty newspapers are published in Turin alone, and while the State Religion is Roman Catholic, the college of that church at Turin has, according to official announcement, but seven pupils, and that at Geneva but one !

My companions had some business with General
Charles Beckwith, the English soldier, who has won a
world wide and honorable reputation as the firm
friend of the Waldenses of Piedmont, and we accordingly called at his pleasant home in one of the main
streets of the city. Some thirty years ago this benevolent Christian espoused the cause of the Waldenses,
and after living at La Tour in the valleys for some
time, recently removed to Turin, thinking he might
do his favorite people better service here. His conversation entertained us exceedingly. Though advanced in life he possesses all the ardor of a young
soldier, and looks as though he might yet endure a
long campaign. He lost a leg at Waterloo. The
General deprecated the scheme of emigration to
America, as urged by various Mormons who had trav-
ersed the valleys. He thinks the habits of the Waldenses are such as to incapacitate them for enduring
the severe hardships attending emigration and settlement in a strange country.

Nearly opposite Gen. Beckwith's house, we saw
the neat edifice recently completed for the Waldensian Church of Turin. This is the first Protestant
house of worship built in Italy since the Reformation.
The Roman Catholics made a desperate effort to prevent its erection, but an appeal was made to the King,
who, with his usual liberality, said "the Waldenses

should have a church when and where they pleased. Many of them had proved his best soldiers." After this the "Board of Inspectors," whose duty it is to examine all buildings in course of erection, endeavored to prevent its resemblance to a church, and to have it like an ordinary dwelling-house. Another appeal being made to the King, he promptly said "the building should be of any style of architecture the Waldenses might desire." Finding their evil hopes all frustrated, the Romanists threatened to blow the building up, but the King kindly stationed a guard about it until their rage had subsided.

General Beckwith collected funds for its erection, and superintended it. It is a handsome Gothic structure, prominently situated, and must be looked upon as one of the most interesting buildings in Europe. Service is performed every Sabbath, in the Italian language, as most of the residents of Turin are Italians. A good congregation is always to be had, and the existence of such a home of Protestantism in the midst of Romanism should be the cause of great good. The corner-stone was laid by the Hon. William B. Kinney, of Newark, N. J., who, I was glad to hear, during his residence in Turin as American Minister, had thrown his influence in behalf of the Waldenses, and being an esteemed friend of the King, had secured to them certain privileges which no other person could

have obtained. It is very generally regretted that
Mr. Kinney's health forced him to resign his important position, and remove to a more genial clime. The
people of Sardinia have had few better friends, the
United States few representatives of greater dignity
and intelligence.

PIEDMONT AND THE WALDENSES.

The sympathy of American Protestants for their brethren in the valleys of Sardinia, is such as to render any account of the Waldenses acceptable, and without the pretence of advancing any novel or extraordinary information concerning this most interesting people, I have concluded to write a few particulars of my tour among them.

From Turin to Pignerol there is an admirable railway. After an hour's ride I found myself with my companions safely landed at the spacious depot at Pignerol, twenty-two miles distant. The seats in the omnibus being all engaged, we chartered a coach, and with an energetic post-boy and lively team were driven to La Tour in an hour and a half. The scenery by the way was fine, but the evening air harsh and penetrating.

La Tour, the chief town in the valleys, is a place of little beauty, though handsomely located. It is about ten miles from Pignerol, and lies just at the entrance to a romantic valley, under the shadow of the highest mountain, the one in which is the large cave, where so many of the inhabitants fled in the days of persecution. The snow clad peaks looked strangely, beside the smiling, sunny valley-scenery. Winter and summer never stood so closely together, and yet so good-naturedly. It is not at all difficult to reach the Waldenses, and we were surprised to find that so few of our countrymen travelling on the continent had made it a point to visit them.

From Great Britain the visitors are more numerous. The Hon. and Rev. B. W. Noel, of London, had lately spent a month at La Tour and vicinity. He manifests the deepest interest in the Waldensian Church, and as one of the prominent members informed us, " knows as much or more of its history than they do themselves."

The morning after our arrival was the Sabbath morning. We were anxious to make the best of the day, and bearing letters to the Rev. B. Malan, professor in the college at La Tour, called upon him at an early hour. The professors reside in a plain but tasteful row of cottages, adjoining the new church, and nearly opposite the college building. We found the Professor ready to give us a cordial welcome, and to offer us the information we desired. He proposed that we should attend morning service at one of the churches in the adjoining valley, Angronia. The walk of three or four miles up the steep mountain path was full of interest, more so for the explanations offered at different points by our esteemed guide. We passed cottages at every few rods, snugly located on the hill-side, and charmingly enveloped in vines. These humble dwellings are mostly of stone, two stories in height, with spacious piazzas and flat stone roofs. The morning was warm, and delightful as one of spring. For some distance before we came to the church, we met the unpretending worshippers thronging the way, and when we arrived, were much surprised to find so large a gathering. A military company composed of the residents of the valley, was being trained near the church-yard, but when the hour for service had come, the music ceased, the arms were stacked, and with a reverential air the uniformed men entered the sacred walls. It was strange to see so much of martial bearing marking a devotional assemblage.

The pastor, the Rev. Matthew Gay, is considered one of the ablest of the Waldensian preachers. His discourse was at once timely, eloquent, and powerful, and withal so simple that a child might understand every word. The closest attention was shown by all present, and when, after the singing and benediction, the large audience quietly parted, every countenance told that the good man's faithfulness had made an impression time should not wear away. ·

The chapel was of the most humble order, the seats rude in the extreme, the floor paved with stones. The women sat at the right of the preacher. No elegant silks or de laines were to be seen. A species of dark blue, coarse, but comfortable looking muslin, was the richest article worn, and snow-white caps, with very large erect ruffles or frills in front, covered the heads of all.

The men were attired in a homespun cloth, plainer than that worn in any secluded agricultural district in America. The singing was conducted by a precentor, as in England. We were introduced to the pastor, and to several of the elders. One of them said, "Americans have done much for us, they have given us a college;" and all gave us a most hearty welcome to Angronia, and evinced deep interest in our far-off native land.

After we had passed from the chapel, Prof. M. suggested that we should devote a moment to a visit to an interesting spot near at hand—the rock over which so many of the devoted Waldenses were hurled to instant death in the time of the persecutions. Shaded and adorned with verdant foliage, we could scarcely realize it as a point where cruelty had once developed its most terrible forms. Plucking a few leaves from the trees at its edge, and breaking off several bits of the rock itself, as mementoes more substantial, we paused for a moment to observe the valley at our feet and the overshadowing hills, and then turned into the roadway and slowly walked to La Tour. The people were wending their way homewards from the service. Ever and anon a party would disappear in some side cut which we should not have imagined passable, much less the road to the residences of human beings. Many of the men had their guns upon their shoulders, and we were employed much of the time in returning the salutations, as every man, woman, and child we passed made it a point to wish us a " good morning." Nowhere in our travels have we found a people so universally polite.

The new church at La Tour reminded us of a New-England house of worship. Its pure white spires and neat exterior contrasted strongly with the dingy looking ecclesiastical structures we had seen in France. We were present at the afternoon service. A large audience was in attendance. The Rev. George Appia, a young graduate, preached, in the absence of the pastor. The sermon was full of love—a fervent appeal to an increase of brotherly affection, one toward another. The house is commodious and tasteful in its interior. During the delivery of the sermon three or four irreverent dogs kept marching to and fro in the aisles with the utmost *nonchalance.* No one appeared to notice them, however.

In the evening we were invited to a reunion of the professors and students, held at the house of Professor Malan. The younger boys read an able article upon the "State of Religion in America," from the erudite pen of M. Roussel. The selection was a happy compliment to our presence. After singing and prayer, P. and R., my travelling companions, offered a few remarks expressive of their great satisfaction with the evening's entertainment, and their sympathy in all the movements of the Vaudois, when I had the pleasure of giving a brief account of the operations of Young Men's Associations, as established throughout the United States, and in which both the professors and students evinced the liveliest interest. Tea was passed round, and, after a half-hour of informal conversation, we parted.

Early on Monday morning we were off to the college. We found all the professors in the library, but did not see the students, as the sessions were suspended, and had been for some time, by order of the Government, on account of the prevalence of the cholera, though its ravages had been mainly confined to Turin. The college-building is of stone, large and substautial, and surrounded with a liberal plot of land. It was erected in 1837 with funds collected in Great Britain, by General Beckwith and Rev. Mr. Gilly, the two indefatigable friends of the Waldenses. The library is well stocked with French and English books, many of them rare and valuable. Philosophical apparatus, and all the appointments necessary to the study of the sciences are supplied. The number of students averages nearly one hundred. A theological department will shortly be opened in this institution, and two or three professors appointed. Hitherto, the young men of the Waldensian Church have been under the necessity of going to Geneva, Lausanne, or Berlin, to pursue their theological education. This has been attended with much inconvenience. Hereafter, they will be able to pursue *all* their studies for the ministry at *home* as it were, and in doing so, they will perfect their knowledge of the Italian language, and thus be better fitted for the missionary work to which many of them will certainly be called by the state of things in the kingdom of Sardinia, where there is now an " open door" of usefulness set before this church.

Leaving the college, we met Moderator Ravel, who had come in from a long distance to meet us. Dr. Ravel and his estimable lady spoke in terms of enthusiastic praise of American institutions as they found them during their visit last year. The sympathy manifested in the New World in behalf of the Christians of Piedmont, has undoubtedly proved a source of much encouragement to them. Dr. Ravel inquired particularly of the New York pastors, and the many warm friends made in America.

At the hospital, a few moments' walk from the college, toward the mountains, we met Joseph Malan, of Turin, the representative of the Waldenses in the Sardinian Parliament. He is the only Protestant in office, and was elected by the union of a few liberal-minded Catholics with the Vaudois—an affable gentleman, who spoke English, and gave us much information as to the character of the Government.

There were only about a half-dozen patients in the hospital, and they were improving. I learned that none but Protestants were admitted unless in extreme cases. The hospital is supported by funds received from England.

Spacious grounds are attached, and tastefully arranged. A more retired or agreeable retreat for the sick could not be conceived. Dr. Ravel and Mr. Malan accompanied us to the young ladies' school. Miss Appia, a sister of the young preacher whom we had heard on the Sabbath, is the Principal. She received us cordially, and the scholars, (about fifty in all,) went through a variety of interesting exercises much to our gratification. We were pleased with their intelligence and perfect order. General Beckwith was the founder of this school.

The Waldensian valleys contain a population of about 22,000 Protestants and 5,000 Roman Catholics. The French language is generally spoken. There are fifteen churches and four preaching stations. The lowlands and many sections of the highlands produce in good quality all the kinds of vegetables grown in the United States. The grape crop has signally failed for three years past, and I was sorry to learn that the potato disease prevailed to an alarming extent. In the shops at La Tour we saw as fine apples and pears as we could wish for, and at our hotel we were served with as great a variety of meats, vegetables, and fruits as the most fastidious epicure could desire, and the charges were reasonable; the rooms neat and commodious. Indian corn is grown on the mountains in large quantities. The bright yellow ears may be seen hanging out to dry, at nearly every dwelling. Hominy and Indian meal are coming into general use. The people are industrious, honest, and frugal, though not what we would call enterprising. They appear content with a little, and satisfied with their country. They are mainly agriculturists. A few are employed at the silk manufactories near La Tour. Many mulberry trees are grown, and chestnut trees cover the

10*

hill-sides. An old writer called the chestnuts the manna of the Waldenses.

The large Roman Catholic Church at La Tour was erected by the Bishop of Pignerol. It contains a number of rich paintings, but is free from the super-fluity of gilt decoration found in most of the churches. A crafty priest has been selected as the pastor, and every means is taken to win converts from the Waldenses. The Sabbath was quietly observed. The shops were many of them open, but there was less confusion and traffic than in most continental towns. The people looked clean, and were excessively polite. We saw no beggars, and were told that among their one hundred and thirty institutions, for social discipline, there is neither a prison nor a poor-house, and it is probably the only community in Europe, certainly the only one in Italy, of equal num-bers, without a beggar or a drunkard.

We were inquired of concerning the proposed line of American steamers from New York to Genoa. All united in expressing the greatest desire for the estab-lishment of such a communication, so they might hear more readily from their American brethren. I sincerely hope the capitalists who have long had the matter under consideration, may conclude to try the experiment. At present the passengers and mails from Italy, Southern France, Switzerland, and Sardinia, have all to go to Liverpool or Havre, before they can secure steam conveyance to the United States. A heavy loss of time and much expense would be saved by a line from Genoa, and there can be no doubt that quantities of merchandise would be forwarded by such route, and many worthy emigrants find their way to the western world.

We continued to enjoy the company and kind attention of Messrs. Malan, Ravel, and other friends during our entire visit, and returned to Turin well satisfied with our tour in the romantic and historic valleys.

FLORENCE.

"In Florence," says Willis, "one lives like a prince and pays like a beggar," and the assertion is comparatively correct. We have our quarters at the "Grand Hotel de New York," directly upon the peaceful Arno. Spacious and well furnished rooms, with unexceptionable beds, are given us at about twenty-five cents per day. A substantial and well-cooked breakfast of eggs, continental beef-steak, (very different from that of old England), potatoes and coffee, costs but forty cents, and a Table-d'Hote dinner, with innumerable courses, good enough for any one, is provided for sixty cents—vastly cheaper this than any comfortable hotel yet found in our continental tour. At the restaurants, and the city abounds in them, a refreshing breakfast may be had for twenty-five cents, and a tempting dinner for thirty to forty cents, but one cannot well endure the company. We have experimented at various places, but never to our

(252)

satisfaction. Once we went with some artist friends to one of the leading saloons, but in additon to the clatter of the slatternly servants, a dozen rapacious pedlars entered in rapid succession. Their great trays of fancy wares were literally poked under our eyes, and refusals to purchase needles only provoked urgent appeals to buy pins. Absolute denials to liberal offers of matches brought persistent proposals to take soap. First came a wily Italian lad of perhaps twelve summers, round faced and black eyed, who seemed bent by every ingenious persuasion to make us his customers. We begged him to retire, and appealed to the waiters to expedite his removal, but to no effect. Then followed a Jewish gray beard, with sallow cheek and hook nose, who with all the pertinacity of his despised and unfortunate race besought us to select hose and handkerchiefs from his varied stock. An obstinate old fellow indeed, from whom it was hard to escape. Then an aged woman with glittering trinkets came to annoy us, and while we were heartily wishing her away, a flower girl sought to tempt us with bursting rose buds, but save this last intrusion which, owing perhaps quite as much to the beauty of the fair seller as to that of her dainty merchandise, we were willing to excuse, our meal time was an hour of continued and provoking interruptions, and henceforth we preferred eating in the quiet and agreeable saloon of our hotel.

The streets of Florence are generally narrow, but well paved and decently clean. One may walk or ride in them with ease and comfort, and not very often lose his way, for their intricacies are not to be compared with those of many of the older British cities. Coach hire is very cheap, marvellously so, and the drivers unusually polite, a pattern for the hardened " cabbies" of London and Paris.

I must not venture to tell of all the fine buildings in this city of palaces; in architectural grandeur it has much, very much to boast, and I make no wonder that lovers of art so richly enjoy both the exterior and interior magnificence of its State and Ecclesiastic structures. The Pitti palace, the present 1854) residence of Leopold, Duke of Tuscany, is a wonderfully massive building, a perfect fortress in itself. The front, which seems full five hundred feet in extent, is composed of rough blocks of brown stone, many of them ten and fifteen feet in length, one that I particularly noticed measured over twenty feet. The effect of this unhewn facade is grand beyond description. The whole edifice looks as though it had been quarried from some gigantic Gibraltar. Several stalwart men, attired in rich uniforms, and wearing huge cocked hats, the Duke's porters, met us at the main entrance, and having signified our desire to examine the palace, or the state apartments, we were directed to a sprightly servant, who speedily opened to us the mysteries of the place. The apartments consist of a reception room, ball room, saloon, and an endless variety of square rooms, about fifty by fifty feet in size, and splendidly furnished— such as we have seen in every royal palace, but the use of which has never been satisfactorily explained.

These rooms open one into another, and when all the doors are left ajar, as they are in a parallel line, the *tout ensemble* is very fine. Rich carpetings, and elegantly frescoed ceilings adorn each room, and the walls are more or less decorated, but not so elaborately as those of the state apartments at Turin. The mosaic tables are beautiful beyond any we have seen, and are said to be worth untold gold. But after all there is an air of stately desolation about these spacious halls, and about all the royal palaces we have visited. Mayhap the crowned residents would be far happier in some vine-clad cottage. Here amid the stiff forms of courtly etiquette and relentless fashion,

> " There's sic parade, sic pomp and art,
> The joy can scarcely reach the heart."

Yet how tenaciously are the baubles of royalty held, and how much ambitious men undergo and endure for the sake of getting and holding power over their fellows.

In the private chapel of the Pitti Palace, in an out-of-the-way corner, we saw Carlo Dolce's " Madonna," and for one, I thought it worthy to compare with Raphael's master-piece, the "Madonna della Seggiola." The artist's mild modest style of coloring—especially the mellow blue of which he was so passionately fond, and introduced in most of his paintings—is greatly to my liking—although critics deal very harshly with poor Dolce. The picture is elegantly framed, but why obscured so, no one could tell. It is deserving a place beside Raphael's, which we had paused to admire with many other gems of art, in the saloons through which we had passed. Artists are constantly copying it, and applicants often have to wait several years for an opportunity. The picture galleries are the chief attraction of the palace, and in some respects the finest in Europe—too wealthy almost for concentration at a single point. The grand old artists whose works are here preserved, all seem to have mixed their colors with brains, and that without stint.

The Boboli gardens behind the Pitti palace are well worth visiting, and have occupied our careful attention. They abound in every floral attraction.

Opposite the palace, or nearly so, is the residence

of the Brownings, whose mysterious poetry is as well-known in America as in Britain. They are permanent residents here, and often met at the house of our esteemed countryman, Mr. Kinney, who since his withdrawal from Turin, has made Florence his home —and with his accomplished lady dispenses a refined hospitality exceedingly grateful, not only to the artists and residents, but to all their countryfolk who pass through the city. Mr. Kinney has kindly accompanied us in our walks, and greatly interested us by his ready knowledge of all places of interest. He has made the city a study, until its every street, house, historic and art association, is apparently as well-known to him as to the oldest and most intelligent resident. But you will have premised all this from his admirable letters to the *Newark Daily Advertiser*, of which he was so long the able and respected editor.

We rode out the other afternoon, to the Cascine, the Hyde Park of Florence—a long strip of beautiful land and forest interspersed with enchanting roads and shaded paths. Passing out at the city gate and by the railway station, we were soon on the confines of the grounds. The drives are very long but never tedious. Midway in the main route of pleasure riders is a large building, a saloon or hotel, on the broad piazza of which a military band was playing gay tunes to the gossiping throng. The Cascine is one of the most lovely public parks we have yet met. The great rivalry between Rome and Florence, can never seriously disturb the latter until the eternal city has a Cascine.

Sunday is a dazzling holiday in most continental cities, in none more so than in Florence. The streets are crowded from early morn with giddy pleasure seekers, and all manner of amusements are indulged without restraint. After dinner I inquired, of one of the waiters at our hotel, at what hour the English church service commenced. He could give me no information, but with apparent delight announced that a balloon would go up at 3 o'clock, and already the streets near the point of ascent were thronged with an eager assemblage, copiously interspersed with the military, whether from fear of a disturbance or from simple curiosity I did not learn. . After a deal of delay, and any number of false and mischievous reports, the airy messenger was cut loose and soared gracefully toward the clouds, amid the enthusiastic cheers of the excited multitude. It was nearly sunset when the crowd tired with gazing at the fast receding balloon, began to disperse, and as the surging throng passed beneath my window, my mind instinctively reached across the Atlantic to the quiet Sabbath-keeping villages of New England, where, and in other parts of my native land, the sacred day was profaned by no such unblushing desecration, no such childish amusements, no such forgetfulness of the divine command touching its devout observance. And to this gross disregard of the Sabbath, we may reasonably charge no small portion of the vice and crime of the continental cities. Where there is no observance of the Sabbath, there is no regard for the Bible, and where the Bible and its teachings are ignored, there are few restraints upon the human passions. It requires the experience of but one Florentine Sabbath, to dissipate all wonder at the recent cruel imprisonment of the righteous Madiai. If there is an alarming apprehension regarding the annual arrival in America of thousands of adventurers from Europe, it is that they will bring with them an habitual disregard of the Sabbath. Americans should see to it that, under the guise of innocent rest and necessary recreation, the Sabbath of their fathers is not ruthlessly prostituted to a mere season of revelry and license, and that by those who should cheerfully uphold, rather than unblushingly infringe the laws and sanctities of the land so prompt to shelter them from the poverty and oppression of the old world.

* * * * * * *

A curious Florentine custom—an excellent one by the way—is that of designating the houses of historic

note by inscriptions neatly carved in marble slabs
usually placed upon the fronts of the buildings.
Many of the residences of the great men of medieval
Florence are thus distinguished, much to the interest
and convenience of the curious stranger, who might
otherwise even with the lucid light of Murray pass
them by unnoticed.

The house of Michae Angelo is carefully preserved
—a narrow building, but deep, and with many continuous rooms, teeming with mementoes of the great
artist. I viewed them with much of genuine reverence, for Angelo has ever held a high place in my
estimation. It was Allston, I think, who said, " there
is something in his works that so lifts one above our
present world, or, at least, which so raises one above
ordinary emotions, that I never quit the Sistine chapel
without feeling it impossible to believe any charge to
his discredit." Hilliard has well denominated him
" the Columbus of Sculpture." There is a striking
boldness of originality in all his works.

In the church of San Lorenzo several of Angelo's
master pieces in marble are shown the visitor, and in
the church of Santa Croce, the Westminster Abbey
of Florence, his remains repose, with those of Machi-
avelli, Galileo, Leonardo Breuno, Lanzi, and Filicaja.

The cathedral is a sumptuous building, and in the
same square the Baptistery, and Campanile or Bell

Tower, excite the traveler's admiration. The tower is nearly three hundred feet high, and the bronze doors of the Baptistery, or the two made by Ghiberti, are those which Angelo, with pardonable enthusiasm, pronounced worthy to be the gates of paradise. They are not very large but ornate in the highest degree, and take front rank among the Florentine wonders. An incalculable expenditure of time, taste, patience, and gold must have been involved in their production.

I have already made incidental allusion to the flower-girls. They are scarcely attractive enough to warrant matrimonial advances, else we should often hear of romantic matches, and many a young American would return to his native heath with more than one trunk! Nevertheless, their avocation is a pretty one, and their manners are, with an occasional exception, unobtrusive and pleasing. When you first nestle by the sluggish Arno, they greet you with a merry *bienvenu*, and filling your hand with fresh-cut and fragrant flowers, hie away ere you are through wondering at their feminine audacity. Every day as you walk or ride through the streets, or loiter in the Cascine, they crowd your button-holes with delicious buds, and blossoms, and when at last you repair to the diligence or railway office to depart from fair Florence, they as by instinct stand by your side to bid

you a *bon voyage*, and press upon you a boquet larger
and better than all you have had before, and then
when you reluctantly say good bye, and not till then,
the patient creatures expect a liberal doceur. Need
I say, they are seldom disappointed: after the slov-
enly and importunate beggars, their modest manners
and quakerly cleanliness, no less than their floral
favors, make refusal quite impossible—and thus they
earn an honest and merited livelihood, and the good
wishes of all who have seen their rosy cheeks and
lustrous eyes.

The streets of Florence at all hours present a motley
mixture of military, church and civil dignitaries, and
the sonorous bells of the grave old cathedrals ring
with an endless melody, distasteful to many, but to
my campanalogical ear never annoying. The church
doors, as in all continental cities, are always open,
and worshippers go to and fro often with sincere
devotion, but frequently with a formality and indifference but illy concealed.

The other night I was startled by one of those peculiar Italian exhibitions, the funeral procession of an
ecclesiastic. Suddenly as I stood opposite a large
hall near the cathedral, the doors burst open, and a
number of carefully cowled "brethren of the Miseri-
cordia" filed silently forth in grim array. Each carried a flaming candle or torch, and as they bore the

body of their departed brother through the dark narrow streets, the glaring light, the strange wild chant, no less than the melancholy grotesque dress of the pious mourners, combined to make the nocturnal scene one long to be vividly remembered.

* * * * * *

It is with much of honest pride, the American traveller finds his countrymen so accomplished in art as their studios in Florence abundantly reveal. All the world pays willing homage to Hiram Powers, the Buckeye Sculptor, whose cunning chisel wrought the "Greek Slave" and "Proserpine." Mr. Powers is not only a skillful, but a most diligent workman. It is now nearly twenty years since he left the land of his birth, and not once has he found time to revisit it. His fame is the result of untiring perseverance, and as such is doubly honorable. He has frequently as many as twenty visitors in a single day, and it is highly complimentary to his good-nature, to say that he receives all with the utmost cordiality. Fame is not without its perplexities: a man cannot enjoy greatness undisturbed.

Hart, of Kentucky, is fast winning an enviable position, and my Virginia friend Barbee, my fellow-passenger from New York to Liverpool, has already far advanced his exquisite work, the "Coquette." Mr. Powers, who is *au fait* in such matters, and not apt to speak flatteringly, says " it is the best first effort he has ever seen."

I am surprised to find good marble both scarce and dear in Italy. I had always thought a chief induce-ment to artists to locate here, was the abundant supply, and cheapness of the article. The price usu-ally received for completing a bust is from $400 to $600. Hart is to get the latter amount for one or two of those in his studio. Powers now asks $1000.

Gould, whom you will remember as the painter of the best portrait of Kossuth, is driving a good busi-ness. He has been to the East during the summer, and is now amusing himself with a sketch of oriental life—a scene at Constantinople. His works are all highly creditable : his copy of Raphael's Madonna is said to be the finest in Florence.

Kellogg has also been spending the summer, or a portion of it, in the Orient. He has several fine pic-tures in hand, but is mainly engaged on a life-size painting of two English girls, and if they are nearly as pretty as he represents them, it would be danger-ous for a bachelor to venture in their neighborhood. Kellogg bears a very high reputation, and justly.

T. Buchanan Read, whom you know as a Pennsyl-vania poet of some fame, has two or three really charming pictures in hand : the " Rescue of Undine," and the " Lost Pleiads," would either of them do credit to any living artist. The conception and coloring of the former is truly exquisite. Another work, nearly completed, the "Trial of Culprit Fay," as described in Dr. Drake's well known and happy poem, will also tend to increase the artist's renown.

It is fortunate for the artists that living is so cheap in Florence. It is on many accounts preferable to Rome as a place of residence. It is impossible to remain in Rome during the summer months, while a regard for health and comfort does not require that Florence should be abandoned at any season. Occasional summer days are rather hot, and cold winds prevail in the autumn, but to those who work in doors, these peculiarities are not objectionable.

There are so many American students of art now in Florence that the natives take all who speak English for children of the new world. A young English painter tells me he can scarce make any one believe he is not a Yankee!

Besides artists, there are at all seasons not a few Americans resident in the beautiful villas about the city, and delightfully they live at an economy quite incredible.

12

"THE HOLY CITY."

HERE I hang out my latch string from the topmost story of a very comfortable hotel, demi-French, demi-English, named the "D'Amerique," and yet more Italian than anything else. They say it is unhealthy to live anywhere near *terra firma*. It is certainly fashionable, in modern Rome, to abide up stairs, and of course I must do as others do.

I congratulate myself on passing safely through the regiment of *gens d'armes* and cocked hats of every order, that have stuck their bristling bayonets at me ever since I left old England. I have been so fortunate as to avoid being arrested as Kossuth, or locked up as Mazzini, or hauled before the police on suspicion of being in communication with the revolutionists. The trouble which I have taken to have my passport scratched at every few miles, should insure me exemption from all trouble. It may not however. Tottering kings and haunted dukes must keep an eye

(266)

on the harum scarum Yankees that impudently invade their dominions. May the fates save me from incarceration in any of the continental dungeons. If their internal air is half as gloomy as that of their exterior, one might as well be killed off at once.

The agents of his Papal highness took my passport from me when I first entered the city gates, and will probably restore it when I make up my mind to move on; that is, if I pay them enough. Everything here goes by pay. One may have his trunk loaded with incendiary documents, but if he will pay the officers even a reasonable sum, he need not give up the key.

One wants two things above all others, to accomplish continental travel : a passport, and a well filled purse. These requisites secured, he may go anywhere with comparative ease ; without them, he may smoke his pipe and whistle anything but the *Marseillaise*, but make no progress. Good looks, or good manners are of no avail.

Since the genuine Romans went by the board, everything in Rome seems to have degenerated. There is nothing modern at all creditable, and the people are about as destitute of the poetic fire and genius, the intelligence and enterprise of their noble ancestors, as the insignificant donkeys that crawl through the narrow streets. Now and then you meet an intellectual countenance, a life-like eye, but a filthy lazzaroni constitutes the main feature of the population of modern Rome, and in the rural districts the beggars seem to have sole and undisturbed possession; every other man you meet sticks out his unwashed hand for a baocchic, or some larger coin of the country. The diligence drivers won't go unless they are well fed with extra coppers. In fact it is dangerous to look in the face of man, woman or child. I have dared to do so once or twice, and been instantly besieged for alms.

The streets of Rome are more cleanly than I expected, but the people swarm in them like drones. The houses look gloomy and uncomfortable: one might live in Italy a month, and never get a smile, for were you to bestow pence or shillings upon every mendicant, you would insure their continued demands rather than gratitude. The pretty girls, and they are precious few, only now and then put forth a loving look, and I am at loss to discover the Italian beauty of which poets have so long and fondly sung. It evidently does not belong to the present day.

You have heard of the down-easter who in answer to the inquiry, how he liked Rome, replied it was a fine city but he thought *the public buildings very much out of repair.* I can readily conceive how a monied Yankee, traveling, as too many do for fashion's sake rather than a love of the grand or beautiful, could make such an expression. The propinquity of the ancient and the modern, the almost indiscriminate commingling of the ruined, half ruined and unbroken edifices, give to the whole city a strangely dilapidated air. The ruins are many of them stupendous and convey to the most skeptical mind abundant evidence of the superior architectural taste and skill of the early Romans. It is impossible to disappoint the most exalted expectations in a survey of these remarkable relics.

How immensely grand and suggestive the remains of the Colosseum :

"That noble wreck in ruinous perfection."

And how instructive the crushed and fallen palace of the Cæsars.

Of course I have paid due attention to St. Peter's. Midway between St. Paul's and St. Sophia, it is in many respects more wonderful than either. Its gigantic proportions are not fairly realized at the first visit, but soon impress their reality upon the surprised beholder. As a stately monument of the wealth and superstition of Rome, and an architectural wonder, it will ever be the central attraction of the Holy City. From its roof in the clouds we looked with delight upon the far spread landscape and its dotting villas, and within the copper ball surmounting the dome, which from the street looks no larger than an apple dumpling, some half dozen curious Americans, more patriotic than reverent, sang "Hail Columbia" with the utmost nonchalance.

I dropped in at St. Peter's on Sunday morning, and found a whole company of soldiers on their stiff knees before one of the priests. What they had been about I did not learn; that they have at all times very much to repent of, there can be no doubt; they always will while they remain in the service of one of the greatest of earth's despots. But their penance was wonderfully brief. In half a shake, they bounced on their feet, shouldered their arms, and walked off. Gaunt and cowardly looking chaps they were; better suited to squatting on their indolent knees in St. Peter's, than standing up to skirmish with a handful of truly courageous men.

The sumptuous art galleries of the Vatican have been so often described that I shall not refer to our visit to them further than to remark that weeks rather than days may be spent in examining their wealth of wonders. The present government cannot preserve them too sacredly as indubitable proof of the former glory of Rome. As a recreant descendant boasts of his ancestral dignity, and thereby hopes to cover his own shame, so to a certain degree may these noble galleries plead a lenient criticism of the present fallen and forlorn condition of the papal states.

In the mosaic manufactories attached to the Vatican we saw, in process of completion, a number of mosaic portraits of the popes, for the new church of St. Paul, (without the walls.) What patience and care with little things it requires to prepare these conglomerate and valuable works of art. I never before realized the labor and consummate skill necessary to combine 'the ten thousand distinct pebbles in a grand and accurate whole. But commensurate with the toil and time given to the perfection of these portraits will be the truthfulness and endurance they are likely to enjoy.— To this day the elegant mosaic representations of the Apostles remain in St. Peter's as clear and undimmed as when first completed.

From the patient mosaic workers of the Vatican we may draw a golden lesson, viz : that in the undertakings of life, strict and scrupulous accuracy in every detail, however insignificant or tedious in itself, will alone insure a career of perfect and enduring success. It was shrewdly observed by Michael Angelo—" Trifles make perfection, but perfection itself is no trifle."

It is rather a singular coincidence, that his Grace Archbishop John Hughes, or " *Sa grandeur Monseigneur Hques, Archveque de New York,*" as here announced, and your very humble correspondent should have entered the Holy City on the same day. Cardinal Wiseman is also here, and one of the Hungarian Cardinals, having never visited Rome since his appointment until the present time, has to-day been formally confirmed. The ceremony of giving him the hat, or cap, was celebrated this morning at the Vatican. I feasted my republican eyes on the great display of uniformed State and Church authorities in attendance. Cardinal after cardinal rolled up in the rich coaches, and entered, followed by rows of gaudily attired servants. The Swiss guard, the Pope's life preservers, with their harlequin dress looked dashy enough, as they mingled with the ecclesiastics.

I managed to get several admirable glimpses of the Pope, as he sat at the far end of the chapel under his mammoth mitre, surrounded by guards and red-coated Cardinals. He is a fair-looking man, rather younger than you would suppose, and possessed of fine eyes and a good voice. The necessary oath having been administered to the new Cardinal, the small red cap was given him, and instantly he was saluted with a kiss on each cheek from each of the Cardinals present. Indeed these venerable dignitaries kiss one another like school-girls. I saw them at the feminine work all the morning, while passing from room to room, and very good-natured and complacent they appeared.— If common rumor be true, there is little of humility and self-denial practiced by these high-living ecclesiastics. They quite ignore the old proverb—"A true Cardinal should have his soul in sackcloth, though his body be in scarlet."

In Rome you see all the extremes to which the papal faith tends. How much less of odium would attach to the Pope and his religion had he no temporal power—no concern in the uncertain and even vexatious political movements of his hot-headed countrymen—no state battles to fight—no hireling army to cajole. I quite agree with Coleridge, " The Pope ought never to have affected temporal sway, but to have lived retired within St. Angelo, and to have trusted to the superstitious awe inspired by his character and office. He spoiled his chance when he began to meddle in the petty Italian politics."

Since the return of Monsieur Bedini, the American papers are subject to a more intolerant censorship than ever. One of the bankers here tells me that his Boston and New York files are frequently mutilated. P. received a copy of the New York Observer this morning. It had been detained at the office a long time, and shows the marks of censorship ; an article from the " Irish Correspondent," speaking rather plainly of the Holy Church, is rendered unintelligible by the grating of pumice stone ; you cannot decipher the correspondent's remarks at all, but a long extract from

one of the Pope's latest bulls which he had introduced
to comment upon, is left untouched ! P. says he is
much obliged to the gentlemanly inspectors for deign-
ing to use pumice stone rather than the scissors, as he
is thereby privileged to read a most interesting article
printed on the back of the unbearable communication.*

Speaking of newspapers, perhaps in no other way is
the supreme darkness and superstition of the Church
of Rome more glaringly exhibited than in the surprising fact, that here in a city numbering its residents by
tens of thousands, the boasted centre of ancient and
modern art, but two newspapers are published, and
those with a paucity of materials, and editorial impo-
tence, of which the most obscure rural district in England or America would be heartily ashamed. Thanks
to the liberty-loving Charles Albert and his worthy
successor, Sardinia is kept in no such barbaric night.
There are, as I have already written, some thirty well
conducted newspapers published in Turin alone.—
How much of the intelligence of that Capital,
and all Sardinia, is due to their influence.

* " Postal arrangements at Rome are slightly out of joint. A comedian recently applied for a letter at the post-office, and was told there were forty cents
to pay for it. ' I can't pay that,' said he, ' for I know what's in it.' ' Well,
how much will you give ?' asked the postmaster. ' Four sous is all it is worth
to me,' said the comedian. ' Well, take it then,' replied the postmaster, ' for I
have read it, and it's only a love letter.' "

The strictest surveillance is kept over all who are suspected to be anywise interested in advancing the Protestant faith, and yet not a little would appear to be annually done to expose the fallacies of the established Church. My friend R. has been making inquiries concerning the circulation of the scriptures in Rome. His inquiries have elicited many interesting facts. One of the most efficient agents, is a Jewish Rabbi, who, although making no pretensions to Christianity, says he considers Romanism closely akin to idolatry, and that observation has satisfied him that there is nothing so well calculated to reveal its absurdities and improve the condition of the degraded Italians, as a knowledge of the revelations contained in the Old and New Testaments. That he is sincere in his statement we may judge from the activity which he has long shown in favor of Protestantism.

Another individual, recently a Roman Catholic priest, is constantly engaged in circulating the Word of life, though every step must be taken with great caution, the police being always on the alert, and every other man a governmental spy. The time *will* come when Rome shall no longer be sealed to the entrance of the gospel light. May God hasten the day!

The hotels of Rome are unexpectedly comfortable, not only cheap, but one gets an equivalent for his money in excessive attention. Indeed one is obliged to spend much of his time in acknowledging the salutations of the well trained waiters. Ranged on every floor, standing by the doors and doorways, you can't move a step without seeing a half-dozen hats jerked off, and a scraping and bowing beyond parallel. Better be this way than surly or rude, as too often the case with American servants.

The weather is exceedingly whimsical; thermometer stood at 38 degrees at seven yesterday morning, and we had a regular snow-storm in the afternoon! The natives stared as though a Daniel had come to judgment. I was with a party of friends at the new church of St. Paul's, when the furious storm commenced, but succeeded in getting back to the hotel dry and comfortable, thanks to the good cover of our carriage. Vivid lightning and stunning thunder accompanied the snow, rain, and hail—for all came down in liberal quantities.

Strange weather for southern Italy; but I found, some time since, that the boasted climate was about as changeable and severe as our own. In some respects it is really much worse. I think I never suffered from more acute or penetrating winds. Not content with irritating one's skin, they strike to the very vitals. One never goes out at night unless absolutely necessary. The sun, moon, and stars have no better lustre than in America, and the skies are seldom more gorgeous than you may see them after an April shower.

As in Florence, so here, the American artists occupy a very creditable position. We have visited nearly all the studios, beginning with that of Crawford, who seems to rank first, and is unquestionably worthy the wide reputation he enjoys. It is a pleasing indication of the growing taste for art in our young country, that the greater portion of the wealthy Americans who visit Rome from year to year leave with our artists generous orders for the best fruits of their patient and skillful industry.

The suburbs of Rome abound in interest and must be carefully studied to complete the understanding of its former glory. Others have so oft and well described their wonders that I shall not enter upon any recapitulation of the same, but close my letter by a reference to a visit to the graves of Shelley and Keats—two English poets, each of whom with positive errors often wrote with transcendant beauty.

Shelley, you remember, was drowned off the Italian coast, and had not completed his 29th year when he died. His body was consumed on a funeral pyre, in the presence of Byron, Trelawney, and other of his sorrowing friends. A curious coincidence happened in connexion with this ceremony; when the flames were extinguished, and they proceeded to gather up the

poet's ashes, it was found that every part of him was
consumed except his heart, which was untouched.

A little way out of the city we found the Protestant
or English cemetery. There is an old portion and a
new. In the former à dark flat marble slab, near to
the back wall, marks the tomb of Shelley. It bears
the following curious inscription:—

> PERCY BYSSHE SHELLEY,
> Cor Cordian
> Natus IV. Aug. MDCCXCII.
> Oblit VIII. Juli, MDCCCXXI.
> " Nothing of him that doeth fade,
> But doth suffer a sea change
> Into something rich and strange."

But it was to the grave of the youthful Keats in
the same yard, that my especial attention was attracted.
His poetic romance "Endymion," to the memory of
Chatterton, has ever been to me,

> " A thing of beauty."

His last words were "I am dying: I shall die easy:
don't be frightened, be firm and thank God it has
come." No doubt he looked to death as a glad relief
from the cares and malice of earth, which alas, his sen-
sitive nature was but too poorly fitted to endure.
There was much to admire in his character, and many
an earnest tear is dropped upon his quiet grave—
where amidst rich, glossy, and clustering ivy, a small

white marble slab, ornamented·with a harp and broken strings, bears this striking epitaph :

This grave
Contains all that is mortal
of a
YOUNG ENGLISH POET,
who
on his death bed
In the Bitterness of his heart
At the Maliciousness of his enemies
Desired
These words to be Written
On his tomb-stone &c.
" Here lieth one
Whose name was Writ in Water."
FEB. 24TH, 1821.

As I scattered a few fresh buds o'er the tomb of
this unfortunate son of genius, who at the early age
of twenty-four passed from life's battle, I could but
wish that, in the pretty imagination of his hours of
illness, he might feel the daisies, he loved so dearly,
growing over his silent resting place.

NAPLES AND POMPEII.

WE are delighted with Naples. It is a really lovely and bewitching place, despite the stupid and ragged lazzaroni crowding its every street, alley and lane. It amply sustains the high character claimed for its grand and enchanting bay, and surrounding gorgeous landscapes. Let prejudiced tourists, (and there are such) doubt and hesitate as they may, where, where, oh! where, can they find a spectacle so unspeakably resplendent as Naples and its vine-clad vicinage, when seen from the deck of the steamer entering from the tossing Mediterranean, or better, from the summit of Vesuvius on a cloudless day? There is a magnitude of grandeur, a striking variety and completeness of romantic beauty in the dazzling and marvellous panorama, that must inevitably satiate the most critical eye.

The sun shines gaily and warmly at Naples, prying into every nook and corner of the long high-walled

(280)

streets, sweeping across the rich suburban country, gaily tinging the blue restless waves, playing on the ever throbbing bosom of the great volcano, and audaciously peering into the awful jaws of the fathomless crater.

The streets of Naples are long, and many of them straight to a degree quite unusual upon the continent. Tall, dark-faced, black-haired, large-eyed men crowd in at every corner; commerce commands its votaries; trade has its disciples, and crafty they often are. Naples is not an idle city. He who brands it such has no knowledge of its characteristics, or willingly misrepresents. Go into the main streets, turn into the by-ways, and the din of honest industry everywhere rings upon the opened ear. True, Naples deals lightly in great articles of commerce. Her manufactures are not such as the world talks loudly of, but yet just such as every man, woman and child feels happy to patronise. What dandy would go without his " kids," Paris gives them to him in style. Naples, if not quite so chaste, certainly at half the price, for Naples is economical. Pennies do the work of shillings—copper goes where silver would in Britain. At a well-kept, clean, light, well-aired, quiet hotel, with good waiters, good meals, and a landlord full of smiles and skilled in half a dozen useful languages, we have rooms, fronting the bay, for the reasonable charge of a dollar to two dollars per day, as we happen to eat, drink, and get merry.

Good pavement and good gas lamps make a ride through the streets of Naples highly agreeable by day or by night. For something like fifteen cents per hour, we are rattled about the city at a trotting-course pace, in a more comfortable than attractive looking two-wheeled vehicle, with a small ebony pony, driven by a tall whiskered, amiable Neapolitan, a man of unusual capacity for his position.

Naples has many curious street customs. Here, for the first time, I have seen herds of goats driven about, and milked at the doors of the customers. The lactific and sprightly creatures appear to heartily enjoy going the rounds, and most accommodatingly "stand and deliver" wherever required, and no one can question the freshness or purity of the milk.

The maccaroni eaters have duly exhibited to me their capacious and wonderful gullets, but it would be supererogant to dwell upon their hackneyed characteristics. They form an amusing faction of the lazzaroni, and draw much small change from the traveler's pocket, and for this very reason, perhaps, refrain from any thing like labor.

, When it rains here, it certainly rains. None of your London drizzling or Scotch mist, but an out-and-out pouring, such as we have found quite too severe for our out-door enjoyment during nearly all the present week. The streets are deluged, and sometimes impassable. But they perhaps get no other thorough cleansing, and it is a wise provision of Nature thus to wash and purify them. Returning from a visit to the catacombs, we were caught in one of these terrific showers, and found the streets speedily transformed into canals through which good-sized boats might pass at ease. It was only by the kindly provision of impromptu bridges made at the crossings by the obliging guardsmen and others, that we were enabled to make any progress whatever.

In churches Naples has much to show. The cathedral known as St. Gennaro is said to occupy the site where originally stood a pagan temple of Apollo.— Many of the churches contain very rare works of art, and all are well worth visiting—though less vivid in interest than those of Florence and Rome. What with the crowds thronging to worship, such as it is, the swarming of the lazzaroni, the bustle of the busy shopkeepers, and the net-work of soldiery, Sunday is made a very lively and eventful day.

The population of the city is about five hundred thousand, and the number of visitors (tourists) is said to annually average about twelve thousand :—they come chiefly from Great Britain, France, and the United States, and none are welcomed more heartily than the money-spending, curiosity-hunting Americans, whom I have every day met in the shops, especially in those for the sale of lava and coral ornaments or jewelry, of which the most beautiful specimens are made by the ingenious Neapolitan artisans.

The British chapel here is a neat affair, attached to the palace of the Embassy, but in common with all American tourists, we have been alike surprised and indignant to find it necessary to pay four carlini (about thirty-two cents) each for a seat. If the Church of England, with its vast wealth, and the large British population of Naples, cannot sustain the preaching of the gospel, except by this petty and contemptible course, they had better abandon the field until they can control sufficient means to do so. Their present custom is disgraceful, and unworthy an intelligent and generous people. I was sorry to find it practiced at Florence, where there is even a larger number of permanent English residents of extensive means.

The King of Naples* is said to be the largest as well as the ugliest man in the kingdom. He holds his chief strength among the *gens de peu*, while with the more intelligent classes he is very generally unpopular; and if his character is as reported, it is strange that his wife or children entertain the slightest affection for him. I was standing in one of the streets of Portici

* The late King Bomba.

one morning, when loud cries of the king! the king! attracted my attention to a plainly built carriage, drawn by a pair of horses that would have made Snediker's eyes sparkle. Three portly individuals were the passengers; they all smoked long segars with evident gusto. The stoutest man was pointed out as the king. His dress was slightly military—small bands, gilt buttons, and a fatigue cap. He made a very low bow when I tipped my Yankee beaver. A royal summer house is located at Portici, and to this his Majesty was going, in company with two friendly scions of imperial blood.

The Neapolitan army numbers 180,000 men, all blessed with good appetites, but by no means excellent soldiers. If half the idle fellows were at school, the prosperity of the kingdom would be infinitely more certain. Fortified by men of sound education, by institutions of learning, by sound religious principles, a land may bid defiance to ugly men of war and frowning castles. Strange does it seem, that with the prosperity attending education and Protestantism, (as developed wherever these important advantages are enjoyed,) staring in the very eyes of the Italian rulers, they yet hesitate to permit their introduction, and cling with an incomprehensible tenacity to the false power of ignorance and Rome.

*   *   *   *   *

A railroad to Pompeii! Ye gods, what an idea!—
But it is an iron reality. We found ourselves at the
station just in time for the train, bought our tickets,
and took seats in cars quite as comfortable and elegant
as any in England or America. With a thrilling
whistle, we move on; our long train, well crowded,
mainly with third-class passengers. The outskirts of
the city are soon passed, and we dash along the edge
of the lovely bay—the angry waves seeming ready to
inundate the road at every surge. Vesuvius nears;—
the great black volcanic pile rears up a lofty, striking
picture. We shudder lest the coarse black cinders
fall upon us, and ever and anon start as though the
ever-expected eruption had come; but all is quiet.—
The grape yards and picturesque gardens decking the
base of the mighty mountain, look doubly beautiful as
the sun suddenly glitters from his dishabille, bringing
into bold relief every charming leaf and flower. Gar-
dening under the shadow of Vesuvius! Does it not
seem like rearing lambs on a lion's bosom? Who
knows but that at any moment the liquid rock may
rush into the heart of the apparently secure garden,
and make a Pompeii of it, and a Pliny of its proprietor? For the time, danger may be distant; but who
would not rather live a hundred miles than a hundred
rods from seething, treacherous Vesuvius?

A few moments, and we stop at Herculaneum, or

the station adjoining it. The rocks hereabouts show their volcanic nature. The stones all appear like lava—they are of lava. Two or three additional brief stoppages, and the Pompeii station is reached—just sixty minutes from Naples. An unwashed, uncouth vagabond addresses us in broken English, and conveys us a few rods to the entrance to the long buried city. A government guide is here introduced—a brown-faced old fellow, with dark blue trowsers, a heavy cloak, and blue naval cap, trimmed with faded scarlet. Passing a guard of indolent soldiery, we wind around a narrow pathway, and soon enter the well-paved streets of ancient Pompeii, which are even with the surrounding country, and not below, as those of Herculaneum. The house first examined is said to have been the residence of Diomedes. It was the first discovered, and there is enough remaining to satisfy the most skeptical of its surpassing splendor. Extensive rooms, halls and gardens, elaborate fountains and baths, prove its proprietor a man of taste and wealth. In the long cellars may still be seen the ancient wine jars, and at one point the imprint on the wall of the skeletons of the suddenly smothered family. The apartments on the ground floor appear to have been exquisitely decorated with delicate stucco and elaborate paintings.

We walked leisurely through the vacant streets,

ever and anon halting to listen to the monotonous explanations of our guide, who was particularly attentive. The streets are remarkably straight, much more
so than those of many of the modern cities and towns
of Italy.

The pavement consists of irregular shaped flat stones
of large size, admirably preserved. Sidewalks remain
in most of the streets, and, in all, the curb-stone is perfect. The crossings consist of three large stones; but
gutters do not appear to have been in vogue. What
strange sensations filled our minds as we gazed

> " On the wheel-track worn for centuries
> And on the stepping stone from side to side,
> O'er which the maidens with their water urns
> Were wont to trip so lightly."

Many street wells or fountains remain, and from the
public baths and bathing rooms in the private mansions, we may presume the city was well supplied
with water, and the people given to cleanliness.—
Around nearly all the houses open courts were built,
and there are numerous indications of a devotion to
floriculture on the part of the citizens. Beautiful mosaic floors still remain, though it is to be regretted
that nearly all the choice relics of a moveable nature
have been carried off to the Neapolitan and other museums. The walls of all the palaces, and many of the
more humble abodes, were frescoed. But few of the

buildings were above one story in height, and all were built up to the line of the street. At one place we saw a barber's shop; the actual post or stand upon which his chair had been placed. A number of razors were found on the premises. The ancients knew enough to shave. Pliny observes that up to the 454th year of Rome, precisely the most uncivilized period of their empire, the Romans had no barbers; but that at that epoch P. Ticinius imported a supply of those artists from Sicily. He gives to Scipio Africanus the credit of introducing the fashion of shaving every day.

The Tragic theatre is one of the finest edifices in Pompeii, where the characteristics of an ancient theatre may be closely studied. It is evident that the surviving inhabitants returned after the destruction of Pomeii, and carried away the decorations from the buildings as far as possible. The Comic theatre must have been a splendid affair; the stone seats and mammoth stage are yet visible. The building was roofed which was by no means common. Few theatres of the present day are so strongly, handsomely, or conveniently planned as this.

The temple of Isis is one of the most interesting relics. It measures about sixty-eight feet long by sixty wide. The penetralia are shown, where the priests concealed themselves when delivering their oracles.—

13

Our Italian guide grew irreverent when designating this, and to our venture that the priests were hardened characters in those days, boldly intimated his belief that they were not a whit better at the present time! "But are you not a Roman Catholic?" we asked.— "Oh, yes; but I believe in the religion, not in the priests!"

We found our greatest pleasure in a careful examination of the ruins of the amphitheatre—a colossal edifice containing thirty-two rows of seats, capable of containing twenty thousand spectators. A wide corridor, paved with lava, leads down to the entrance, from which branch the passages to the arena, used for the ingress of gladiators and beasts, and the egress of the dead In many respects this building is more interesting than the Colosseum at Rome. The massiveness of its masonry can but be admired, and remains an imperishable monument to the skill of its trusty builders.

Excavations are constantly being made at Pompeii, though it is known from the old charts, that the main portions of the cinerulent city have been found. It was one of the finest cities of the Romans, and its temples are surpassed by no modern erections.

We continue our walk up the deserted streets, noticing on either side the remains of buildings bearing to this hour clear indications of the variety of purpo-

ses to which they were once appropriated. Here is
an inn, and here a stable ; and here, in close proximity, a row of tombs, in several of which are to be seen
the niches in which were placed the urned ashes of
the dead. We enter the shop of a baker, and are surprised to find implements of his trade, resembling
closely those used by his craft at the present day.—
There is the oven, the kneading trough, the tank for
water, and the marble counter ; and yet more, for the
bakers of Pompeii seemed to have united the trade of
a miller with their proper calling, the huge stones by
which the grain was ground. Here are several wine-
shops, in which are still to be seen the large earthen
wine and oil vessels, places for cooling wine, and what
is very curious, the stains discoloring the marble from
which the wine was sold. And here is a dungeon, in
which were found the remains of a prisoner, the chains
of his captivity still clinging to the bones of his wrists
and ankles—useless fetters for the captive of death.

It were easy to fill a volume with a description of
what may be seen at Pompeii, and more than a volume to record the impressions and to picture the melancholy images with which its desolations thrill the
soul. We look upon a city once filled with the pride
of life—the abode of luxury, the resort of the gay and
licentious, the mart of an extensive commerce, and
the receptacle of treasures of art of unsurpassed value.

Now, it lies in silence before us a city of the dead, its
ruins remaining like sepulchral monuments, to bear
witness to the manners and employments, the luxuries
and vices, the woes and final doom of the vast population which once thronged its streets.

After visiting the city of Pompeii, the traveler naturally repairs to the Museo Borbonico, in Naples, in
which storehouse of things curious and rare are many
apartments, in which the government preserves the
articles found at Pompeii. Here may be seen works
of art in mosaic, painting and sculpture, dug from the
ruins, which show that its inhabitants were as fine in
their artistic taste as they were corrupt in their morals.
Here, too, are articles of jewelry, finely wrought in
gold and precious stones ; bracelets, necklaces, and
rings, some of these latter yet encircling the bony fingers they once adorned. Many of these ornaments are
as exquisite in their workmanship and as tasteful in
their style as any which are to-day to be found in the
shops of Rome. The lapse of eighteen centuries has
witnessed little improvement in the art of the jeweler.
Here, too, are articles of domestic use, lamps and can-
delabras curious and graceful in their construction ;—
kitchen furnaces, with all the conveniences of modern
articles of the kind ; steel-yards and weights, tea-urns
and water pitchers of bronze, vessels for cooking, and
dishes of all kinds ; also many articles of food, in some

cases partly cooked; bread, bearing yet the name of the baker; walnuts and prunes charred by the heat; eggs, and honey, and olives. In fact, such is the variety of things of this sort in this vast repository, that one may form an idea of the domestic life of the Pompeians, almost as perfectly as if to-day the city were living, and he a guest within its walls.

HERCULANEUM AND VESUVIUS.

AFTER Pompeii, or even before, the now subterranean city of Herculaneum, and the burning mountain of Vesuvius merit, and abundantly remunerate the most careful survey. They are genuine wonders whose interest it would be difficult to exaggerate, and the study of which must remain among the traveler's more vivid and agreeable remembrances of Southern Italy.

Like the Acropolis at Athens, or the castle of old Edinburgh, but with far more of savage dignity, the huge volcano o'er-shadows the fair city of Naples, and is alike an object of fear and admiration. Fear lest at any moment its sulphurous mouth may open and vomit hot destruction over the land, and irrepressible admiration of its colossal proportions and royal bearing, no less than the wildly beautiful glare of the fiery smoke ever, even in its most peaceful moods, escaping from the belching crater. A dark night brings this lurid flame into bold relief and furnishes an

(294)

awful light, whereby, for many leagues around, the noctivagant landsman or mariner may know his course and bearing. This friendly office has naturally won grim Vesuvius many grateful friends.

Herculaneum is in the same direction though not so far from Naples as Pompeii.

The scattered ruins of the buildings of that ancient city, lie directly within the modern, and not at all attractive, town of Portici, some fifteen minutes' ride by railway from Naples. A guide met me at the railway station, and in ten minutes we had walked to the gateway to the old theatre, the most grand of the buildings yet discovered. An odd old genius, wearing a faded military uniform, proceeded to light three wax candles; taking two to himself, and giving me the other, he beckoned me to follow. We made the descent of a long flight of modern stone steps, and came to the stage of the building. There it stood, perfect and grand, apparently none the worse for its age. With a dexterous move, the acquirement of great experience, the old guide fastened one of the candles to the wall at one extremity of the stage, and bid me walk with him to the far end, to get an idea of its size. Then we passed into the galleries, dressing-rooms, rear passage ways, and a variety of well-preserved nooks and corners, all of which served to increase my admiration for the genius, ingenuity and taste of the ancient architects. The whole structure was buried in lava to the depth of some fifty feet, and now buildings stand directly over it. On several points in the walls were remnants of choice frescoes, and though most of the ornaments have been taken off to the museums, enough of sculpture remains to tell that the edifice was one of great richness of decoration. A few rods from the theatre, in another street, we visited the discoveries of cottages recently made. The remains are quite as interesting, though not nearly so extensive, as those at Pompeii.

"You will have to pay one piaster for the pony, and one for the guide," said the Frenchman to whom I had made application for an outfit to Vesuvius. Knowing this to be merely an asking price, and far more than generally paid, I offered the fellow half the amount, and the proposal was quickly accepted. He certainly provided an excellent pony. Trotting up narrow streets and lanes, with the guide close behind, swinging his long mountain stick, I soon reached the outskirts of Portici, and struck upon the trail for Vesuvius. Here we were surrounded by a score or more of young and old men, all claiming to be guides, and capable of rendering material assistance. The reiterated assurance that one guide was quite sufficient, did not at all allay their impertinent offers, nor prevent them from following in rude procession. The bad weather had kept all visitors away for a number of days, and the leeches were anxious to bite. Putting the pony to speed we soon cleared the whole party, save two resolute fellows, who, though terribly hurried, managed to catch up, after we had somewhat reduced our speed. They rendered us a little service in the ascent, but did not make any thing great of it.

The pathway from Portici is one of the worst over which I ever drove a horse. At spots it was only by cat-like climbing and clinging that the little nag got along. Repeatedly it seemed as though he could go no farther, but he never even hesitated or missed his footing during the entire distance. Those who have made the perilous ascent of Mount Washington may form some idea of the precipitous journey.

In a little more than an hour we arrived at the hermitage, the famous old inn where all voyagers halt and refresh. A few rods on, and we passed the neat observatory building, recently erected by the king. A grand view of the mountain may be had from this point, and the fine building, surrounded with its curious fences of lava, seems to stand like a defiant work of art, daring the very jaws of one of nature's most furious creations.

On, over perhaps a mile of desolate roadway, in the heart of the plains of the lava, and we come to the foot of the cone where the horses are left to rest, and

the more difficult part of the ascent commences. Two
or three large chairs were lying near, and the guides
wanted to take me upon their shoulders. I much
preferred to walk, and the task was immediately commenced. It proved no joke; at every step my boots
would plunge nearly a foot deep into the fine sand or
gravel, and, combined with the dreadfully steep
ascent, made it hard work to get along at all. Three-
quarters of an hour, and an unusual stock of perseverance and patience, brought us to the top. A slight
fog, which had overtaken us when part way up, now
changed to one of startling density. A few moments'
rest, and we set off for the crater, not without some
doubt, however, as to the propiety of venturing near
such a fearful opening without a clear sky and considerable less wind. Walking around the top of the smoking mountain, the wind so strong that on one or two
occasions we had positively to cling to the lava, to keep
from being blown heels over head, into the crater, or
somewhere else—scrambling and scratching, hanging
on to the guide, and he hanging on to me—I tumbled,
rather than otherwise, to the very edge of the boiling
abyss. Hurling a huge stone down the dreadful opening, the distant echo told us loudly of its mighty
depth. At times the sulphuric vapor came into our
nostrils at such a rate as to make us quite despair of
ever regaining our breath. From the seams of the

rocks issued forth steam and hot air, hot enough to boil an egg; while, to my infinite surprise, at a few feet distant, and actually within the crater, I stuck my boots into two feet of snow, or accumulated hailstones! This was a union of fire and water more strange than any I had ever encountered. Think of it—two feet of snow in the calorific crater of Vesuvius, and that, too, in Southern Italy, in the month of November!

But with so much of sulphur, fog and wind, it was judicious to think of a return to lower regions, and with much difficulty we made our way up from the crater, (for we had with perhaps undue temerity, descended full an hundred feet into its very jaws,) and taking one more survey of the chaotic mass around —for the fog would permit us to see but a few feet off —started on the descent. Such a getting down hill cannot be described. Really it seemed as though we were going by telegraph. Such strides; yards instead of feet at a time. Less than ten minutes, and we were down to the pony's stall. At about midway of the descent I made a brief halt, to enjoy the superb view of Naples and the surrounding country—the world renowned bay, and its blooming islands,—scenery, which the best pens of the world have ever praised without bounds. The sun's bright rays—for the fog had only visited the heights of the mountain—threw a golden hue over everything, which added to the rainbow tints of the foliage, the peering spires of the city, and the dancing waves of the bay, rendered the *tout ensemble* one of rare and boundless splendor, equal to any I had enjoyed in all Italy.

At the bottom of the hill we found pony all right, and hoped for a speedy and comfortable return to Naples, but when near the hermitage, a dreadful storm of rain and wind overtook us. So hard did the wind blow, that at times the pony had to stop abruptly in the road to catch his breath. Arriving at the hermitage, we were soaking wet from head to foot. A gloomy stone shed sheltered pony from the pitiless storm, while I retired with the guide to the house, which proved almost as rude as any Irish cabin I remember to have entered in "ould Erin." Here we met a clownish old fellow, and a more decent soldier, but neither could afford satisfactory information as to its clearing up. So, after a half-hour's delay, and a taste of very poor *Lacrimi Christi*, we made off. If the ascent seemed impracticable, the descent appeared doubly so; but pony never winced at the rocky pathway—now rendered more difficult than ever, by the fearful current of water rushing over it. Step after step, down, down, down we came, all as wet as sop, and sadly forlorn. The rain continued, and at times poured with increased vehemence. At last we reached

the village of Portici, where every one seemed determined to add *eclat* to our return, and as I pushed the
pony to a Gilpin pace, and plunged through alley and
lane ;

> " The dogs did bark, the children scream'd,
> Up flew the windows all :
> And every soul cried out, well done !
> As loud as he could bawl."

Whether every returned pilgrim from the crater, is
thus cheered, I cannot tell. Certain it is that in my
excursions in Italy, I enjoyed nothing more than the
pellmell return to this town, from whence I took the rail,
and in a very short time was back safely at the hotel in
Naples, well satisfied with the day's adventures, though
rather uncomfortable from the dampness of my gar-
ments.

The ascent of Vesuvius though by far the most
hazardous and fatiguing excursion to be made in the
vicinity of Naples, should not, as I have intimated, on
any account be neglected. Better leave Paris without entering the Louvre, or Florence without a stroll
in the Cascine, than quit Naples without scrambling
up the cone and venturing at least a reasonable distance down the mouth of the crater, which with its
sulphurous fumes and impenetrable blackness, is more
eminently suggestive of the infernal hereafter than
any place short of the great original.

"THE CITY OF THE SULTAN."

ORDINARILY the approach to the " City of the Sultan," either by the Marmora or Euxine is exuberantly
superb. Travelers of all nations have literally
exhausted the vocabulary of extasy in attempting to
portray its bewildering romance. But we were doomed
to misfortune, and forced to forego our anticipated
raptures, by the stern decree of the storm-king, who
reigns in the Orient quite as imperiously as in the
Occident.

It was a night full of shadows, starless and dreary,
as our crowded steamer ploughed the tumultuous
waves of the angry Marmora, and with the morning,
the dense mist which had filled the atmosphere since
the going down of the sun, changed to a drenching
rain, penetrating to every nook and corner of our rolling home, and completely shutting out the view of
the distant and longed for city, which the captain's
careful reckoning assured us would otherwise · be
plainly visible.

(302

We were nearly opposite the Seraglio point, when we caught the first glimpse of the graceful minarets of ancient Byzantium and its clustering suburbs.

As the anchor was dropped opposite the Custom House, and the great valve of the boiler opened for the escape of the surplus steam, the boatmen swarmed about the vessel like so many industrious fleas, and the comparison will not be thought inapt by those who have had to submit to their sharp biting, for more unblushing extortionists are not to be encountered even among the flagrant swindlers of Italy.

Making the best bargain we could, we were soon taken bag and baggage to the Custom House, a verminous rookery, jammed with an indiscriminate mixture of goods in box, bale, and parcel, and vocal with the cries of excited porters, and vexed merchants and clerks. Under the peculiar circumstances the air of cool indifference and ease assumed by the cross-legged officials who sat around the building was as amusing as provoking. Not one that I noticed in answer to the torrent of inquiries and complaints, offered a response at any length without pausing to take several distinct and prolonged puffs upon his chiboque. But luckily we were detained but a moment, and *mirabile dictu!* had nothing to pay.

A stout hamel, or porter, undertook the double task of guiding us and transporting our luggage to Misserie's Hotel, the St. Nicholas of Constantinople, but only resembling the great American caravansary in the exorbitance of its charges. Now began the ascent of the steep streets from the landing at Galata, for Con stantinople has no wharves or piers, and in the graphic language of that prince of French travelers, Gautier, "the town every where plunges its feet into the water." And such streets as we were forced to climb! even the contracted Italian towns had failed to give us a premonition of their infamous character. It was truly amazing to find the hamel making good progress with his burden, while we without incumbrance found it next to impossible to keep upon our feet, for the

" Pavements fang'd with murderous stones."

The holes, the sloughs, the ups and downs, were worthy a prairie trail, rather than the leading streets of a metropolitan city. But these were endurable when compared with the test to which they put our nasal organs. The two and seventy stenches Cole-ridge counted in the streets of Cologne, could not possibly have been more horrible than the effluvias exhaling from the offal and garbage, left to decay in these cumulous by-paths. How those doomed to permanently tread their stifling mire, manage to survive, is a question fit to puzzle the most intelligent sanitary student. Little wonder that when an epidemic developes itself here its victims fall like grain before the reaper's sickle. Even for that favored class of the population, the dogs, (of which I shall have more to say anon,) who have the best portions of the streets for their hunting grounds, the accommodations are far from inviting, and not at all in accordance with the spirit of the Koran.

As you may presume much of the vapory enchantment which the city presents from the harbor, is dissipated on entering its rude and nauseous streets, and ere the traveler reaches his hotel he is satisfied that its unique buildings and novel customs, its filth and irregularity are to say the least a very disagreeable and discreditable feature, and one which must greatly lessen the pleasures of his visit.

A very slight expense would provide several thoroughfares of which any city in Christendom might well be proud. I know of no place so susceptible of improvement, and yet more inexcusably neglected. If Abdul Medjid would devote only one-half of his palace and harem expenses to the improvement of the streets, his name would henceforth be far more grateful in the ears of all the Frank population and tourists, if not in those of his own subjects, a portion of whom at least, have a progressive tendency.

Pera, the district to which we had been directed, is the new Edinburgh of Constantinople. It is now the main place of residence of the foreign population, that is to say the English, French, Italians and such Americans as may be here from time to time. It is higher and usually more cleanly (if cleanliness is known here at all,) than Stamboul, and in many respects a better district, while the influence of its large Frank population is at once perceptible. There are even yet streets in Stamboul where the giaour can not walk without being liable to insult, while here he is, in the day time at all events, as entirely free from molestation as the most venerable Mohammedan.

*　　*　　*　　*　　*　　*

We were at Misserie's and the Globe Hotel for several weeks, but are now more economically and comfortably located in private apartments with an Armenian family, and I make the city and its peculiarities my daily study. Of course it is vastly different from any of the strictly European capitals, and presents many novelties which none of them can boast.

All travelers have written elaborately of the Bazaars, and I have found them an entertaining, if not profitable resort. In the vast concourse of eager traffickers you encounter every variety of face, from that of the fanatic dervish and timid Jew, to that of the Armenian belle, fresh, rosy and laughing—and the goods and wares have all the gaudy and unique finery of finish peculiar to the East .

"A dazzling mass of gems, and gold, and gliter,
Magnificently mingled in a litter."

The cafes cannot be compared to those of Paris or
Marseilles. Furnished in the most ordinary manner,
and often positively filthy, they offer little to attract
the stranger, until by dint of much perseverance, he
shall have acquired a taste for the "dark and turbid
coffee" of which the Orientals are so extravagantly
fond.

It was Bentikoe, a Dutch physician, if I remember
rightly, who said that *two hundred cups* of tea might
be drank in a day by a single person, and with great
benefit to the individual! and Horace Smith was persuaded, as all the English people appear to be, of its
"benign influences upon vitality, hospitality, convivi-
ality, comicality and all the 'alities.'"

The Turks substitute Java and Mocha for Young
Hyson and Oolong, and drink morning, noon and
night, though nothing can excite many of the "alities"
in their staid and decorous nature. The coffee is
served in small cups at an incredibly low price, and
to those who cannot endure its strength, furnished as
it ever is without milk or sugar, there is not a little
pleasure in seeing the solid comfort with which the
lounging Moslem sips cup after cup, and smacks his
unctuous lips, as though fully and gratefully accepting
the Bentikoe-ian theory.

The cafes take the place of the porter houses of New York, and the gin palaces of London, and are an excellent substitute, for coffee, however strong, does not entail " woes and mischief, wounds and sorrow, sin and shame" upon those who partake of it even to apparent excess.

London is famous for its street cries and pedlars, but I have nowhere met more motley and persistent hawkers than here. Before we are out of bed in the morning our ears are filled with their stentorian shouts, for all the Orientals have powerful lungs and do not allow them to suffer for exercise. First comes the coffee dealer, for, as if the cafes were not numerous enough, the liquid is a common street commodity. He will sell us a cup or a gallon all scalding hot, and if we may believe his story, immensely palateable. Then follows the blancmange merchant and the sherbet vender, with his cool and popular beverage, in a warm day very refreshing. And amid a swarm of other peripatetic tradesmen, the confectioner approaches, and much of the confectionery is delicate and good. The Orientals have a sweet tooth, and in the shops great quantities of sugar mixtures are daily disposed of. The fig paste or *rahat-el-hulkum* often sent to America, is a standard article, though not so much sought as the *hâlva,* which is consumed like bread and butter and largely relished by all classes. It is prepared in largo forms, and sold by the slice or by weight, and much resembles molasses candy.

Perhaps the most novel of the street brokers are those who shake their bags of coppers in your face, and beg to exchange for a small discount any coin or bill you may hand them. These nomadic cambists are callid enough to shave a Wall street bear, and yet every Frank must have found them a great convenience, especially if he sallied forth to the bazaars, with his pocket full of paper piasters.

The bakers have a curious fashion of supplying many qualities of bread from that as nearly black as soot, to a fair Genesee hue, and the loaves are retailed slice by slice and at a price to which the starveling cannot demur. The industrious bakers work with a will, and in many cases their shops are so exposed to the public gaze that every step of their labor, from the kneading of the dough to the selling of the loaf, or its fractions, can be plainly seen by all. Perhaps such public exposure would insure better bread from bakers in other and more refined communities.

It is a belief of the Moslem that when the blessed are all received into Paradise, then the earth will become one vast loaf of bread, which the hand of the Almighty will hold out to them like a cake.

The stores and shops are usually small and unpretending. There are no great windows, and showy

cards as in English and American cities, and advertising except by word of mouth, is evidently unknown.
The women never appear as shop-keepers, though
they are apparently as fond of shopping as their
Occidental sisters, and crowd the bazaars almost to the
exclusion of the other sex.

Constantinople may be said to be in a constant
cloud of smoke, but it does not arise above the house-
tops, and comes from the universal pipe, rather than
the industrious chimneys, as in Liverpool and London.
Everybody carries his tobacco with him, and should he
perchance forget his pipe, there are pedlars ever ready
to supply him; indeed he can at any corner have a pipe
filled and lighted at a moment's notice. Smoking has
been pronounced "necessary to the existence of the
Turk." From the zeal with which it is practiced one
would think it a catholicon for every ill Oriental flesh
is heir to. It is a strange thing, says Gautier, "that
tobacco now in such universal use throughout the
East, has been the subject of the severest interdiction,
on the part of many former Sultans. More than one
Turk has paid with his life, for the luxury of smoking: and the ferocious Amurat IV., more than once,
made the head of the smoker fall with his pipe."

The tobacco and pipe shops are very numerous,
and the social position of the Turk is easily told by
the value of his pipe, or its amber mouthpiece, which

to be unexceptionable, should be of a pale lemon color, partly opaque, and without spot, or flaw, or vein. Such a one will command from one to three hundred dollars, and sometimes much more.

A collection of pipes worth from twenty to thirty thousand dollars, is said to be not unusual among the high dignitaries and richer private persons. It is in fact an Oriental mode of displaying the possession of wealth.

It is perhaps not remarkable that a custom so prevalent in the East as smoking should grow apace upon all who linger among the Orientals. Let the stranger abhor tobacco as he may, if he remain here a few months, he will as inevitably take to his chibouque or nargilhe as to his kaique, and the fragrant fumes incident to the burning of the weed, will become his daily and indispensable solace and delight. Even the dignified missionaries give way to the universal passion, and vary their sacred duties with frequent recourse to the seductive narcotic.

The foul American habit of chewing tobacco is made the subject of much derision by the Moslems.

The Bazaars, the post office, and the public buildings generally, are in Stamboul, which is divided from Pera, by the Golden Horn, a branch of the sea, bridged at several points, and always alive with small boats, or kaiques, as they are called—a graceful sort of canoe, by far the prettiest water conveyance I have yet seen; propelled by one, or two, or more sturdy oarsmen as the case may be, they cut the blue waters with surprising velocity, and offer a means of travel at once expeditious, agreeable and inexpensive. We have made many excursions in them and always to our great enjoyment.

But I was about to tell you of the Post office, where with diligent search we failed to discover a single letter; though the other appointments were generally good. The correspondence of the country is by no means extensive, the postage high, and the department consequently not of the first importance. All about the building were stationed letter writers, a useful class of men, who, furnished with pens, ink, and paper, and a good supply of brains, for a small compensation, direct, write or translate a letter in almost any language you may suggest. I have thought such public chirographers and translators might prove an exceeding convenience even in New York, where those who have stores adjacent to the Post office are constantly annoyed by requests to write, read, answer, direct, or interpret letters, for those who are themselves incapable to the task, and who often express as much surprise at receiving a letter as did Mr. Weller, who you will remember, said, he didn't know as how any of the gentlemen of his acquaintance could write.

I confess to no little surprise at the stalwart and graceful physical bearing of the Turks. Nowhere, have I seen such uniformly well developed and muscular men. Those from twenty to thirty years of age, are extremely athletic and powerful, while those farther advanced in life hold their strength to a degree that must surprise the robust and broad shouldered European.

In a company of an hundred Turks not ten will be found to measure less than six feet in height, indeed the small of stature, deformed and weak, are apparently a smaller proportion than in any European nation. The face is often very finely formed, the eye sharp and brilliant, the hair dark and glossy, and the cheeks tinged with a bronze hue glowing with health and vigor. As a race, though of less swarthy complexion, they much resemble in figure, and nobility of carriage, the North American Indian. This will not hold true however of the epicurean pashas and state dignitaries, who are often disfigured by an unnatural corpulency, the result of indolent habits and inordinate appetites.

The Armenians, whom Dr. Dwight denominates, the " Anglo-Saxons of the East," are a shrewd clear-headed race, in appearance not so sturdy as the Turks

14

but nevertheless well proportioned, and often positively handsome. They form nearly a third of the
whole population of the city, and it is among them
that the American and other missionaries, have met
the greatest success in their work of evangelization.

Most of the crime and disorder of the city is
attributed to the Greek population (which is very
large), and not without reason, for it is the lowest and
most unscrupulous. Nearly every night the dark
streets and by-ways of Galata, the district along the
water's edge, are the scene of robbery, assault and
assassination. The Greek ruffian has the least possible
regard for human life, and would cut his fellow's
throat from ear to ear with as little hesitancy as he
would plunge his glittering stilletto to the heart of a
dog. And in turn the Turk has so little respect for
the Greek, that when he is caught in any of his mis-
demeanors, his punishment is prompt and terrible.
A short time since, several Greek pirates were caught,
and brought to Stamboul, and this morning their
headless bodies were exposed to the public gaze in
the chief thoroughfares. A ghastly spectacle and a
fearful warning to all transgressors. Turkish justice
is usually speedy and severe. An English gentleman
had reason to suspect a few days since that certain
articles of wearing apparel had been pilfered from his
trunks by his Mohammedan servant. He brought

the case before the court, but quickly withdrew it when after a brief examination the presiding justice was about to sentence the culprit to have his mouth slit from ear to ear, and afterwards the ears taken off close to the head.

The Turkish females and many of the Armenian, still rigorously adhere to the provoking *yashmak*,* which makes it next to impossible to satisfactorily define their facial lineaments, but no language can do justice to their great kohinoor eyes, black, brilliant and captivating, though not so wicked as those of the French and Italian coquette. Their stature is often short and dumpy, and in this particular they form a striking contrast to the men, who by the by, though allowed (the Turks) to have four wives, seldom have more than one.

Only the Sultan, the viziers, pashas, beys and other persons of great wealth or high rank have large harems, as the luxury is enormously expensive.

The Turkish pasha will never allow a word of conversation regarding his domestic affairs, and his home is never open to the male giaour, consequently little is known as to what sort of wives or house-keepers' the women make. They are certainly out

* The *yashmak* is not a mere semi-transparent veil, but rather a good substantial petticoat applied to the face : it thoroughly conceals all the features except the eyes.—*Eothen.*

of doors a great deal, and for this should look more
ruddy and healthful than they usually do.

Of course I have not been in the imperial harem,
but on two or three occasions have met the court
ladies riding in their cumberous araba's through the
main street of Pera. Once I saw them at a photo-
graphist's, evidently much pleased with the specimens
of his skill. Their fine veils were scarcely sufficient
to hide their pale features, which had all the characteristics of the passive Oriental beauty, strikingly set
off by the large penetrating eyes.

In all their excursions these houris are attended by
stalwart eunuchs, who are very prompt to clear the
way, and so far as possible shield their fair charge
from the public gaze. They are not always successful, however, and I am half inclined to think the
eloquent eyes rather desire than otherwise to escape
the closely drawn curtains of the araba, and hold
converse with the outer world, so repulsive to the
ebony gentlemen.

The habitual covering of the face throws a romance
about all the fair Orientals and adds immensely to
one's desire to know them better. Debarred, however, by the stern rule of the land, an outside
barbarian can only interchange glances with the
gentle houri, and reserve his heart for the less restrain-
ed and more beautiful daughter of his own land.

THE SULTAN AT WORSHIP.

FEBRUARY, cold, dreary, and boisterous in the States, is exceedingly quiet, sunny, and bland in the oriental world. Friday last was one of the best days imaginable, and R. and I concluded we might as well improve its inviting noon by a look at his serene highness, Abdul Medjid, the reigning Sultan of all the Turkeys. Neither of us had the slightest idea as to where he thought of going to perform his devotions, as he vacillates from one mosque to another with strange irregularity—first favoring Stamboul, then Top-hana, then Orta-keuy, and so on. By dint of intense perseverance, and the aid of two Turkish words, all we could command, we finally got a boatman to understand we were anxious to see the Sultan, and we wished him to take us to him, wherever he might be, intimating at the same time that by doing so, we would assign him a liberal *backsheesh;* but failing, he would in all probability go home with

(317)

his pockets comparatively empty. With a peculiar expression of satisfaction at our intimations, of which he probably did not understand a word save the ever welcome "backsheesh," we jumped into the frail kaique, stretched ourselves on the smooth floor, and greasing his great white oars, unshifting his bright calico jacket, and attending to other duties always rigidly observed by those of his profession, he quickly pulled us out into the deep channel of the broad, gay Golden Horn. Skillful indeed were his movements, as we swept swiftly through the throng of huge black steamers and sailing craft anchored on every side— the winged representatives of nations far and near. R. smilingly said he meant to take things easy, and getting the good-natured kaiquejee to fill his long cherry-stick pipe, he went to puffing as though he were born and bred in the land of the prophet. I turned to the pages of "Christianity Revived in the East," a copy of which I had just received from Dr. Dwight. For a long time we were gliding rapidly along, as softly as though upon a sea of paper. No discordant ripple appeared on the fair bosom of the oriental waters: and when R. had cleverly exhausted his tobacco, and I raised my eyes from my interesting volume, we were opposite the grand palace of the Sultan, at the pretty suburb Beshiktash, some three miles from our starting point. A long row of royal

kaiques moored to a pier adjoining the palace, served
to assure us that we were in ample time to see the
imperial departure, and getting out at the landing-
place, we had a fine opportunity to inspect the splendid boats and athletic boatmen. The "Sultan's own"
was a majestic-looking kaique, some seventy-five feet
in length, painted a snowy white, and ornamented
with an abundance of carving both chaste and elegant. The Sultan's apartment was upon the after-
quarter, under a rich canopy of scarlet broadcloth
and velvet, trimmed with golden fringe. His seat
was a superb sofa, with richly embroidered cushions.
His kaique, and five others nearly as large and magnificent, were moved up to the palace gates. We re-
entered our boat, and bid our kaiquejee pull out opposite the palace, that we might deliberately view the
embarkation. The boatmen all ranged themselves
with their faces toward the grand gate, and a large
band of musicians, with brass instruments, was stationed on the beautiful stone platform. In a few moments a middle-sized, calm, cool and collected-look-
ing gentleman came slowly down the wide garden
pathway, with a most dignified step. No attendants
were visible, save two or three eunuchs, with startling black faces, who walked at a good distance in
the rear. As soon as the Sultan (for the plain gentleman was no less a personage) came opposite to his

kaique, the band struck up a pleasant and popular national air, the brace of cloudy eunuchs bowed almost to the ground, and five or six singers in livery shouted with anything but delectable emphasis— " Long live the Sultan !" or something of the sort.

The six and twenty oarsmen brought their heads nearer to their feet than they are wont to do on ordinary occasions, and the Sultan took his seat, and seemed quite as comfortable as though in the grand saloon of an Albany steamer. At the instant the royal kaique started, a Turkish war vessel near by, let her guns off at a rapid rate, and in a minute the great ships up the Golden Horn caught the sound, and the whole harbor was darkened with gunpowder smoke, while the noise was fairly deafening. We urged on after the Sultan (the other five kaiques had been filled by members of his household, pashas, and other attendants, and were in his wake,) and passed right under one of the land batteries, which poured forth its warlike salute directly over our heads ; then the batteries on the Asiatic side took up the echo, and it seemed as though we were in the midst of the final bombardment of Sevastopol.

The Sultan was but a very short time in reaching the new mosque at Orta-keuy. His boatmen were unusually powerful fellows, and plied their long oars with great vigor and precision. They were dressed in a tasteful uniform, long trowsers and long shirts, with flowing sleeves, all white and nice and clean. Each one wore a well-regulated moustache, which, as such, was rather graceful than otherwise, and all appeared quite young and handsome. At the prow of the boat, which was elevated and gorgeously gilded, a man was stationed with a long pole to clear the way, or assist in stopping when desirable; another stout fellow acted as steersman. At various points along the shore, all the way from the palace to the mosque, (perhaps a mile,) companies of the gray-coated Ottoman troops were drawn up in good order, and at the mosque landing stairs, a guard carefully kept off the intruding subjects. When we reached the place, or the nearest point where we could get our kaiquejee to go, (who seemed to have a profound reverence for the Sultan, so much so, as to be unwilling to mention his name in a tone above a whisper,) the illustrious ruler and his train had already entered the mosque. We forced our way through the guard, and R. had got pretty well into the religious edifice, and I was close at his heels, when a portly pasha chanced to espy us, and ordered his servant to say we could not be admitted. We were in long enough, however, to get an idea of the service, which consisted of of the usual superabundance of bowing, and crying Allah! Allah! The Sultan occupied a private box in

14*

the gallery; the principal pashas were near him, and
the mosque was thronged with devoted worshipers.
We spent some time in roving about the mosque yard,
and the landing platform, which was spacious and of
stone. The military gentlemen offered no opposition
to our approach, and that of some half dozen French
naval officers, though the masses were ordered to
remain at a distance and roughly dealt with.

As we were straining our eyes to see the Sultan
come out in awful pomp, thinking he ought to be
through with his prayers, an order was given that the
royal kaiques should retire, and as quick as a flash,
all but one, the smallest and plainest, were hurried
away. The troops were also dismissed, save a few
guards. We were disappointed, and began to surmise
we were "done for," and that his Majesty had
slipped out the back door, or gone off in disguise;
but seeing there was evidently something yet in
the wind, we tarried, secured a good post by the
remaining Kaique, and kept our eyes very wide open.
In a little while there was a marked sensation among
the officials; the boatmen sprang to their feet, and
soon the Sultan came out in the same dignified style
we had before noticed. He took an easy survey of
everything around him as he paced measuredly along,
and seemed wholly unaffected by the homage paid
him. The aldermanic-looking pashas stood in a row,

and bowed exceedingly low as he passed; while the guards jerked their heads up and down like top-heavy sun flowers in an autumn gale.

We could but admire the simplicity of the Sultan's dress; black trowsers, a black coat, and black cloak, with an ordinary red fez cap—the same as worn by thousands of his subjects. His countenance was rather downcast, and his face somewhat worn with disease and care. Next to the President of the United States, I think him the most unostentatious-looking ruler of any considerable territory I have ever seen. No feather or diamond glittered about his person. How different from my school-boy notions of a Sultan. How changed from the custom of even a quarter of a century since.

As he stepped into the Kaique, a black soldier came rushing up with a petition. The pashas and guard succeeded in arresting him before he reached the imperial presence; but as the Sultan hoisted his red silk umbrella, and rowed off with his two plainly dressed servants, and dozen oarsmen, I heard him say a few words to one of the guards. It was probably his acceptance of the petition; as by an old law, the Sultan must never neglect to notice a request made at any place, even from his humblest subject.

After the Sultan had gone, the pashas' boats were drawn up, and one by one the dignitaries went their

way. Among the number we saw the Capitan Pasha,
or Secretary of the Navy or Admiralty, and Ali
Pasha. All the pashas seemed to be in excellent
health and spirits. They were dressed somewhat like
the Sultan, though nearly all wore diamond stars, or
other decorations. They were fat and hearty, and
evinced an intimate acquaintance with good living—
a familiarity with turtle-soup and champagne, or their
Turkish equals. Each pasha had a long retinue of
servants, and as he entered his Kaique, two riflemen
took seats by him as a body-guard, and the other
attendants crowded around him. Long pipes were
promptly produced, and the pipers had a fresh supply
of tobacco in hand. The pashas appeared very intimate with each other, and laughed like ordinary
men!

After all the illustrious officials had decamped, we
thought it well to try to get a good view of the
mosque, so jerking off our overshoes, we marched in.
The building is one of the latest order, having all
the modern improvements. Fine marble, and richly
variegated composition work, gives the interior an
attractive appearance. Neat carpets cover the floor.
In the gallery we saw the Sultan's seat, and those of
the pashas, and also a sitting-room with chairs, sofas,
and tables in regular Christian order, with washing
rooms, and on the lower floor, at one side, we found a

reception and private coffee-room, where the Sultan had just been indulging. The outside of the mosque is very chaste, purely white. The minarets, with gilded points, look exceedingly beautiful at a little distance on a sunny day.

Again in our own kaique, we ordered our oarsmen to pull to the new palace of the Sultan. At first we were refused admittance, even to the grounds, as the Sultan had adjourned from the mosque to an examination of the building; but impressed with our importance, from our near approach to the royal mosque, our Kaiquejee insisted that we should be allowed to land. We did so, but found that it was against the rules for visitors to enter during the Sultan's presence, and accepted a very polite invitation to call some other day. Steering for Top-hana, we soon reached the miserable wharf, and again stood upon *terra firma*.

A half-crown, or about sixteen piastres, (fifty cents,) satisfied our faithful kaiquejee, who, to our infinite amazement, never even winked for *backsheesh*. We allowed him some in our settlement, and hurried home through the mire, the dogs, and the donkeys; exceedingly well pleased with the morning's results, and quite ready to extol the amiable Abdul Medjid. In the words of his courtiers, "May his virtue increase! May his honor be increased!

*　　*　　•　　*　　*　　*

I have just returned from a visit to the Sultan's new palace at Beshik Tash, adjacent to Top-hana, and near to Pera; indeed, it lies between the Bosphorus and the eastern extremity of the latter suburb. It embraces the choicest view of the Seraglio point, the mouth of the Marmora, the Maiden's Tower, Scutari and its peering framework of mountain grandeur: old Olympus, "high and hoary" forming the prominent jewel in the continuous chain. And here with this superb combination of exquisite land and waterscape, ABDUL MEDJID has chosen the site for a new and gorgeous palace. The most skilful and ingenious artisans have been gathered from among his own subjects, and those of other sovereigns throughout Europe, and no expense is to be spared to render the construction perfect beyond parallel : far outstripping in the extent of its accommodations and the magnificence of its finish, the most elaborate and costly erections of his illustrious predecessors.

With a bevy of sprightly friends, among whom were a number of the younger members of the missionary families, I appropriated the better part of this brilliant morning to a careful examination of this imperial structure now in course of rapid completion. Our appearance at the grand gateway, *minus* anything approaching to a pass, or shadow of authority for entering, was the signal for sturdy opposition to our admission upon the part of the guards and attendants generally, but with resolute indifference to all their attempts at hindrance, we urged forward and soon stood unmolested, in the tasteful grounds surrounding the building; a fresh and extremely satisfactory triumph of our national perseverance, and assurance. Several acres of admirably arranged ornamental grounds are attached to the palace, and with the growth of a few years, the grass and shrubbery must become an elegant addition to the loveliness of the situation, enabling it to rival in its beauties the far famed charms of the old and romantic Seraglio gardens. The front of the palace is parallel with the Bosphorus, and at a distance of not more than one hundred feet from the boundary of its azure tinted waves; the intermediate space being gracefully decorated with fountains, flower beds, and smooth walks. A wall of granite, massive, and well built, suggestive of the superior masonry of the famous docks of Liverpool, receives the laving of the rolling flood, and nobly confronts its foaming power. Steps extending the entire length of the wall and pier, facilitate the embarkation and landing of the members of the royal household and such other parties as are allowed to touch their kaiques to the hallowed precincts. A tall iron railing, of heavy but beautiful design, and English manufacture, protects the gardens from the pier, and from the posts of several capacious gates, gas lamps of rich patterns, shed their brilliant rays over the bosom of the clear waters, when the better light of day is no longer present.

The eminent luxury of gas light is as yet known in Constantinople only to the Sultan's establishments, and to but few of these. The contrast of the dazzling flame, as it beams over the Bosphorus, from the palace burners, side by side with that of the flickering olive oil tapers suspended from the gate-ways of the private mansions crowding its banks, is such as to inspire the frank traveler with a deeper admiration for the perfection of artificial illumination as enjoyed in his own land—and to my own mind is strikingly suggestive of the variance between the cheerful radiance of evangelical Christianity, and the gloomful shadowings of Mahommedan superstition.*

I was not so fortunate as to secure the precise dimensions of the new palace, and from the irregularity of its outlines, it would be dangerous for one unskilled in such matters to attempt their definition merely from casual observation. It will not be improper, however, for me to suggest a comparison, and if I were to say a frontage of twice the extent of that of our City

---

* A company is now (1860) about to light the streets of Pera with gas.

Hall, (New York) and a proportionate depth, I am persuaded I should not encourage an idea very far from correct. There appears to have been an additional division added to the structure after the main portion had been considerably advanced. The appearance of the whole from the Bosphorus, from which it is seen to signal advantage, and much better than from any other point, is that of a long row of distinct buildings, joined as our city houses are, but without similarity of architecture or dimensions. I was surprised that the architect, whom I heard it stated, was an Englishman of high repute, had not been more careful to secure a symmetrical appearance, particularly for a building of such unusual pretension and magnitude.

Internally this elaborate palace is quite unlike any I have elsewhere visited. Of course the eccentricities of oriental life and taste would not allow of its conformity to those of the Christian world. Here the harem, that lingering relic of barbarism must be provided for, and the accommodations are unexceptionable if an outsider may judge. Large rooms and small ones, all with the close shielding blinds, are in course of rapid completion. A large reception hall or banquetting room is a marked feature, and is the first such room, I believe, introduced in any of the Sultan's palaces. But for the proximity of the harem I should think it suggestive of the early imitation of European

royalty. In truth I am vandal enough to prophesy
that ere a dozen years this finely frescoed hall will
have been witness to many a feast and merry-making
graced by all the refinement and fashion of Continental and British manners. The intelligent Turks
have no thought of eating with their fingers and
thumbs in this age of improved cutlery.

We left the great building by the cellar, a department not materially different from other cellars, unless
in its amplitude: its stout arches and unique pavement
of miniature cobble stones, such as we had seen
applied to the same purpose at the Seraglio, and in
other places, and arranged in tasteful figures looked,
at a distance, like delicate mosaic work, and on a
closer inspection extremely neat and compact.

The outward irregularities of the new palace are
well matched by the interior confusion. The whole
building is little less than a grand maze, and in case
of fire the royal occupants might give over all hope
of escape. The architect should be advertised as a
puzzle maker. Nevertheless the building has many
accommodations and conveniences unknown in the
older palaces, and is in fair keeping with the steady
advance of enlightenment in the East. It will stand
a creditable monument to the pardonable ambition of
Abdul Medjid, and an ornament to the already richly
adorned shores of the Bosphorus.

THE DOGS.

If in his walks about dilapidated Byzantium, and his study of the now imbecile but once powerful government of Islam, the traveler is ready to exclaim *Stat nominis umbra*, he will be careful to except the dogs from his sweeping declaration, for their presence, or omnipresence, is still a reality more palpable than agreeable to the faithless Frank, and worthy the palmy days of the immortal Mahomet.

They serve at least one good purpose in their capacity as city scavengers, for they clean away the offal like the hyenas at the Cape : does a horse, a camel, or even one of their own number die in the open street or road, the carcase is not left to taint the air, but in a very few hours these ravenous creatures have eaten all the flesh, and left the bones picked to perfection. They are a fierce race, but will not usually attack you in Constantinople (in the day time) though dangerous to meet in the rural districts, if one has no

(331)

means of defence : but from a stick or stone they will
fly, apparently knowing the effect of both by experience. An English tourist, some years since, strayed
from Constantinople, and was enjoying his classical
stroll exceedingly, when he found his progress suddenly interrupted by a pack of dogs, all barking at
once, and making a dead set at him : he stopped and
faced them, then they halted too ; he started and then
again the pursuit commenced, until quite exhausted
he sank on the ground to rest ; the dogs immediately
sat down in a semi-circle before him, left off barking,
and patiently awaited his rising, and then the hunt
recommenced until he sat down again, when his
canine foes very gravely did the same. Provoking as
it was he could not help laughing, as it recalled a similar circumstance in the *Odyssey* which he had regarded as a poetical fiction : however most luckily for
him, a shepherd came in sight, who seeing his
dilemma, called off the dogs, and told him how dangerous they were : indeed as he justly observed, the
story of Actæon, who was devoured by his own dogs,
might not be all a fiction.

Ross Browne, that merriest of eastern pilgrims,
provokes us to laughter in his *Crusade in the East*,
by his amusing allusion to the canine population of
the city of the Sultan, whose support he avows, and

whom he introduces to his readers with the following dog-matical defence :

" The dogs of Constantinople are a legitimate part of the population. Without them it would be no longer Constantinople. They are as much a part of it as the mosques, or the Turks, the Armenians, or the bazaars. Dogs are here protected by public sentiment, or some superstition, or by law; so they swarm in immense numbers; they do not belong to anybody, but roam in freedom; enjoying the fullest immunity from molestation. Travelers generally set them down as the great nuisances of the East, and heap unmeasured abuse upon every cur that dares to bark his sentiments. This is unjust; they might as well abuse the' Turks for wearing beards and worshipping Mahommed, as denounce the poor dogs for showing hostility towards Christians."

This may be so, and had the canine brutes one particle of attraction about them the majority of travelers would cheerfully defend them, but of all creatures it has been my lot to encounter, these are by odds the most repulsive. In vain have I searched among them for a generous specimen, for an open-countenanced, free hearted, smiling cur, one to whose acquaintance I might advance with somewhat of confidence and respect, by whom courtesy would be appreciated or at least decently acknowledged. Of a dark yellow, or dingy brown, an indescribably ugly color, with glaring gray eyes, a diabolical grin, and ever grating teeth, there is certainly nothing in their *personnel* to admire, and their habits present no redeeming feature. From the windows of my room upon one of the principal streets, a loathsome group of the carniverous vagrants is always in full view. Sprawling in every conceivable attitude of indolence, over the filthy surface of an open plot of ground, a receptacle for the garbage of the neighborhood, they mingle in great numbers, and with commendable quiet, and harmony, during the day, only now and then growing boisterous in an attack upon a fresh deposit of fragments from the table of some high living Moslem : but at night every soothing propensity of sleep or repose is effectually banished, as from the going down of the sun to the rising thereof, one incessant uproar rings in my susceptible ears, and wantonly riots upon the hours I would assign to Somnus, without let or hindrance.

Now there comes a startling combination of sounds, harsh, thrilling and discordant beyond any that ever ventured to my disturbance, and such as I am irrevocably persuaded only Ottoman canine lungs could produce, and beside which the united vocal exertions of a forest of screech owls, or a wilderness of catamounts would be "like flute notes in a storm."

Then after a momentary mumbling of low croaking growls, as destitute of melody as an Italian hurdy-gurdy, louder, ten times louder, as with the oral powers of Stentor, with all respect for that thundering ancient, bursts forth a fresh volley of the demoniacal yells: a charge is commenced, the victim, a thoughtless cur off his limits, or one of the district temporarily offensive to his guild, is mauled and torn with frightful ferocity, and only makes good his escape from fatal consequences by prompt recourse to his ambulatory powers. Again, a foot passenger of the human community stumbling over the lightless streets, lantern in hand, as the law directs, unintentionally arouses the antagonism of the crabbed whelps, and but for his trusty cudgel and athletic arm, his chances for escaping an impression of their sharp ivory upon his corporeal outlines would be far more dubious than desirable. And so the night, every night, wearies away; fruitful in unmitigated clamor. To sleep through the din is only the privilege of those to whom nature has given the enviable facility of commanding repose amid the most unnatural affinities.

Major B. whose room is just under mine, though long subject to the nocturnal hubbub of the four legged miscreants, has not yet acquired a total indifference to their rioting, and night after night his air

gun, skilfully aimed from the uplifted window beside
his bed, carries silent and summary destruction to
prominent members of the horde, and sends others
limping and howling away; but yet to little purpose,
for like crows, scores respond to the death knell of a
departed comrade, and no perceptible diminution in
the numerical strength of the crew is observable with
the return of day-light.

The mysteries and miseries attending the existence
of one of these Byzantian curs, from the opening of
his eyes in innocent puppyhood, to the closing of the
same in hoary and ill-requited dogdom, would unfold
a tragic catalogue of facts, could they be authentically
recorded, and set off with the descriptive coloring of
a Sue or Dickens, with etchings "from life" in pencil
or oil, by Sir Edwin Lanseer. Think of the days of
fruitless search for breakfast, dinner and tea, the days
even destitute of a consolatory bit of bread and cheese
by way of luncheon. Think of the nights, long, black
and dreary, passed without even the homely shelter
of a damp area, or the lee-side of a stone wall; and
then the battles to be fought, those only of defence,
necessitated defence, from the unprovoked assaults of
cruel and intrusive contemporaries. Reckon the
fractured bones, the bleeding feet, the mangled ears
and aching craniums. What a sorry picture we may
paint without going beyond the ordinary vicissitudes

of the every-day experience of these ill-starred quadrupeds, for whom the partiality of the Koran apparently avails but little.

But amid all the hardships of their seniors many of the juvenile curs lead lives of surprising jollity. Often by the fences, in the corners and under the piles of refuse matter conglomerated on the vacant lots about Pera, have I watched the youngsters studying their way into active life : commencing to scratch for a competency, and that with laudable ingenuity and perseverance. Already though acquainted with terrestrial haps and mishaps for fewer days than they have toes, the little dependents (for parental neglect had abandoned them to their own resources almost at birth), were adroit scavengers and adepts in the invaluable knack of living by their wits. In the clear sunshine of noon-day, lolling lazily on their backs, with heels sky-ward (after more than ordinary success in foraging,) rolling one another over, tumbling here and there in a style truly grand and lofty, and ambling about like petted kids, anxiety seemed to form no part of the nature of these rising members of the generation of Mussulman dogs. Strikingly in contrast with the demure and sombre existence of their adult brethren was this frivolous conduct. A type of the innocence and sprightliness of youth, and comparative freedom from care having

15

its counterpart in beings of a higher intellect and better fortune.

An hundred thousand dogs are said to be constantly wandering about the streets of Constantinople. It would not be unsafe to reduce this estimate one half, and then the city may boast a greater canine population than any I wot of. It is related, although I discovered nothing of the kind, that at Pera the dogs look with more favor on the Europeans than at Stamboul, and that the Turks do not think it strange that there should be a sympathy between the two races! "Should you ever find them to incommode you," says a French writer, (M. Charles Emanuel,) "you must cry ' *Houst!*' the Turkish word for away! "But then," he continues, "you must cry it out *a la Turque*, that is calmly, with dignity, and in a voice issuing from the chest, slightly cavernous. At the first ' *Houst!*' so articulated, they will fly."

A regard for candor compels me to allow that I have not been in a single instance, attacked by any of the numerous gangs by which, by day and night, we are ever surrounded, alike in Pera and Stamboul —and if the virtuous and wise Moslems entertain a kindly feeling for this vast canine population, surely it is not for a giaour, a Christian dog, to complain, however he may differ in sentiment. *De gustibus non disputandum!*

THE ENVIRONS.

THE kaiques have been called the omnibusses of Constantinople. They certainly are a favorite, and, owing to the position of the city, most convenient means of conveyance from one district to another.— Thousands of them are constantly plying to and fro upon the Golden Horn and Bosphorus, and the kaiquejees form a distinct and numerous class of the population—the " cabbies" of Constantinople. They make the best bargains they can, and though often noisy and excited, are seldom unmannered. Constant practice has given them arms of oak, with muscles of iron, and they jump their spicular boats through the water with surprising skill and velocity. The passenger sits on a soft carpet placed immediately on the floor of the kaique, and must balance himself very carefully, or he may capsize the feathery craft.

The most tempting excursions about the city, and

its environs, may be made in the kaiques. Now the traveler explores the broad Golden Horn to its graceful terminus at the " Valley of the sweet waters."— Anon he breasts the Cimmerian waves of the commingled Marmora and Euxine, as he crosses to the "silver city" of Scutari, on the Asiatic shore, where beneath the shadow of

" Olympus high and hoar,"

he may find much to entertain his leisure hours;— where are the dark cypress groves, and the camel trains have their starting point for interior Turkey in Asia.

But his most satisfactory excursions will be up the Bosphorus, to Therapia, to Bebek, to Buyukdere, to the Giant's Grave, to Kulalee, to Tcheranagun, the favorite palatial residence of the great Mahmoud, and to other charming places on either banks of the palace-studded Hudson of the Orient, whose rolling seas

" Lash and lave
Europe and Asia."

After Miss Pardoe, and Theophile Gautier, whom you must have read, to say nothing of an hundred less captivating but capable writers, I will not attempt to daguerreotype the unique and teeming beauties of the Bosphorus. I may say, however, that to my own mind, they have not been over-rated by their most enthusiastic admirers, and that the best hour to scan their wondrous magnificence is that just preceding the going down of the sun, when the rich purple clouds clustering in a thousand fantastic and dainty shapes, form a sublime and fitting peroration to the long, brilliant day. The hum of the busy city falls lightly upon the ear, the glittering minarets sparkle like burnished stars, the vine-robed kiosks reflect the delicate hues of their living drapery, and the rolling seas dance to their own aqueous music and that of the soft South wind.

At such an hour you may well ask the kaiquejee to rest upon his oars, while in mute ecstacy you drink in the impressive and inspiring fullness of the transporting scene.

Let no one talk loudly of Italian sunsets until he has witnessed one of these gorgeous spectacles in the Orient. The celestial Alps with their crystal crowns, could add little, if aught, to the measure of its spirit-stirring and poetic sublimity.

And to the lover of sunshine, in all its enlivening fulgency, the mellow and apricious East offers a perpetual treat. Here assuredly (if it be not so elsewhere,) it would seem .

> " No task
> For suns to shine."

After twilight little if any business is done in Con-

stantinople. Long and wholesome custom renders
unnecessary the " early closing movement," and more-
over, the character of the streets would make nocturnal shopping somewhat unsafe. Those who of necessity venture out, go armed with a trusty lantern
and cudgel wherewith to grope their way and keep
off those who prefer darkness to light for their dubious deeds. Over the face of the Bosphorus ten thousand feeble lamps glimmer from either shore, but the
quiet everywhere reigning indicates a complete ces-
sation of trade and toil.

When, as on several occasions, we have gone late
in the day to visit friends at Hass-Keuy, Bebek and
other districts, we have remained all night; indeed the
early barring of the great gates which divide one
ward of the city from another, would have prevented
our returning, except in case of fire, when at the boom-
ing of the signal gun (bells having no favor with the
authorities) the gates are thrown wide open and remain
so during the night.

Returning quite late from the American Minister's
and other other favorite resorts in Pera, we have always managed to make our way without accident or
molestation, but should have found it very difficult to
make any progress whatever without our lanterns.
The dogs, who in the day time have the good manners
to leave a portion of the streets to their superiors, take

full possession of them at night, and have to be routed up or trod upon at nearly every step. The watchmen shout lustily every few moments, and strike the pavement with their great clubs, with a vigor which serves alike to intimidate the rogues and disturb the honest men. R. has more than once threatened to put a summary end to one of these municipal nuisances who makes it a point to batter his cudgel upon the stones near our domicil, during a great portion of the night.

*   *   *   *   *   *

The streets of Stamboul and Pera are alike unsuited for vehicles; occasionally the clumsy arabas flounder through the widest of them, but in general they are quite impassable. The carriers are men and horses. Of the porters or hamels the most extravagant stories are told. Their broad shoulders do not quake under burdens that would overwhelm an Irishman or negro. It is said they carry with apparent ease, and for long distances, as much as any two laboring men in England or America. The more bulky goods are carried on large poles supported by the shoulders of two, four, or six men as the case may be. Woe to the luckless pedestrian who happens in the route of these trains when under full headway. He might almost as well encounted the Royal express. Not that the speed is great, but the power with which the stalwart men ad-

vance is wholly irresistible. Much of the confusion
of the business streets comes from the piercing shouts
of the hamels to those who chance to obstruct their
way, and an accidental, much less an intended collis-
ion with the nicely balanced load, is a signal for re-
sentment as much fiercer than that attending the
knocking a chip off a school-boy's shoulder, as the
load is larger than the chip.

Mules and donkeys are perhaps more used as porters than horses. They carry wood, building materials, and market truck, and are driven by noisy fellows
with long whips, which they apply with little cessa-
tion. When R. orders a load of wood for his New
England stove, it is brought on the backs of perhaps
an half dozen donkeys, and long before they near the
house we know of their approach by the clatter of
their shodden hoofs on the jagged stones. There is a
lively time in the unloading, and an amusing elevation
of heels, and shaking of long ears when the relieved
carriers trot away at a pell-mell rate, closely followed
by their ragged and hooting masters.

A peculiar and convenient custom is that of station-
ing saddle-horses for hire at prominent points throughout the city. Like the omnipotent cabs of London,
they may be engaged at a moment's notice. The
charges are somewhat exorbitant, but the taking price
is not out of the way. For twenty piastres (about sev-

enty cents) I have had the undisturbed use of an animal of more than usual carriage and speed, for three full hours, and that to go beyond the city limits, for which liverymen usually exact an increased charge.

Near the "Grand Champs des Mort" in Pera, is the equine station which receives our chief patronage. Here for a distance of a quarter of a mile or more, upon the unusually broad and pleasant roadway, may always be seen a group of animated Greek, Turkish, and Armenian men and lads, leading their sleek animals up and down, and keeping a sharp lookout for customers. At the approach of a Frank they clamorously extol the merits of their respective beasts, while the prancing cattle so literally hem you in on every side, that a speedy choice must be made to escape their clustering feet. The attendants, who in most cases are not the owners of the horses, usually make it a point to accompany you on foot, running close behind with whip in hand, and apparently never tiring; but we have made it a rule to decline their attendance. The horses are often very handsome, fat, glossy and agile to a remarkable degree for hacks. They pick their way through the irregular pavement and steep acclivities of the streets with great dexterity. Long custom has given them the sure feet of mountain ponies. Their trappings are for the most part shabby enough, and the saddles uncomfortably

15*

hard. Nevertheless, we have greatly enjoyed our rides both in and out of the city, and of one of the latter made a few days since, I venture to give you a somewhat detailed account, as it took us over much interesting ground :

The day was as mild and balmy as though it were midsummer, and the ever-brilliant sun gave us the smile of his brightest Oriental face. What an almoner of good-cheer is the sun. A Persian visiting Great Britain was taunted by a native of that Island, because some of his countrymen worshipped the sun. "So would Englishmen," was his reply, "if they could see him." Assuredly, the influence of sunshine is productive of joy wherever it penetrates.

Winding our way through the circuitous and crowded streets of Pera, we soon came out into the broad fields behind the great French hospital. For perhaps a mile, there was a way bearing a slight semblance to a road, but afterward we were compelled to force a passage through ravines and gullies bold enough to have startled an Indian hunter. The face of the extended country—for we soon cleared the suburban houses—presented a naked treeless appearance. Hill followed valley in close proximity, and the whole landscape forcibly reminded us of many points in the highland districts of Perthshire and Aberdeenshire, in the East of Scotland, though the hills were never at all lofty. We did not see a single *ferme ornee*, and in only one or two instances could discover any signs of cultivation. The plough and the spade seem almost unknown, even so near this great metropolis. We met a drove of sheep, and another of cattle. The animals were in good condition—healthy, and decently fat. They probably came from some fertile district in the interior, and were better than much of the live stock sent to the Constantinople markets, where it is usually hard to secure a good piece of beef or mutton.

Having remarkably sure-footed and fast horses, we were not long in reaching the little village situated at the head of the Valley of the Sweet Waters of Europe. A long, grassy plain, extends from it for several miles, on either side of the "Waters," which are a narrow continuation of the famous Golden Horn. Handsome shade trees add to the picturesque beauty of the locality, which in spring and summer is the chief place of resort for the Turkish, Armenian and Frank ladies of Constantinople. Here the fair maidens come to enjoy the pure and refreshing air of the open country, and here gossip has its greatest exchange. Here the merits of the city beaux are coolly discussed; and here many a flirtation is as coolly practiced. The Sultan is often in the merry throng; and during the later hours of Friday, the Mohammedan Sabbath, after all the religious forms have met attention, the number of visitors is truly enormous and Felicitas would seem to reign triumphant. Thus you see the hypocritical Parisian fashion, of devoting the morning of the Sabbath to worship, and the afternoon to recreation and deviltry of every sort, has gained favor even among the inhabitants of the staid city of the prophet.

The Sultan has two summer palaces or kiosks, in the Valley of the Sweet Waters, (or, more properly, of " Fresh waters," which Dr. Dwight tells me is the correct interpretation of the Turkish name, and there is nothing particularly sweet in the waters.) They are of wood, in the Turkish style, ornamental and spacious, with the usual araneous windows. One was built by Sultan Mahmoud, and is seldom inhabited, and never repaired, so that it now presents a somewhat dilapidated appearance. It is said that Mahmoud, having built this charming nest for a favorite odalisque, refused again to visit it, after an early death had taken her from him.

At the large gateway leading to the grounds immediately connected with this palace, we asked an aged Turk if we might drive in and have a look at things. " It is forbidden," said he, with the *sang froid* of a thorough-bred Mussulman; but as he offered no serious opposition, we entered, and took a careful survey, finding nothing, however, sufficient to pay for our trouble. A small, but pretty, artificial water-fall, constructed from the stream, was the only feature worthy of note, and that seemed meagre enough after the artificial wonders of Chatsworth.

The roads all around the royal kiosks are of the meanest order, if, indeed, they may be said to be of any order at all. The Sultan generally goes to and from his metropolitan residence in his elegant kaiques, and probably thinks little, and cares much less, for the convenience of those who go on horse or in carriages.

Near to where the waters open into the broad Golden Horn, on their way to the Bosphorus and its connected seas, we saw extensive buildings erected for the manufactory of "tiles," such as are used for roofing many of the Constantinople houses. They are of red clay, brick color, and closely resemble those in use in the States. Turning a little way into the country, in order to cross the waters by the upper bridge, we met several long trains of camels, on their way to the distant inland towns. No sight seems to me more purely Oriental than this. I well remember when I saw it for the first time, on my arrival at Smyrna, how all my juvenile fancies of the East came rushing into mind. These animals are natural

to the East, and to the East only, and are wholly in
Eastern service, though for years there has been a
movement towards their introduction into our great
Western prairies.* They go rolling along at an easy
and dignified pace, as though they had no care, no
want, no regard for anybody or anything. A demure
little donkey is at the head of each train, with the
driver upon his back. Strange customers these
drivers, but always content as they fife some oriental
ditty, or draw on their venerable pipes, and ever and
anon give Mr. Donkey a dexterous poke in the ribs,
for donkeys here as everywhere need such persuasive
arguments.

Once upon the elevated land at the head of the
Golden Horn, we secured a superb view of the great
city, and its countless suburbs; of the beautiful
Bosphorus; of the rolling sea of Marmora, and in the
dim distance, the foaming, ever-restless waves of the
turbulent Euxine; while the high hills behind
Scutari, and all along the Asiatic coast, loomed up
in all their encrimsoned grandeur. Constantinople
looks remarkably well a little way off. 'Tis essentially
true, that

" Distance lends enchantment to the view."

The evergreen cypress groves that shade the vast

* I think the dromedary preferable to the camel. It is a more hearty animal,
and can stand almost anything, as I have witnessed in the Crimea.

burial‘grounds throughout the city, give it a rural
aspect, quite unlike that of any other city I have
seen ; and the unnatural absence of large mercantile
establishments, and huge factories with their sky-
pointing chimneys, does much to increase the distinction.

It cannot be denied that the Golden Horn makes
one of the best harbors in the world. I may compare
it to the East River, if you can suppose that that
great stream came to a quiet termination somewhere
in the vicinity of the Novelty Works. Where the
" Horn" first branches off from the junction of the
Marmora and the Bosphorus, seamen complain that
the water is altogether too deep for safe or ready
anchorage ; but when you come near to the first
bridge, beyond which merchant vessels seldom go, it
is in every way suited to port use. War ships pass
up above the second bridge, to the navy yard, which
is admirably located. The width of the Golden Horn
averages about a quarter of a mile from beach to
beach. As there are no docks, the vessels all anchor
pell-mell in the stream, and the sight of the mingled
spars from our point of observation was enough to
delight the heart even of an amateur sailor.

We soon struck an old road. The large flat stones
proved very troublesome to our ponies, and we could
not urge them into anything like a decent pace, for

the many irregularities of the ancient pavement. It was the old highway to Adrianople, and by it, for a mile or more, we passed through great fields of the dead—acres of tomb-stones, many of them showing the marks of time's abuse. At last we reached the city walls at the Adrianople gate. Having carefully examined this, we entered the broad and rudely paved road, following immediately along the outside of the walls. It extends for nearly a league between the mass of ruins, and a great cemetery. The walls are sadly mutilated and destroyed : they were originally three in number, and flanked with tall square towers, but scarcely a tower remains in sufficient perfection to afford an idea of its former grandeur. The walls appear to have been composed of stone and brick, carelessly combined, and were probably very strong. Even now it would be difficult to overturn them.

An intelligent continental writer (Gautier,) has well described their present condition:

" These are the walls of Constantine, at least ; such as has been left of them, after time, sieges and earthquakes have done their worst upon them. In their masses of brick and stone, are still visible breaches made by the catapults and battering-rams, or by that gigantic culverin, that mastadon of artillery, which was served by seven hundred cannoniers, and threw balls of marble of nearly half a ton in weight.

"Here and there, a gigantic crevice severs a tower from top to bottom; farther on, a mass of wall has fallen into the moat: but where masonry is wanting, the elements have supplied earth and seed; a shrub has supplied the place of a missing battlement, and grown into a tree; the thousand tendrils of parasitical plants sustain the stone which otherwise would have fallen; the roots of trees, after acting as wedges to introduce themselves between the joints of the stones, have become chains to confine them; and the line of wall is still (to the eye) continued without interruption—raising against the clear sky its battered profile, and displaying its curtains and bastions, draped with ivy, and gilded by time, with tints by turns mellow and serene.

"As you pass along the outer road it is difficult to realize, that a living city lies behind the defunct ramparts. It would be easier to believe one's self near some of those cities of the Arabian legends, all the inhabitants of which had been by some magical process, turned into stone. Only a few minarets rear their heads above the immense circuit of ruins, to testify that there is life within, and that the capital of Islam still exists."

The conqueror of Constantine XIII., if he could

return to the world, could make again, with striking appropriateness, his celebrated quotation from the Persian :—

" ' The spider shall weave her web in the palace of emperors, and the owl cry by night from the towers of Ephrasaib.' "

We rode a number of miles on the antiquated road, and finally arrived at the shore of the dashing Marmora, but found no gate, and had to return to the last or Narli-Kapur, or pomegranate gate, in order to enter the city. Immediately on the right we came upon the " Seven Towers," or rather the spot where the " Seven Towers" used to be :—

> " He saw with his own eyes the moon was round,
> Was also certain that the earth was square,
> Because he had journeyed fifty miles, and found
> No sign that it was circular anywhere.
> His empire also was without a bound ;
> 'Tis true, a little troubled here and there,
> By rebel pashas and encroaching giaours ;
> But they never came to the Seven Towers "

Three of the towers have disappeared, and the whole building or inclosure which appears to be connected with the old walls, is in a ruinous state. The towers were formerly very high and secure, they were used as prisons. One is now a powder magazine. We were at first refused admission, but evincing a determination to go in at all hazards, the guards loitering about the doors in goodly numbers, gave way without delay, but with evident reluctance. It is said to be against orders to admit visitors, without a firman, or some official authority. Creeping up the dilapidated stairway, to the top of one of the towers, we secured a capital survey of the city and surrounding country. Our promise of *backsheesh* had produced a favorable impression on the part of the two Turkish military gentlemen, who officiated as guides, (one of them was about as black as ebony,) and they lost no opportunity to carefully point out and describe every famous locality within our gaze. Several old cannon were lying about the top of the walls. They seemed as much used up as the Ottoman government at the present day—perhaps a trifle more so.

Descending, we found that the gates and doors, excepting one very small one, had all been closed, and that a swarthy sentinel was stationed at the main entrance. We were not prevented from passing out, and our *backsheesh* seemed to give much satisfaction to all hands, although the grim sentinel looked as though he would not let in another party of " Christian dogs" on any consideration.

Again on our faithful horses, we plunged into the narrow city streets, and commenced a rapid transit through the Greek quarter. The streets were even more contemptible than those of Pera. The houses

gloomy and closely jammed : the projecting windows
almost coming together over our heads. The pavement unusually rough ; the mud deep and dangerous ;
the dogs numerous and vicious. We rode for a long,
long distance, without meeting anything whatever, to
relieve the tedious monotony, save now and then an
èloquent girlish eye peeping from those coquettish
overhanging windows; and there was a degree of
modesty, and innocence in the " sly glance," we
could but admire. Most of the dark-eyed Grecian
witches were knitting or weaving, with much apparent industry.

Passing the Greek quarter, we came to where the
Turks and Armenians congregate. The streets wore
a commercial air, shop followed shop, and stall
crowded stall. Our iron shod animals fairly made
the welkin ring with their sharp clatter on the hard
stones ; while the dogs of every degree, even the lowest, came yelling after us.

We passed under the venerable aqueduct of Bosjo-
han-Kemeri. A double row of forty gothic arches
remains in condition, and puts to blush much of the
masonry of to-day.

Crossing the Golden Horn by the second or middle
bridge—a well built modern structure—and passing
through the road over the little burial ground back
of the main street of Pera, we came to the high walls

around the new British Palace, and soon after to our own appreciated home, where we delivered our serviceable horses to their waiting owners, and sat down to a sumptuous repast at our friend Van L.'s hospitable table, which we relished no less than a jovial recapitulation of our animated adventures.

ST. SOPHIA.

It has been aptly said, " the stranger, as he views the glittering minarets and innumerable domes that rise above the streets of Stamboul must forget for awhile that this was once the patriarchal throne of John Chrysostom : he is not prepared at the first sight of Constantinople to recognize the city which contended with Rome for ecclesiastical dominion."

If Rome has her seven papal basilicas, Constantinople has her seven imperial mosques, which with their satellites engross the whole atmosphere of external religion, and while I am as loth to take part in the hackneyed chaunt about " mosques and minarets," as was the matter of fact author of " *Eothen*," you would account it very strange were I to pass these remarkable structures in utter silence. They are a prominent feature in every Mohammedan city and the chief pride of Islam. In architecture they have the facility of external showiness and interior

(358)

simplicity, but usually neither will stand a very critical examination.

I have already referred to one of the latest built, in speaking of the Sultan at his devotions, but it was by no means worthy to compare with those of Stamboul.

The chief of the imperial mosques, originally a Christian temple, and dedicated to the Divine Wisdom, " Agia Sophia," (as personified by the Greeks, and, according to their teaching, mother of the three theological virtues,) attracts the traveler's early inspection. It was converted into a mosque the very day on which Mohammed II. took possession of Constantinople and its magnificent crescent, gilded, it is said, with fifty thousand gold pieces, and mounted upon the dome by the successor of the Caliphs, can be seen dazzling in the sunbeams an hundred miles at sea. It is only within a few years that .St. Sophia has been accessible to the Frank without an imperial firman, the obtaining of which involved a very considerable outlay of patience and piasters. Now, however, the sacred temple may be entered as readily as St. Paul's or St. Peter's, the only expense being the reasonable *backsheesh* with which the keepers are content.

The position of St. Sophia is unfortunate as is that of nine-tenths of the superb ecclesiastic edifices of the old world. Instead of a great open space all about the ponderous pile, it is literally crowded and obscured by a world of shops and petty bazaars, which ever attract to the neighborhood a swarm of chattering buyers and idlers whose confusion is at times intolerable. There are also groups of pilgrim merchants ever lingering in the vicinity, venerable men with huge green turbans and flowing beards, who expose for sale "all descriptions of chaplets, perfumes, relics from Mecca, charms against the Evil eye, amber and ivory mouthpieces for the chibouque, and dyes, and toys for the harem."

Passing all these, with a deaf ear to their importunities, and the graceful fountain where the faithful perform their vodu, a necessary preliminary to prayer, (Mahomet says, the practice of religion is found in cleanliness, and that it is the key of prayer,) we enter the mosque, not however without the jealous glance of the pious Moslems ever lolling about the grand doorway. Nor can it be accounted at all strange that these devout disciples of the prophet and the Koran should be thus apprehensive of our entry into their "holy of holies." The cool irreverence of the Western giaour, and his obvious contempt for the traditions and customs of the Moslem religion, give abundant reason for a suspicion of his every movement. But we are offered no insult, having duly left our shoes in the broad vestibule—an Eastern practice, to neglect which would be alike ill-mannered and hazardous.

Judged by the richly furnished churches of France and Italy, St. Sophia is well calculated to disappoint the visitor at first sight. Islamism has little partiality for the pictorial and plastic arts. Nevertheless the structure is amazingly grand, and upon careful inspection impresses the beholder with its gigantic proportions* and its lofty columns of jasper, porphyry and verd antique. The majestic dome is unquestionably one of the finest in the world, and must have shone "like a sun of gold and mosaic" before its splendors were despoiled by the Moslems.

Many costly carpets cover the floor, all apparently awry, but this is that they may be in the proper direction toward Mecca, as St. Sophia was not originally intended for a mosque, and is wanting in that particular.

Manuscript and richly ornamented copies of the Koran are disposed about the mosque carefully supported on wooden tressels. As you are aware the Koran is held in the greatest possible respect among the Mohammedans. They never touch it without being first washed or legally purified ; and lest they

---

* About 25,000 persons can stand within the building.

should inadvertently do so, they put an inscription on it, " Let none touch it but those who are clean."

From the dome, cords to which are suspended tufts of silk and ostrich eggs, sustain lamps wherewith the vast edifice is occasionally illumined. Green disks presented by the several Sultans, and bearing selections from the Koran, ornament or disfigure the walls according to one's taste.

About the only *bona-fide* curiosity shown the visitor is a small piece of rusty carpet, said to be one of the four carpets on which Mahomet knelt to perform his devotions. It is unnecessary to say that this modest relic is valued beyond all price by the Turks.

Strange as it may appear, the side chapels of the building, which are not used for purposes of worship, are stored with trunks, and goods of all kinds, for, the mosques serve as store-houses, and those who are going away on a journey, or who fear being robbed at home, deposit their wealth under the immediate protection of Allah; and Gautier is responsible for the statement, that there has never been an instance of the loss of a farthing under such circumstances.

At the hour of our visit a venerable priest was preaching from one of the slightly elevated pulpits. Before him on the floor sat a score of devout hearers, including several women. What was the precise tenor of his discourse we were unable to learn. As in the Roman churches there is a constant going and coming of worshippers, and here and there all over the carpets (for there are no seats,) pious Moslems are to be seen with their faces Mecca-ward offering their humble prayers. There is no wandering of the eye, no turning of the head, to indicate any abstraction of the thought, but an intense and profound devotion. Nor is the duty of prayer confined to the mosques. Throughout the empire at various places beside the highways, are square enclosures of stone, called Nas-nasgirk, with ground inside, as high as the top of the walls; annexed to them are fountains for ablution, and here daily prayers are offered by passengers. When there are none such, the kebla, or direction to Mecca, is pointed out by a table which every Mussulman carries about him. A small carpet is spread, and the person, turning his face to the Holy City, prostrates himself with his forehead touching the ground, occasionally rising on his knees, and again laying his face to the ground, during his prayer. When done he folds up his carpet and proceeds on his way.*

Of course in this legendary and superstitious land a structure so venerable, historic and eminent as St. Sophia, must be the centre of many strange and thrill-

* Dr. Walsh's Constantinople.

ing traditions. Of these I will only repeat one of the most current. Thus it is told. When the doors of the ancient Christian temple were forced by the barbarous hordes of the Sultan, there was a priest at the altar engaged in saying mass. At the noise made by the hoofs of the Tartar horses upon the marble pavement and the shouts of the Moslem soldiery, the priest interrupted in the holy sacrifice, took up the sacred vases, and proceeded with slow and solemn step toward one of the lateral naves. The soldiers, brandishing their cimeters, attempted to reach him, when he suddenly disappeared in the wall which opened to receive him. They believed at first that he had escaped by a secret passage, but the masonry was solid, compact, and impenetrable. Sometimes it is said the listening ear will catch the murmur of vague psalmodies within the wall. It is the priest still living, like Barbarossa in the cavern of Kiefhausen, and muttering in his sleep the interrupted liturgy. When St. Sophia shall be restored to the Christians, the wall will open and the priest, leaving his retreat will again appear at the altar to finish the mass begun more than four hundred years ago.

Sheldon and Company.

A Select List

OF

PUBLICATIONS.

Messrs. SHELDON & COMPANY beg leave to say that their publications can generally be found at all Book Stores, News Depots, and Religious Depositories. When not obtainable at these places, any book on the list will be forwarded, prepaid by mail, on receipt of the retail prices annexed to each book.

Special attention is called to the list of School and College Text Books. Samples of these are sent to Teachers and Educators by mail prepaid, on receipt of one half the prices annexed.

NEW YORK:

SHELDON & COMPANY, 115 NASSAU ST.,

Publishers and Booksellers.

1860.

J. P. Thompson, D.D

The Christian Graces. 16mo., ... 75
Memoir of the Rev. D. T. Stoddard. 12mo., . 1 00
A new volume (*in press*).

S. Irenæus Prime, D.D.

The Bible in the Levant. 16mo., . . . 75
Switzerland (Illustrated). 12mo., . . . 1 00

William J. Hoge, D.D.

Blind Bartimeus. 16mo., ... 75

Rev. W. P. Balfern.

Glimpses of Jesus. 16mo., . . . 60
Lessons from Jesus. 16mo., ... 75

Rev. Henry M. Field.

From Copenhagen to Venice. 12mo., . . 1 00

Mrs. Maria T. Richards.

Life in Israel. 12mo., . . . 1 00

Manton Eastburn, D.D.

Thornton's Family Prayers. 12mo., . . . 75
"   "   "   Fine ed., red edges, . 1 00

John Dowling, D.D.

The Power of Illustration. 18mo., . . 30
The Iudson Memorial. 16mo., . . 60

James B. Taylor, D.D.

Baptist Ministers of Virginia. 1st Series, . . 1 25
" " " 2d " . . 1 25

W. C. Duncan, D.D.

The Tears of Jesus. 12mo., ... 75
Pulpit Gift Book. 12mo., ... 1 00
History of the Early Baptists. 12mo., . . 75
Life of John the Baptist. 12mo., . . . 75

Geo. C. Baldwin, D.D.

Representative Women. 12mo., . . . 1 00

Rev. Alfred S. Patton.

Losing and Taking of Mansoul. 12mo., . . 1 00

George Gilfillan, LL.D.

Third Gallery of Portraits. 12mo., . . . 1 25

Mrs. Augusta B. Garrett.

Precious Stones of the Heavenly Foundations, . 1 00

Mabel Sharman Crawford.

Life in Tuscany. 12mo., ... 1 00

David Benedict, D.D.

History of the Baptists. 8vo., sheep, .　.　.　3 50

Fifty Years among the Baptists. 12mo.,　　1 00

E. T. Hiscox, D.D.

The Baptist Church Directory. 16mo.,　.　.　50

Rev. D. C. Haynes.

The Baptist Denomination. 12mo., .　.　.　1 00

J. B. Jeter, D.D.

The Life and Writings of Rev. A. Broaddus,　.　1 00

Campbellism examined. 12mo.,　.　.　.　1 00

The Mirror. 16mo.,　.　.　.　.　.　60

Rev. J. D. Fulton.

The Roman Catholic Element. 12mo.,　.　.　1 00

John Clarke Marshman.

Life and Times of Carey Marshman & Ward,　.　5 00

Edward B. Underhill.

Struggles and Triumphs of Religious Liberty,　.　75

William Dean, D.D.

The China Mission. 12mo.,　.　.　.　1 00

Mrs. Macleod Wylie.

The Gospel in Burmah. 12mo.,　.　.　1 00

Rev. Jacob Abbott.

The Rollo-Books.

14 vols., illustrated. 16mo., each, . . .		50
14 " " Cheap ed. 18mo., each, .		38

The Rollo Story Books.

12 vols., illustrated. 18mo., each, . . .		25

The Florence Stories.

Florence and John, 7 illustrations. 16mo., . .		60
Grimkie, 7 " " . .		60
The Orkney Islands (in press).		

Abbott's American History.

Aboriginal America, 18 illustrations. 16mo., .		75
Discovery of America (in press).		

Rev. George B. Taylor.

The Oakland Stories.

Kenny, 5 illustrations. 16mo., ...		50
Cousin Guy, 5 illustrations. 16mo., . . .		50
Gustave (in press).		

J. T. Trowbridge.

The Old Battle Ground. 18mo., . . .		50
Father Brighthopes. 18mo., ...		50
Hearts and Faces. 18mo., ...		50
Iron Thorpe. 18mo., ...		50
Burr Cliff. 18mo., ...		50

HOUSEHOLD LIBRARY.

Life and Martyrdom of Joan of Arc. By Michelet,	50
Life of Robert Burns. By Thomas Carlyle,	50
Life and Teachings of Socrates. By George Grote,	50
Life of Columbus. By Alphonse de Lamartine,	50
Life of Frederick the Great. By Lord Macaulay,	50
Life of William Pitt. By Lord Macaulay,	50
Life of Mahomet. By Gibbon,	50
Life of Luther. By Chev. Bunsen,	50
Life of Oliver Cromwell. By A. de Lamartine,	50
Life of Torquato Tasso. By G. H. Wiffen,	50
Life of Peter the Great. Compiled by the Editor, 2 vols.,	1 00
Life of Milton. By Prof. Masson,	50
Life of Thomas A'Becket. By H. H. Milman, D.D.,	50
Life of Hannibal. By Dr. Arnold,	50
Life of Vittoria Colonna. By T. A. Trollope,	50
Life of Julius Cæsar. By Henry G. Liddell, D.D.,	50
Life of Mary Stuart. By A. de Lamartine,	50

SUNNY-SIDE SERIES.

Peep at No. 5. By Mrs. E. S. Phelps,	50
Tell Tale. " " "	50
Last Leaf from Sunny-Side. By Mrs. E. S. Phelps.	50
City Side. By Cara Belmont,	50

Mrs. Thomas Geldart.

Daily Thoughts for a Child. 16mo.,	50
Truth is Everything. 16mo.,	50
Emilie the Peacemaker. 16mo.,	50
Sunday Morning Thoughts. 16mo.,	50
Sunday Evening Thoughts. 16mo.,	50
Popular History of England. 16mo.,	75

S. G. Goodrich (Peter Parley).

The Cottage Library. 10 vols., 18mo.,	3 75
Picture Play Books. 4to.,	75

Francis L. Hawks, D.D., LL.D.

Richard the Lion Hearted. 16mo.,	75
Oliver Cromwell. 16mo.,	75

Aunt Mary's Stories. 12 vols.,	3 00
The Little Commodore. 16mo.,	75
A Treasury of Pleasure Books. Gilt,	1 50
Indestructible Pleasure Books, each,	20
The Illuminated Linen Primer,	20
The Farmer Boy's Alphabet,	20
The Scripture Alphabet,	20
Little Annie's Ladder to Learning.,	40
Child's Pleasure Book,	75
The Pretty A. B. C.,	20
Pleasure Books in Colors, each,	13

Eliphalet Nott, D.D.

Lectures on Temperance. 12mo., . . . 1 00

Robert Turnbull, D.D.

. Life Pictures from a Pastor's note book, . 1 00

Rev. Matthew Mead.

The Almost Christian. 18mo., . . . 45

John Frost, LL.D.

Wonders of History. 8vo., ... 2 00

The Wife's Trials and Triumphs, . . . 1 00
Life of Spencer H. Cone, D.D., ... 1 25
The Life and Works of Lorenzo Dow, . . 1 50
Father Clark, the Pioneer Preacher, . . . 63
The Napoleon Dynasty. Illustrated, 8vo., . . 2 50
Marble Worker's Manual, ... 1 00
Memoir of Thomas Spencer, ... 60
The N. Y. Pulpit, Revival of 1858, . . . 1 00
The Baptist Library. 8vo., sheep, . . . 3 50
The Living Epistle. Tyree, ... 60
Rollin's Ancient History. 8vo., ... 1 50
The Words of Jesus and Faithful Promiser, . 37
Roman Orthoepy, ... 50
Young Men of America, ... 40 .